Comprehensive
High School
Reading Methods

The Charles E. Merrill
COMPREHENSIVE READING PROGRAM
Arthur W. Heilman
Consulting Editor

Comprehensive High School Reading Methods

DAVID L. SHEPHERD

Professor of Reading

Hofstra University

CHARLES E. MERRILL PUBLISHING COMPANY

A Bell & Howell Company

Columbus, Ohio

Published by
Charles E. Merrill Publishing Company
A Bell & Howell Company
Columbus, Ohio 43216

Library of Congress Catalog Card Number: 72-96847

International Standard Book Number: 0-675-08959-X

1 2 3 4 5 6 7 8 9 10—77 76 75 74 73

PRINTED IN THE UNITED STATES OF AMERICA

Preface

The use of language to think and to express ideas has been characterized as a uniquely human phenomenon. Certainly the interaction between teacher and learner uses language. Indeed, each person who teaches a body of subject matter is also a language teacher. He teaches the language as it is used in the subject of his expertise.

Here we are primarily concerned with one aspect of language usage—reading as it is used in different types of subject matter. The effective implementation of this idea rests upon philosophical premises. First, the ability to read and understand the language of a subject determines the learner's competency and mastery in that subject. Second, the changes taking place in our society as well as the individual's functioning in the democratic society require his independence in gaining and communicating ideas through language—reading. Third, the teaching of any content and the ability to read the language of it are fused. Content and reading are an interwoven entity. Fourth, the learner must be cognizant of the learning processes in order to become independent and self-directing.

Consequently, specific ideas and techniques are presented to show how instruction in the reading skills can be incorporated into any subject area. The first chapter develops a rationale—a philosophic base. Next, techniques of diagnosis are discussed so that instruction can be adjusted to the specific needs of the learner. This is followed by a discussion of the skills the learner needs to read effectively, with subsequent discussion of classroom techniques. Ways to individualize the instruction are emphasized. The major subject areas are investigated to show a more detailed implementation of the fusion of content and reading skills. Finally, the characteristics of a total high school reading program are discussed.

Essentially, this book emphasizes specific and practical methods a practitioner can employ to fuse reading and content. Throughout, the teacher is held as the key for effective instruction.

v

The persons who contributed to this book are many. They are the high school students in various parts of the United States who have felt the need for instruction in reading in different disciplines. The concerns and ideas of many teachers have also contributed. All through the years they have expressed their desire to know how to fuse instruction in reading with the teaching of content more effectively.

Contents

CHAPTER ONE

The Rationale

Reading is an intrinsic part of the classroom teaching of content. A cursory review of content curricula will show the importance of teaching students how to obtain information along with teaching subject matter. All subject matter learning depends in large measure on the student's competence in the language of the subject. He must understand the vocabulary and syntax used in each subject, and be able to use language skills to aid his own internalization of the information, and to communicate it to others. Competence in the language of the subject requires the use of various aspects of the language arts as they apply—reading, writing, speaking, and listening.

Teaching students to apply the language-reading skills to each of their content areas comprises the basic premise of this book.

THE PURPOSES OF THE CONTENT AREAS

Any content area teacher can list a number of values of learning the subject he teaches. Reasons that may be given will range from a statement that the subject is required by a state or school curriculum or that it is good mental discipline for the student, to statements that note the values of expanding the student's background of knowledge about his heritage. Whatever the reasons, most content teachers are convinced about the value and pertinence of their subject.

We must look more closely at the aims of education of which the aims of content teaching are integral. A review of educational goals over the last quarter century shows common threads. Sidney Hook stated seven educational ends.

1. Education should aim to develop the powers of critical, independent thought.
2. It should attempt to induce sensitiveness of perception, receptiveness to new ideas, imaginative sympathy with the experiences of others.
3. It should produce an awareness of the main streams of our cultural, literary and scientific traditions.
4. It should make available important bodies of knowledge concerning nature, society, ourselves, our country and its history.
5. It should strive to cultivate an intelligent loyalty to the ideals of the democratic community.
6. At some level, it should equip young men and women with the general skills and techniques and the specialized knowledge which, together with the virtues and aptitudes already mentioned, will make it possible for them to do some productive work related to their capacities and interests.
7. It should strengthen those inner resources and traits of character which enable the individual, when necessary, to stand alone.[1]

The sum total of these ends points toward the development within the individual of the abilities to think independently and to conduct himself as a sane, perceptive and knowledgeable person. A review of these ends does not reveal information and basic skills alone, but also the powers of critical thought, perceptive sensitivity, imagination, awareness of man's development, receptiveness to new ideas and the development of inner resources. Therefore, teaching in the content fields must be concerned with more than the learning of knowledge, important as it is. Techniques of thinking and the effective use of language must also be taught.

Frederick Mayer defined education and pointed out what the results of it should be.

> Education is the supreme embodiment of morality. It is based on man's awareness of himself and his potentialities for development—scientifically and aesthetically. It is a perennial hope which can never be defeated by actuality. It is a timeless aspiration which gives meaning and illumination to human existence. It represents man's yearning for status and significance. It represents man approaching utopia if he has the faith and enthusiasm and the insight to anticipate the future with an open perspective.[2]

This broad view of education envelops far more than the mere acquisition of content. It involves an outlook upon life—man's faith in the control of his own destiny. We may infer also that Mayer is concerned with man's ability to view new ideas with an open mind.

London and Spinner look at education and its ends for the twenty-first century. They cite the information explosion which is upon us now in many aspects, and emphasize the need to develop critical thinkers.

> In the future information exploded world the primary need will be for critical people; all people must be critical. They will have to be critical so that

---

[1] Sidney Hook, *Education for Modern Man* (New York: The Dial Press, 1946), p. 2.
[2] *The Goals of Education* (Washington, D.C.: Public Affairs Press, 1960), p. 98.

they will be able to sort out the valid from the invalid information bombarding them. They will have to be critical so that they can discard old solutions and uncover the new ones demanded in a rapidly changing ever more complex society. They will have to be more critical of all proposed solutions because in our increasingly interrelated interdependent society all errors and mistakes will be more serious and the consequences more far-reaching. This need for critical people will encompass all areas of life—social, political, and economic. Business and industry, in other words, will need critical people—not personnel. They will need them in order to survive.[3]

The theme which is apparent in these three views of education is the need to develop independent, perceptive thinkers with powers of critical evaluation. Though the full meaning of the three statements encompasses far more than the province of this book, they do contain implied direction for the study of the content fields. They point emphatically to a broader base than the learning of content or skills only. They imply the need not only for developing knowledge through the skills but for the evolution of values within each individual. All three views note the need for an awareness of man, of his background and of the current knowledge developing around him. But this is not enough. Man must know how to use the knowledge to become critical and independent in his thinking.

These general statements of the aims of education can be related to the teaching of content and specifically to the teaching of reading in the content subjects. We must aim to:

1. help the students acquire a better understanding of the various facets of the society around them;
2. provide the background of knowledge about the history of peoples, the arts, ideas, discoveries and inventions which affect our ways of living—the heritage of the world's civilizations;
3. develop insights into and critical evaluation of the concerns and issues of society;
4. strive toward an understanding of the interdependence of science, nature, technology, society, and the individual;
5. enable the students to acquire basic knowledge which will lead to vocational skills;
6. develop the capacity of students to adapt to change and growth in information and institutions;
7. help the students in their use and understanding of the techniques of communication; and
8. strive with the students to develop their critical independent thought, their personal values, and a concern for the responsibilities of others as necessary prerequisites for intelligent democratic living.

These outcomes are intangibles. They involve the formulation of attitudes and the nature of the individual's perception of himself and of society. There is no

---

[3] Herbert London and Arnold Spinner, eds., *Education in the Twenty-first Century* (Danville, Illinois: The Interstate Printers & Publishers, Inc., 1969), pp. 8–9.

direct road to these outcomes. We cannot be sure that our teaching will guarantee them. We can, however, work toward them as the student becomes proficient in specific skills and can apply them in different situations.

The teacher will have to plan specifically for the accomplishment of these desired outcomes. Behavioral objectives in both the cognitive domain (those objectives which are concerned with the students' knowledge, its use and application, and its analysis or synthesis) and the affective domain (those objectives which are concerned with measuring the students' interests, attitudes, and values) will need to be stated, which will specify precisely what the teacher intends to accomplish in each lesson.

THE INTERRELATIONSHIPS OF THE LANGUAGE ARTS SKILLS

When the goals of teaching are accomplished, they seem to be reached through a series of steps. Fundamentally, the aims of content teaching evolve from the formulation of ideas which in turn are based upon information—knowledge.

The sources of knowledge are derived from both direct and indirect experiences which an individual has throughout his life. They stem from the activities of living in society, i.e., from discussion and interaction with others, actual experience, reading about information and men's activities, and from other sources encompassed by all of the communications media—television, films, radio, and pictures. Ideas seem to grow from internalization—the thinking an individual does about the information he has acquired.

In order to make effective use of these sources, the student needs competence in specific skills of communication and thinking. He needs to apply skills of language usage in speaking, listening, reading and writing. In fact, the student's degree of competence in the skills determines his level of effectiveness in the use of knowledge sources. Table 1 (below) shows the interrelationships of the language arts skills.

TABLE 1
SKILL CORRELATIONS

Speaking (doer)	*Listening* (receiver)
1. Knowledge of word sounds.	1. Recognize word sounds.
2. Knowledge of the meaning of words to express a specific thought.	2. Knowledge of the meaning of words used.
3. Understand how to formulate various sentence patterns and how to express meaning through them.	3. Understand how to get thought from various sentence patterns used.
4. Know how to speak coherently to express a desired meaning.	4. Understand conversation and denote the desired meaning.
Be able to speak to a main idea.	Note the main point (idea).
Organize ideas according to purpose.	Note the speaker's plan of organization.

Speaking (doer)

5. Include details to fit purpose and content of the communication.
6. Be able to support a main idea with appropriate details; have coherence among details.
7. Use clue words to indicate a pattern of thought.
8. Present information to indicate inference.
9. Foreshadow.
10. Choose words, idiomatic and/or figurative language to express thought.
11. Know purpose.

Reading (receiver)

1. Knowledge of word structure.
   meaning clues
   sound clues
2. Knowledge of the meanings of words.

3. Understand how to get thought from various sentence patterns.

4. Understand functions of sentences in paragraph; recognize logic of sentence arrangement.
   Recognize the main idea.
   Recognize paragraph types.

5. Read for details—note type and function.
6. See interrelationship of main ideas and details and of details to each other.
7. Note clue words indicating pattern of thought.
8. Note inferences.

9. Anticipate outcomes.
10. Note and understand styles of writing (figurative speech, metaphors, mood, etc.).
11. Recognize author's purpose, bias, type of structure.

Listening (receiver)

5. Listen for details—note type and function.
6. Listen for interrelationship of main ideas and details.
7. Note clue words that indicate a thought pattern.
8. Listen for information organized to indicate inference.
9. Anticipate outcomes.
10. Interpret figurative speech, idiomatic language.
11. Recognize purpose, bias.

Writing (doer)

1. Know how to spell words, prefixes, roots, suffixes, inflectional endings, syllables.
2. Knowledge of words to express a specific thought.
3. Understand how to formulate various sentence patterns; to express meaning through them.
4. Know how to arrange sentences in paragraphs to express a desired meaning.
   Be able to formulate a topic and/or main idea sentence.
   Understand paragraph types; be able to construct them.
5. Include details to fit purpose and content of paragraph.
6. Be able to support main idea with appropriate details; to relate similar details.
7. Use clue words to indicate pattern of thought.
8. Present information to indicate inference.
9. Foreshadow.
10. Choose words, idiomatic and/or figurative language to express thought.
11. Establish purpose, bias, type of structure.

THE FUNDAMENTAL PLACE OF LANGUAGE

Effectiveness in the skills of communication and thinking is intimately interwoven with effectiveness in the use of language. For instance, to understand a simple sentence, the student needs to understand the words used as well as the syntax of the sentence. In speaking and writing, his knowledge of language enables him to formulate the sentence. He needs to know which words to use, their proper order, and the interrelationship of the words in order to express precisely what he wishes. In listening and reading, the student needs the same basic skills except that he is not the originator but the receiver; he must perceive the meanings of the words and their interrelationship in order to comprehend the thought. Evelyn Jan-Tausch writes:

> The language-reading communication at the first level of "something taken in" involves the receiver (pupil), the sender (author) and the teacher who clears the lines for transmission of the message by careful assessment of both the receiver's capacity and the frequency level at which the sender is communicating. Without skillful intermediation on the teacher's part, the reading or communication may fail to occur or the message received will be garbled and misleading. Evaluation of the perceptual strengths of the receiver aids the teacher in selecting the appropriate method of conveying the message.[4]

In speaking of reading as language, the relationship of reading to the content fields is readily apparent. Each subject uses language in accordance with its own nature; it has its own mode of using a language. Word usage and structure are adapted to the ideas pertinent to a particular area. For instance, we know that the language in mathematics is terse and spartan with all important details connected by a specific relationship. Not so with a story which may be filled with descriptions designed to give the reader a general mood or tone, in which the individual details are not important.

Melvin Michaels noted in his study that students have difficulty in acquiring subject matter independently. His listing of students' reasons for their difficulties in various content fields shows, almost exclusively, problems with language.[5] It is interesting that the students did not say that the *facts* were incomprehensible. Rather, an analysis of the responses shows a high percentage of difficulty with both vocabulary and comprehension. We could deduce, then, that the major sources of difficulties students have in the content fields lie not in the disciplines themselves, but in the language used to express the information. If we could somehow circumvent language in the content fields, we might hope to eliminate difficulties in teaching the pertinent concepts. Obviously this cannot be the case. The ability to read is essential to success in school subjects, and the only solution is to help the student with the language used in each content field.

---

[4] "Reading as Language," *The Reading Teacher* XXIV, No. 2 (November 1970): 153.

[5] "Subject Reading Improvement: A Neglected Teaching Responsibility," *Journal of Reading* IX, No. 2 (October, 1965): 16–20.

Students may not be aware of the function of language when studying content. For purposeful study, they need to be made aware of the central role of language and the skills which enable them to use language. It is only as they understand the process of learning and the fundamental role of language that it is possible for them to see their relationship to the process of education. Beatty and Clark point out that "human learning is the changing of relations between a self and its perceived world as the self is expressed in striving to become adequate."[6]

APPLYING PRINCIPLES OF LEARNING TO READING

Coupled with competence in language are other conditions of learning. One is the individual's "striving to become adequate," the inborn motivation to learn. But the student must see the connection between what he is learning and the effect of the learning upon him as he responds to the world around him. This is basic to the development of interest. Further, his learning must relate to his background of knowledge obtained through many sources, the new information tied to that previously learned. Bruner writes:

> Let me suggest that in general, material that is organized in terms of a person's own interests and cognitive structures is material that has the best chance of being accessible in memory. That is to say, it is more likely to be placed along routes that are connected to one's own ways of intellectual travel.
> In sum, the very attitudes and activities that characterize "figuring out" or "discovering" things for oneself also seem to have the effect of making material more accessible in memory.[7]

There are many avenues open to the learner which can lead to discovery. He learns through participation in activities, from discussion with others, from observation, from listening, and from thinking about the situations which come to his attention. Reading is an imporant one of these avenues.

We are constantly bombarded with the idea that our society is a reading society—that to achieve one must be literate. We also learn and read that a child's success in school is aligned in large measure with his success in reading. Few in our society doubt this. Therefore, we need to gear our instruction to incorporate a mastery of reading all kinds of material. Smith and Dechant state that reading is so interrelated with the total educational process that educational success requires successful reading. They go on to say that experience has taught us that those who fail in school usually have failed first in reading.[8] Roma Gans expands this idea by

---

[6] Walcott H. Beatty and Rodney Clark, "A Self-concept Theory of Learning: A Learning Theory for Teachers," in *Readings in Educational Psychology,* ed. Henry Clay Lindgren (New York: John Wiley & Sons, Inc., 1968), p. 171.

[7] Jerome S. Bruner, "The Act of Discovery," in *Readings in Educational Psychology,* ed. Henry Clay Lindgren (New York: John Wiley & Sons, Inc., 1968), p. 193.

[8] Henry P. Smith and Emerald V. Dechant, *Psychology in Teaching Reading* (Englewood, N.J.: Prentice-Hall, Inc., 1961), p. 470.

saying that emphasis is on continuing one's quest for information and pursuing reading as a regular way of learning. She says this emphasis is relatively new but that
reading instruction must be planned to whet the appetite to read widely and carefully, and to read for decision making—all in a classroom atmosphere which develops the powers of thought.[9]

Effective teaching procedures follow two well-known principles of learning:
You must know how to incorporate principles of learning into daily teaching procedures; and, you must guide the students daily in techniques and habits of efficient
learning.

Obviously, since the skills of reading must be learned just as subject matter
must be learned, you will apply the principles of learning to the student's mastery
of the reading skills. Some principles of learning as they apply to reading are:

The Students Must Have a Purpose and a Motivation to Learn

This is very true in reading. A student who does not read because of a lack of
motivation does not get the practice he needs in reading skills. In such instances
any instruction he may get in the skills of reading will be of little use to him, since
practice is a necessary part of skill development. Having a purpose for reading is a
part of effective motivation. When the student reads to get some information—when
he has a purpose—he reads to that point. The effect upon comprehension when
there is a lack of both purpose and motivation is apparent.

Learning Must Have Meaning for the Learner

The goal of reading is to enable the reader to get meaning from the printed
material. The reader must be able to understand the information and to determine
its significance to himself. Though his motivation may be high and his purpose well
delineated, the reader will accomplish little if he fails to understand the ideas. Likewise, there is little point in a student being able to recognize the words if the meaning of them and the ideas shown through their interrelationship elude him. The
student reader despairs in this situation, and if he regularly fails to get meaning his
comprehension will suffer along with his motivation to read.

A Background of Experience and Knowledge is Necessary for Learning

New ideas must be connected to existing ideas and information. A background
that provides a basic understanding of the vocabulary and enables the student to
apply concrete illustrations of the new ideas forms the base on which he can build
the new information. This principle is of immense importance in making study
assignments. Further, the skills of interpretation and critical reading are more easily
applied when the reader has an experiential background in the subject about which
he is reading. He then has a base for comparison and evaluation.

The Learner Must Be Active in His Learning

Learning to read is not a passive process. It is nearly impossible to teach skills
to a student if he puts forth little or no effort. You can teach techniques but the

---

[9] "Greater Reading Power Needed Today," *Childhood Education* XXXVIII, No. 3 (November, 1961): 104–107.

student must practice and apply them. Fortunately, nearly all students do apply the techniques they are taught and are successful in getting meaning from the printed page.

Learning Requires the Forming of Habits

When a student learns how to use reading skills and how to attack a reading assignment he is learning techniques—habits—that will insure success and efficiency in his efforts. For the student to become an efficient reader, many of the skills must be so well developed that they function smoothly and simply. When a student reads he should not need to think about reading technique but rather concentrate on meaning. The technique should become so ingrained that it becomes automatic for him.

Much Learning Is By Association

Learning to read is no exception. The student learns first to use and understand language through listening and speaking. Reading is one additional form of using language. When he reads he recognizes the words and attaches meanings to them from his oral knowledge about them. Also, a new meaning for a word may be easier to remember if the student already knows the word by another meaning. An example is the word *revolution* as it is used in science (revolutions per minute) and in social studies (The French Revolution). Both meanings are different but both have an underlying similarity.

Learning Requires Practice

This is particularly true of learning to read. The student does not learn an effective reading technique merely by being shown. He must use it. It is the same as a coach telling and showing a baseball pitcher how to hold the ball in order to throw a curve. The pitcher has to practice what he has been shown if he is to become competent in the technique.

Favorable Attitudes Toward Learning Foster Effective Learning

Students who have difficulty in reading and who develop negative attitudes toward the reading act will find it difficult to use reading as an effective learning tool. Their whole mental set will oppose this avenue of learning.

Students Learn at Different Rates and in Different Modes

You cannot expect all students to have the same abilities, needs, and levels of reading. Humans vary in their traits, capabilities, and development, and the teacher must take these differences into account. Classroom procedure, to be effective for each student, must provide for each student's needs.

Learning is More Effective if the Learner Knows the Reason for What He Is Learning

In reading skill development the student needs to understand the importance and usefulness of each skill. He needs to understand how the skills can increase his reading competence. Such realizations will not only help his improvement in reading, but his motivation will also improve.

It would seem that the goal of reading instruction in school would be to develop in the student the competence needed for his independent efforts to acquire meaning from all kinds of printed material. Your goal, then, is to have the student become independent at the stage of development where you are involved with him. Such independence would consist of the ability to acquire understanding of the subject matter and to develop in interpretive, critical, and creative thought. The student must acquire the skills of obtaining information and then the habits of using the information in his thinking. A balance is needed in subject teaching between factual understanding and thinking beyond and about the facts.

BASIC PREMISES FOR TEACHING READING IN THE CONTENT AREAS

Four basic premises provide the underpinning for teaching reading in the content fields. If you accept them, you will have a philosophy and procedure to use in incorporating the teaching of reading into the teaching of content.

Reading in the Content Fields is Part of the Total School Reading Program

Two fundamental considerations are the bases for any viable school reading program. First, you must instruct in the skills of reading. Such instruction should be in printed material of all types of content and styles of writing. Second, the students need to apply the skills through a wide reading program. Skills themselves are not subject matter, but tools with which to obtain information. As with any skill, practice in the appropriate technique is necessary.

Reading in the content fields is but one part of a total program. Other parts of a school reading program would include: *first,* classes to teach the skills of reading which in the elementary school would be the classes where reading is taught as a subject, and in high school possible elective classes for those students, at all levels of reading, who wish to sharpen their skills; *second,* the application of reading in the content areas to expand the range of material so that skills can be further developed and applied; *third,* both a library program in the school and supplementary classroom collections to foster research skills and opportunities for wide reading; and *fourth,* provision for those students who need both corrective and remedial help. These four aspects of a total school program implement the dual prongs of skill teaching and wide reading.

All Teachers Are Responsible for Helping Students Read Their Specific Subject

This premise follows logically from the first. Logical reasoning about reading instruction in the content subjects points to the fact that the teacher, who has a background and expertise in a specific subject, is the one best qualified to adapt the reading skills to it. Reading cannot be taught in a vacuum. When instruction is given in the reading skills, the material must include some sort of information. The reading skills are supposed to help the student get from the language used by the author the information pertinent to the subject. Therefore, for instance, the mathematics teacher is the best qualified person to extract the mathematics content from the language used to express it and to show the student how to do so.

Further, it is generally accepted that a student's competence in a reading skill grows best when he is instructed in its use at the moment his need occurs. Therefore, when a student is reading a mathematics problem, help is needed at that time.

The Focus of Teaching Is Changed From Teaching Content to How to Read and Understand the Content

This premise has been implied in the first two in that the teaching of reading is not an activity separate from the content but a part of it. The procedure incorporates the techniques which show how information can be attained. You no longer teach just the "what" of content, but also the "how"; and of course, in teaching the students how to obtain the content the content itself is learned.

There is a Commonality of Skills in All Content Subjects Just as There is a Pertinent Application to Each Content Field

Obviously the basic techniques of learning vocabulary or of mastering essential points are essentially the same for each content field. However, the vocabulary in each field is different and the styles of writing peculiar to each content field suggest different approaches. For instance, the type of writing used in fiction is different from that used in the highly detailed factual prose of science. If a student learns how to find the main idea of a story, he may not be able to apply the same skill in studying science materials.

In 1957 L. L. Krantz conducted a study with ninth and eleventh graders to see which reading abilities would be predictive of later success in the content fields. A general conclusion was reached that study skills, comprehension, and vocabulary correlated highest with subject achievement in both grades. Krantz also showed that each area of content did require the use of certain skills which were specialized to that field.[10]

When you decide to incorporate the teaching of reading in your content area, you must undertake certain preparation. First, discern those reading skills which are pertinent to your subject and how they apply to it. Second, you need to know ways to diagnose each student's proficiency in applying the skills to your subject. Thus, you will know the skill emphases you need to make with each class. Finally, you need to evolve procedures for fusing the instruction in reading with the teaching of content. The procedures must enable you to accomplish your traditional charge to teach content as well as the additional charge of developing students' reading skill in the subject.

---

[10] "The relationship of reading abilities and basic skills of the elementary school to success in the interpretation of the content material in the high school," *Journal of Experimental Education* XXVI (1957): 97–114.

QUESTIONS AND PROBLEMS TO BE CONSIDERED IN REFERENCE TO YOUR OWN CLASSROOM

List A (For readers who are training to be teachers.)

1. List the behavioral objectives in both the cognitive and affective domains for each topical unit in your subject.
2. What skills of speaking, listening, reading, and writing must the student be able to use with competence in your subject?
3. Consider the implications of the statement, "Each subject teacher is a teacher of the language of his subject." How will the implementation of this statement affect your classroom teaching procedure?
4. Consider ways you may motivate the student to learn.
5. What degree of student independence in learning and student direction do you wish to achieve? What approaches will you use?
6. What provisions do you have for different learning rates and modes?

List B (For readers who are teaching.)

As you view your teaching, how would you answer the following questions:

1. What are your purposes? List specifically what you wish to accomplish.
2. How will you implement your purposes in your classroom procedure?
3. What skills do you plan to teach in reading, writing, speaking, and listening?
4. What background and skills do your students need for success in their study?
5. How will you relate your subject to the students so that they will see its relevance?
6. What degrees of student involvement do you plan? How will you develop and direct it?
7. How will you accommodate your teaching procedures to the differing needs of the students?

CHAPTER TWO

Effective Teaching
Through Diagnosis

Effective teaching encompasses more than the transfer of information from the teacher to the student. It also includes adjusting the instruction to the needs, desires, and capabilities of the students. Effective teaching requires diagnosis. You must investigate, determine needs, and plan for the optimum development of students. Information gained through diagnosis of the student's mode of learning, his strengths, and his limitations enables you to adjust both the content and method of instruction to the individual student. A balance must be maintained between the demands of subject mastery and the characteristics of the student. Good instruction must consider the individual, to fit the curriculum to him in the manner through which he learns best. This is not possible without diagnosis.

THE GENERAL NATURE OF DIAGNOSIS

In diagnosis we collect and judge relevant information about the student and his modality of learning. To be effective, diagnosis must be individual. Basically you want to know how the student learns. Then you have a basis on which to work in applying teaching procedures.

Diagnosis takes place in a continuum which ranges from daily teaching activities in the classroom to the highly technical investigations into deficiencies of the severely retarded reader. At one end of the continuum is the general appraisal of the student's daily classroom work and at the other end is the application of psycho-medical-educational tests in a clinical situation. There are levels or stages of diagnosis within the continuum. Strang listed seven:

1.   Information describing the student's reading performance obtained through classroom instruction and from informal and standardized reading tests.

2.   Investigation which seeks clues to other aspects of the student's behavior that influence his reading performance. Such clues are noted through observation, interviews and personality tests.

3.   An analysis of the student's reading process to note specific strengths and deficiencies so that specific remedial measures and practice can be prescribed.

4.   An analysis of mental abilities which underlie success in reading such as visual memory and association.

5.   A clinical analysis of personality traits and values which may provide insight into the student's reading performance and may indicate need for psychotherapy preliminary to or concomitant with reading instruction.

6.   Neurological examination to determine the possibility of brain damage.

7.   Introspective reports by the student stating his view of his reading difficulties and how he attempts to accomplish various reading tasks.[1]

Obviously, as a classroom teacher you do not perform diagnosis at all levels. The first level, that of providing diagnosis through daily classroom teaching, is well within your responsibility. Burnett makes a strong plea for the teacher as a diagnostician. He states that

effective classroom instruction can take place . . . because there is a teacher, who, within the framework of his classroom organization, is looking for individual problems that come up in the course of instruction. He varies his instructional approach enough from day to day to strengthen weaknesses that become apparent, and to expand and reinforce certain basic learnings that have been covered before but now need expansion and reinforcement. This effective kind of teaching approaches what has been called "diagnostic teaching."[2]

This level of diagnosis incorporates the factor of prevention. As we work with individuals and reteach, expand, and reinforce as necessary, possible areas of difficulty are corrected before they become remedial problems for the student.

Level two is also within the classroom teacher's province—especially the skillful observation and the interview. For both these techniques you need to know what to look for and how to interpret the evidence gathered.

The remainder of the levels, for the most part, require the time and technical skill which classroom teachers do not have. However, some may be able to begin an analysis of a student's reading strengths and weaknesses, specifically through

---

[1] Ruth Strang, *Reading Diagnosis and Remediation* (Newark, Delaware: International Reading Association, 1968), pp. 4–6.

[2] Richard W. Burnett, "The Classroom Teacher as a Diagnostician," in *Reading Diagnosis & Evaluation,* ed. Dorothy L. DeBoer. Vol. XIII, Part 4, Proceedings of the Thirteenth Annual Convention (Newark, Delaware: International Reading Association, 1970), p. 4.

purposeful classroom activities and evaluations. For instance, during class discussion you may begin to note areas of difficulty by identifying the skill needed to obtain answers to the most important questions asked during the session. This, of course, involves preplanning and an analysis of the reading material.

Level seven can be used to gain insight into the student's mode of reading. In answering questions about how he arrives at an answer, the student helps you gain insight into the method he uses for obtaining and using information. Melnick states

> Among the insights revealing reading proficiency, the teacher may note evidence of the following:
>
> 1. The student's approach to a reading passage;
> 2. His tendency to relate ideas rather than merely seize on isolated details;
> 3. His ability to uncover the author's pattern of thought;
> 4. His ability to organize and show the relation among details;
> 5. His tendency to let his emotions or prejudices and personal experiences influence his comprehension;
> 6. His tendency to relate what he reads to other knowledge he has gained;
> 7. His ability to communicate in writing what he has gained from reading.
>
> Diagnostic questions, then, reveal rather than conceal individual differences.[3]

The classroom teacher is involved with all the students, the superior readers as well as the average and the remedial. The more technical levels (levels three through six) are aimed mostly toward the analysis of the remedial minority of the student body. Our concern in this volume is principally diagnosis for all students and how we may gear our instruction to each individual student.

PRINCIPLES OF DIAGNOSIS

The principles or criteria for producing purposeful and valid diagnosis are basic philosophy implemented by habits of classroom practice.

1. Instruction must be pertinent to each individual child; therefore, diagnosis must also be individual.
2. Diagnosis is continuous and must be paced with the student's development. The individual student is not static but is constantly changing. Instruction for each individual must keep pace with the change.
3. Diagnosis assesses all aspects of the student's physical, mental, and psychological being as they relate to his reading ability. Some reading difficulties may be a manifestation of a deficiency in some other area. For instance, a severe eye difficulty may be a strong contributor to a reading problem. Similarly a negative self-concept may be manifested in the student's failure to progress in reading in accordance with his potential.

---

[3] Amelia Melnik, "Questions: An Instructional-Diagnostic Tool," *Journal of Reading* II, No. 7 (April, 1968): 512.

4. You must understand the limitations of measuring instruments and use discretion in the interpretation of findings. Measuring instruments are not perfect—there is a margin of error. At best even a standardized test gives only an indication of the student's level and areas of strength and weakness. We need to realize that some students do not perform well on a test because of anxiety. The interpretation of diagnostic findings extend beyond those of standardized testing.

5. Diagnosis must determine the general nature of the problem. It seeks to discern the specific areas of difficulty in reading and the degree of the difficulties. Concomitants to the reading problem, such as psychological, medical or environmental conditions, should also be determined if they seem to be causative of the reading difficulty.

6. Diagnosis should indicate where the student can be treated. The degree and nature of the reading difficulty should indicate, within the limitation of the school and the community, where the difficulty can best be treated —regular classroom remedial reading, clinic, or outside agency.

7. The diagnosis should indicate how improvement can be brought about effectively. Suggestions should evolve which give direction to the type of instruction needed, and the type and level of materials to be used.

PRECAUTIONS IN DIAGNOSIS

Diagnosis of each individual student is a personal interaction between the teacher and the student. It should be a mutual seeking for successful corrective action. The student should not be kept ignorant of the diagnostic findings nor authoritatively advised of the corrective plan of action. Rather, you should explain the results to him and involve him in the most logical and profitable alternatives for correction. Indeed, student progress in correcting reading deficiencies increases when he knows what he has to do and the reasons for it, especially if he has been given the opportunity to think constructively about the diagnostic findings.

There are specific precautions for insuring successful diagnosis with the student. They point to an understanding of the personal relationship, with expertise in professional technique. The basic precautions seem to be:

1. *Establish rapport with the student.*   The child should not see the diagnostician as an inquisitor but rather as a calm, helpful, and positive person. The diagnostician should enlist the student's cooperation and interest by being objective, realistic, and hopeful. An anxious student usually will not perform accurately in the diagnostic sessions. Informal techniques should be used in such cases to abate any anxiety.

2. *Study the learning situation as well as the student.*   Note the level of material where the student performs well and where he has difficulty. Note his reactions to the various activities of the diagnosis and note how he attacks words, performs a reading task, and how he implements reading skills.

3. *Take nothing for granted.*   Check on all possible areas, no matter how minute, which may have a bearing on the student's difficulty. No diagnostician jumps to conclusions. Base all conclusions on definite evidence.

4. *Observe traits and habits shown through testing and conversation.*   An ineffective attack on a reading selection can be noted by observing the student in the process of reading. Conversation with the student helps to ascertain his attitude toward reading, his goals, desires, anxieties, and his interests.

5. *Keep written records of the diagnosis.*   The need for records should be obvious. Results of individual diagnosis cannot be trusted to memory. They also provide a basis for measuring the development of the student.

6. *Help the student to analyze his problem.*   You will both get insights: the student about reading and his problem in relation to it and you a better understanding of his mode of thinking.

7. *Use several different types of tests.*   Accuracy in diagnosis is increased when you have more than one source of information about the student's reading status and needs. One may help to explain and/or reinforce the other. Standardized and nonstandardized tests should be used.

METHODS OF APPRAISAL

A complete diagnosis uses many different instruments and techniques of measure, both formal and informal, objective and subjective. Among the many instruments you may have access to or use are:

standard tests
informal tests
school record of progress, developmental history
observation
interview
daily schedule
autobiography

Standardized Tests

The principal purpose of diagnostic testing is to provide a source of information for use in planning relevant instruction for the student. The program chosen must be closely related to the findings of the diagnosis. Standardized tests are one source of information. Even when the primary purpose of the testing is for evaluation, if you are perceptive you will find information which points toward the mode of instruction to be used in the classroom.

A student's answer sheet from a standardized test can reveal more than just a total score of the test or the subscores of the parts. An analysis of the student's incorrect responses, item by item, will show the type of question on which the student has difficulty. Many test manuals include an item-by-item analysis of the test questions that indicate the specific skill the student needs to use for each question.

By noting the student's incorrect responses and the skills the student evidently did not use properly, you can plan programs of instruction in various groupings. It is possible that a class deficiency may be noted, and groups of students showing the same needs will almost certainly be noted. This will give you information which suggests different classroom groupings as appropriate to both level and need.

Another diagnositc use of standardized test scores is in providing insight to the student about his strengths and weaknesses. It is very revealing to a student to see his answer sheet and to plot, or see already plotted, his profile. It gives him a realistic and objective picture of his reading performance. He can see if he really has a reading problem and what the nature of it is. He can note those skills where he is competent, and those where he needs practice. Checking the item-by-item analysis of the questions with the student reveals much about his reading status. Also important, he begins to learn about the reading process and about some of the skills which compose it. Such knowledge can aid his self-direction and motivation.

Though standardized tests can provide diagnostic information for instructional guidance, they are not foolproof and do have specific limitations. Here teachers must be cautious. The test may provide inaccurate scores in measuring a student's reading ability for a number of reasons:

1. It may overestimate the student's reading ability which you will discover when you note the student's inability to read successfully at the grade level of his test score.
2. It may lose validity at certain age levels or competence levels. For instance, a test may fail to measure adequately the reading abilities of a highly competent student because its ceiling is too low.
3. Comparable forms of the same test may not be parallel, thereby failing to show accurate gains or losses.
4. Student guessing may unduly raise scores.
5. The student's speed of work may affect the score as indicated by the slow thorough and accurate student who completes only a portion of the test and thereby gets a low score.
6. The norms for evaluating the score may be based on a population not comparable with your students.
7. An individual's performance differs from day to day because of extraneous causes, thereby affecting the score.
8. Only a limited number of reading skills are measured by any one test. This is particularly true of the skills as applied to the content fields.

The sole use of standardized tests does not comprise a complete diagnosis. The limitations inherent in them preclude this. You must be careful to interpret the results with discretion.

Most of the tests give scores showing general reading comprehension—fiction, factual material, or both—vocabulary, and speed. Very few investigate all of the pertinent skills of any specific content area, though some do have relevant subtests of that type. Some of the most appropriate diagnostic tests for content areas are:

1. *Diagnostic Reading Tests,* by the Committee on Diagnostic Reading, Frances Oralind Triggs, Chairman. (Published by the Committee on Diagnostic Testing, Inc. at Mountain Home, North Carolina, 28758.) The range extends from the K-4 level, lower level (grades 4-8), and upper level (grades 7-13). The lower level is published in four forms (A,B,C, and D) and the upper level is published in four forms (A,B,C, and D) for the diagnostic battery. The test is also published as a survey test which has eight forms (A,B,C,D,E,F,G, and H). The diagnostic sections are untimed while the survey sections take from 40 to 80 minutes.

The upper level survey sections yield a measure of the student's comprehension, vocabulary, and rate of reading. The lower level includes the same general reading skills plus word recognition. For diagnostic purposes the general areas may be further assessed in more detail. At both levels the vocabulary section provides scores on words per minute; general vocabulary; vocabulary comprehension; specialized English literature, mathematics, science, and social studies vocabulary. The rates of reading sections give separate measures of speeded and unspeeded rate of general reading, social studies, and science materials.

2. *Appraisal of Reading Versatility,* by Arthur S. McDonald, Sister Mary Alodia, George Zimny, Stanford E. Taylor, and James Byrne. Published by McGraw-Hill Publishing Company, Educational Developmental Laboratories, Inc. The range extends from basic (grades 6-10) to advanced (grades 11-16 and adults). The basic forms are AA and BB, advanced forms, CC and DD. The testing time is 15-30 minutes. This test measures the student's reading flexibility by comparing the pupil's rate of reading under different sets of instructions.

3. *Iowa Silent Reading Tests, New Edition,* by Harry A. Greene, A. N. Jorgensen, and Victor H. Kelley. Published by Harcourt, Brace and World, Inc. It ranges from elementary (grades 4-8) to advanced (grades 9-13). There are four forms: AM (Revised), BM (Revised), CM and DM. The testing time required is 49 minutes for the elementary level and 45 minutes for the advanced level. This is a group test which measures the student's reading proficiency in work-study type materials. Both levels give subscores on rate, comprehension, directed reading, word meaning, paragraph comprehension, and sentence meaning. In addition the elementary levels include subscores on location of information, alphabetizing, use of index, and the selection of key words.

4. *SRA Reading Record,* by Guy T. Buswell. Published by Science Research Associates. It has one form and ranges from grades 6-12. The testing time is 26 minutes. It consists of subtests yielding scores on reading rate, comprehension, and everyday reading skills: paragraph, directory, map-table-graph, advertisement and index reading. The vocabulary score consists of technical vocabulary, sentence meaning and general vocabulary.

5. *The Traxler High School Reading Test,* by Arthur E. Traxler. Published by the Bobbs-Merrill Company, Inc., Test Division. There are two forms (A and B) and a range from grades 10-12. The testing time is 45-50 minutes. Three subscores are given: reading rate, story comprehension, and main ideas in paragraphs.

6. *The Traxler Silent Reading Test,* also published by the Bobbs-Merrill Co., Inc., for grades 7-10 has four forms (1, 2, 3, and 4). Testing time is 46 minutes. Four subscores are derived: reading rate, story comprehension, word meaning, and power of comprehension.

The brief descriptions of these tests raise two considerations for the classroom teacher. One is that none of them measure all of the skills pertinent to any one content area. The other is that all of them contain subtests which measure skills pertinent to one or more content areas. While you can obtain some diagnostic measures of the student's competence in a few of the skills pertinent to some content areas, there are not any which will give a thorough diagnosis. Therefore, you will need to supplement the standardized tests with informal teacher-made tests.

Informal Teacher-Made Tests

The easiest way for you to find out how students read the materials assigned in class is to make up a test using the material which will be read and studied by the students. Such a group test can be devised for each content field to test the student's competence in such skills as using parts of the book, arriving at word meanings through context, noting main ideas and gaining information from pictorial representations—maps, pictures, graphs, charts. Surveying how the student is able to handle his assigned classroom material is a prerequisite to diagnostic teaching.

The teacher-made group test has many advantages. First, it provides immediate diagnostic information. Second, it can be scheduled whenever you are ready for it. There is no wait for a school-wide testing program or for answer sheets to come back from machine scoring. Third, the teacher-made test is based on material which the student will use and is, therefore, more pertinent. Often the material of commercial and/or standardized tests is not closely related to the type the student reads in class. Fourth, the group test is geared to instruction. You formulate the questions, hence they are similar to those you will ask in assignments to elicit certain understandings. Thereby, you can note a clear relationship between the student responses on the test and the responses he makes in class. Fifth, the test is easy to score. It is wise not to assign any grade to the test but to use it only in noting the students' strengths and weaknesses. Thus, have the students correct their own test in class with discussion about accuracy and appropriateness of specific responses. Sixth, the test becomes a teaching instrument. As specific responses are discussed in class, much teaching can be accomplished informally. For instance, an entire lesson may not be needed for an explanation of the difference between an index and a table of contents. A simple explanation pertinent to one question on the test will often suffice. Also, analyzing specific student responses to various comprehension questions will help to point out the need for using language with more precision. This will help the student develop skill in using language accurately and in seeing when a word has been used improperly. Seventh, the test aids the student in his own self-appraisal. As he corrects his own paper, he sees immediately, and at a time when his motivation is highest, what his strengths and weaknesses in the skills are. Eighth, similar tests can be administered throughout the school year to determine progress. Such knowledge is a strong motivating factor as the student sees his progess.

These tests are quite easy to devise. Though the first one may require some time, subsequent tests become easy and quick to make. There are two areas on which you may need some background. The first is to ascertain those skills which should be tested. The second is to formulate questions pertinent to the skill being investigated. This second consideration is not an awesome one, and becomes easier as you identify the relationship of skill and question.

Detailed directions for making and administering the group tests, called *inventories,* are included here to give specifics from which to work out your own questions.

English—Group Reading Inventory

Directions for the diagnostic survey test are based on an English literature textbook.

I. Use between 34-40 questions.

II. Use questions designed to measure the following reading skills in the proportions shown below.
  A. Using parts of the book (3 questions in all)
    1. Table of Contents
    2. Index of Titles
    3. Glossary
    4. Biographical Data
    5. Introductory paragraph to story
  B. Vocabulary needs
    1. Meaning (7-8 questions)
      a. General background of word meanings
        (1) select correct meaning from several dictionary meanings
        (2) antonyms, synonyms
      b. Contextual meanings
    2. Word recognition and attack (14-15 questions)
      a. Divide words into syllables
      b. Designate the accented syllable
      c. Note and give meaning of prefixes and suffixes
      d. Changing the part of speech of a word (noun to verb, adjective to adverb, etc.)

C.   Comprehension (11-12 questions)
1.   Noting the main idea
2.   Recalling pertinent supporting details
3.   Drawing conclusions, inferences
4.   Noting the sequence of ideas

D.   Reading rate. Have student note the time it takes for him to read the selection. Then, figure reading speed in words per minute.

Example: Words in selection: 4000

Time to read: 10 minutes

$$\frac{4000}{10} \quad \text{equals} \quad 400 \text{ words per minute}$$

Time may be recorded by student noting clock time for starting and stopping or by teacher recording time on blackboard every 30 seconds (1′, 1′30″, 2′, etc.)

E.   Skimming to locate information (2-5 questions)
Use selection different from the one used for comprehension and speed purposes.

III.   Choose a reading selection of not more than four pages.

IV.   In administering the inventory:

A.   Explain the purpose of the inventory and the reading skills it is designed to measure. When the inventory is given, advise the students which skill is being measured.

B.   Read each question twice.

C.   Questions on the use of the parts of a book are asked first. Students will use their books.

D.   Introduce the reading selection, establishing necessary background on the topic and giving the students a question to guide their reading.

E.   Read selection silently. Note and figure speed.

F.   Ask questions on vocabulary. Students will use book for questions measuring ability to determine meaning from context. They will not use the book for other vocabulary questions, and these should be written on the blackboard.

H.   Skimming. Use a new selection. Books will be used.

V.   A student is considered to be deficient in any one specific skill if he answers more than one out of three questions incorrectly, or more than two incorrectly when there are more than three questions measuring a specific skill.

VI.   This inventory, being administered to a group, does not establish a grade level. Nonetheless, anyone scoring above 90 per cent may be considered to be reading material too easy for him. Anyone scoring below 65 per cent may be considered to be reading material too difficult for him. If the material is suitable, the scores should range between 70-90 per cent.

VII.   Form of tabulation of results—see page 30.

VIII. Sample Form of Inventory

Parts
of
book

1. "On what page does the unit (section) entitled *Exploring One World* begin?"
2. "What section of your book would you use to find out something about the author of a story in the book?" (Determines knowledge of section on biographical data.)
3. "In what part of the book can you find the meaning of a word that you might not know?" (Determines knowledge of glossary.)

Introduce
story

Explore student background of experiences on the subject of the story and set up purpose questions. Students read silently. Time required is noted.

Vocabulary

4. "What is meant by the word *crab* as it is used in the story (line_____, column_____, page_____)?"

Contextual
meaning

5. "What is meant by the word *eliminated* (line_____, column_____, page_____)?"

Synonyms and
antonyms

6. "What word means the opposite of *temporary?*"
7. "Use another word to describe the coach when he looked amazed."

General knowledge
of meaning

8. "Select the proper meaning of the word *entice*."
    a.   to lure, persuade
    b.   to force
    c.   to ask
    d.   to caution
9. "Select the proper meaning of the word *initial*."
    a.   the last or end
    b.   the beginning or first
    c.   the middle
    d.   a letter of the alphabet
10. "Select the proper meaning of the word *rectify*."
    a.   to do wrong
    b.   to make right
    c.   to destroy
    d.   a priest's home

Word Recognition:
syllabication;
accents

"Divide the following words into syllables and show which syllable is accented:"
11–12. eliminated
13–14. amazed
15–16. undemocratic
17–18. fraternities

Prefixes and suffixes	19.	"What does the prefix *un* mean as used in *undemocratic?*"
	20.	"What is meant by *pre* in the word *prescription?*"
	21.	"Change the verb *astonish* to a noun."
	22.	"Change the noun *boy* to an adjective."
	23.	"Change the adjective *democratic* to a noun."
	24.	"Change the adjective *slow* to an adverb."

Comprehension: 25.   "What is a_____? What happened when_____?"

main ideas;   26.   (Such questions as applicable here; ask for
27.   only the main points of the story.)

details   28.   (Questions to ask for specific bits of information
29.   about the principal characters or
30.   ideas of the material.)

Drawing conclusions; inferences   31.   (Questions, the answers to which are not completely
32.   found in the textbook. Questions beginning with "why,"
33.   making comparisons, or predicting what may happen. e.g. "Why did Bottle imagine he could perform such astounding athletic feats as setting the state high school record in jumping?")

Sequence   34.   (May be omitted.) Questions asking what happened as
35.   a result of_____, what steps did the police use to solve the mystery, etc.

Skimming   36.   Use a new reading selection. (Questions designed to
37.   have the pupil locate some specific bit of information)

Social Studies—Group Reading Inventory

Directions for the diagnostic survey test are based on a social studies textbook.

I.   Use between 26–30 questions.

II.   Write questions designed to measure the following reading skills in the proportions shown below.
   A.   Using parts of the book (5 questions)
   B.   Using resource (library) materials (4 questions)
   C.   Using maps, pictures, charts, etc. (4 questions)
   D.   Vocabulary (3 questions)
   E.   Noting the main idea (3 questions)
   F.   Noting pertinent supporting details (3 questions)
   G.   Drawing conclusions (3 questions)
   H.   Noting the organization of the material (1 question)

III.   Choose a reading selection of not more than 3–4 pages.

IV.   Have questions of skills D through H—vocabulary, main ideas, details, conclusions, and organization—based on the reading selection.

V. In administering the inventory:
   A. Explain to the pupils the purpose of the test and the reading skills the test is designed to measure. As the test is given, let the students know the skill being measured.
   B. Read each question twice.
   C. Write the page reference of each question on the blackboard as the question is read if the student is to refer to the textbook.

VI. A student is considered to be deficient in any of the skills if he gets more than one question in any of the skills wrong.

VII. Sample form of Inventory

Parts of book

1. "On what page would you find the map that shows (name of map)?" (Shows use of map table found in front of book.)
2. "On what page does Chapter _____ begin? What is the title of the unit of which it is a part?" (Shows use of Table of Contents.)
3. "How can the introduction on pages _____ help you in your study?" (Shows understanding of unit introduction.)
4. "Of what value are the questions, activities, and vocabulary shown on pages _____ to you for understanding the material in the textbook?" (Shows understanding of specific textbook study aids.)
5. "In what part of the book would you look to find the page references of this topic: _____?" (Shows purpose of index.)

Use of Resources

6. "What library aid will tell you the library number of the book, _____, so that you would be able to find it on the shelves?" (Shows knowledge of card catalog function.)
7. "What is a biography?" (Shows knowledge of one type of reference book.)
8. "Name one set of encyclopedias. How are the topics in them arranged?" (Shows knowledge of a type of reference material.)
9. "Name a library guide that will help you find a specific magazine article. If you were to give a report in class and you knew that most of your information would be in current magazines, what guide would you use that would tell you what magazine(s) and what issue of it to use for information on your topic?" (Shows knowledge of a type of library guide to research.)

Use of maps, charts, etc.

10. "What does the map on page _____ show you?" (Shows an understanding of fundamental idea on map.)

11. "What do the black areas (or some other feature) shown on the map on page _____ represent?" (Shows ability to read information from a map.)

12. "Turn to page _____."
    Ask for some specific bit of information that is shown by the chart. Example: chart showing organization of federal government—"What are the three branches of our federal government?" (Shows ability to understand charts, diagrams.)

13. "Turn to page_____."
    Ask for some specific bit of information that is shown by the picture. Ask also for interpretation. Example: picture showing sod house on the prairie—"What is the settler's house made of? Can you tell why that type of building material is used?" (Shows ability to understand and interpret picture.)

"Read pages _____."

Understanding vocabulary

14. "Define _____."

15. "What did So and So mean when he said_____?" (word or term to be defined from the comment must be pointed out) (Contextual meanings)

16. "What is a _____?"

Noting main ideas

17. Questions to ask for only the main points of
18. information—main ideas of the longer important
19. paragraphs.

Noting details

20. Questions to ask for specific bits of information about
21. the principle characters or ideas of the
22. material.

Drawing conclusions

23. Questions, the answers to which are not completely
24. found in the text. Questions beginning with "why",
25. making comparisons, predicting events, measure drawing conclusions. Example: "Why did the pioneers brave the dangers to move west?"

Seeing organization

26. "Each author follows an outline in writing the information in your textbook. In looking through Chapter (one from which the reading selection was taken) write down the author's first main topic." or "If you were to outline the material that you have read, what would be the I, II, III main topics of your outline?"

Science—Group Reading Inventory

Directions for the diagnostic survey test are based on any science textbook.

I.   Use approximately 30 questions.

II. Write questions designed to measure the following reading skills in proportions as shown:
   A. Using parts of the book (4 questions)
   B. Using resource (library) materials (3 questions)
   C. Using vocabulary (4 questions)
   D. Noting the main idea (4 questions)
   E. Noting pertinent supporting details (4 questions)
   F. Following directions (3 questions)
   G. Drawing conclusions (3 questions)
   H. Applying theoretical information (3 questions)
   J. Understanding formulas and equations (3 questions)

III. Choose a reading selection of not more than three pages.

IV. Have questions on skills C, D, E, G, and H—vocabulary, main ideas, details, conclusions, application—based on the reading selection. Items F and J may be based on this or another reading selection.

V. Explain the purpose of the inventory and the reading skills the inventory is designed to measure. As the inventory is given, let the students know the skill being measured.

VI. Read each question twice.

VII. Write the page reference of each question on the blackboard as the question is read.

VIII. Have the pupil score his own paper.

IX. A student is considered to be deficient in any of the skills if he gets more than one question in any of the skills wrong.

X. Sample form of Inventory

Parts of Book

1. "On what page would you find the chapter entitled _____?" (Shows use of table of contents.)
2. "Of what value to you are the questions under the chapter section titled _____?" (Shows understanding of specific textbook study aids.)
3. "How are the chapters arranged or grouped?" (Shows organization of textbook understanding.)
4. "What sections of the book would you use to find the page reference of the topic _____?" (Shows knowledge of purpose of the index.)

Library

5. "How are topics arranged in a reference book?" (Shows knowledge of organization of reference book under consideration.)
6. "What is a biography?" (Shows knowledge of a type of reference material.)

7. "Explain the difference between science fiction and science factual materials." (Shows knowledge of important types of science reading materials.)

"Read pages _____."

Vocabulary

8. (For contextual meanings—Example: "Turn to page
9. ____, line ____. How is the word used by the author?"
10. For recall—Example: "What does this word mean?" or
11. "Use this word in a sentence." or "What is the word I have just defined?")

Main ideas

12. "What is a _____?" (Questions to ask for only the
13. main points of information—main ideas of a longer
14. paragraph; Chapter headings, subheadings, marginal
15. headings, introduction and summary.)

Pertinent details

16. (Questions to ask for specific bits of information about
17. the principle, definition and laws such as descriptive
18. words, aspect of a process, applications of a law, or
19. principle steps in an experiment, life cycle, life of a scientist. Use words that select the relative importance of details—how author shows the importance of specific details. All similar details are grouped around one main idea—each main idea has its qualifying details.)

Following directions

20. (Questions to show sequence of steps or ideas
21. for solving a problem or performing an experi-
22. ment.

Drawing conclusions

23. (Questions, the answers to which are not completely
24. found in the textbook. Questions beginning with
25. "why," asking for the significance of a finding, deciding the value of the finding of an experiment, or the implication of a description of some species or natural phenomena. Cause and effect. What happens if certain natural conditions are present, comparing two or more chemicals, telling chief likenesses, etc.)

Application

26. (Questions that show how scientific laws and principles
27. can be put to practical use, often the same as drawing
28. conclusion questions showing significance.)

Formulas, symbols

29. (Questions showing meanings attached to symbols as
30. given or used in textbook.)

Mathematics—Group Reading Inventory

Directions for the diagnostic survey test are based on a mathematics textbook.

I. Each subject in the mathematics area will require its own constellation of skills. Generally, the skills to be included are listed here.

    A.   Reading verbal problems and stating them in one's own words.
    B.   Adjusting one's reading to the requirements of the problem.
    C.   Translating words into symbols.
    D.   Knowing the meaning of symbols.
    E.   Understanding vocabulary.
    F.   Noting the relationship in formulas and equations.
    G.   Obtaining information from charts, tables, and graphs.

II.   Explain the purpose of the inventory and the reading skills it is to measure. As the inventory is given, let the students know the skill being measured.

III.   It will not be possible to administer this inventory orally. It will have to be duplicated. If there are questions to measure the students' ability to understand explanations in their textbook, and in using special features in their textbook, they should be referred to specific pages in the textbook as necessary.

IV.   Sample form of Inventory (four to five questions per skill)

Restating verbal problems	Use typical verbal problems for the subject. Have students read the problems and write the situations posed by them. Questions may ask also for what is given and what is asked for (detailed reading). Questions which ask students to note the basic mathematical processes may also be used (interpretive reading).
Adjusting one's reading	Students may be asked to state how they would read specific problems, what steps they would use, whether they would read rapidly or slowly, or how they think the reading of mathematical problems differs from story-type reading.
Translating words to symbols	Ask students to underline the words and phrases in a problem that should be converted into mathematical notations. The appropriate symbol may be required of specific words or phrases.
Knowing symbol meanings	Give specific symbols and have the students write the meanings of each.
Understanding vocabulary	Include questions of both generalized and specialized vocabularies. Specifically these would include:

          1.   words representing ideas of quantity (big, bigger, long, wide, etc.).
          2.   words used to represent number figures.
          3.   words used to represent number processes.
          4.   words used to represent kinds of measurement.
          5.   general terms (plus, minus, more than, increased by).
          6.   specialized technical words (radius, isosceles).

Noting relationship in formulae and equations	Use a problem and have the students express the relationship in the form of a formula or equation. Also, an equation may be used expressing the relationship in words.
Obtaining information from charts, tables, and graphs*	Reproduce charts, tables, and graphs and ask questions requiring the pupils to use the graphic representations. Present a problem and have students make a graphic representation of it.

As students score their own papers, they see for themselves their strengths and areas of difficulty in reading the classroom material. As they correct their inventories, they tabulate on the front of the paper the number wrong (or right, as preferred) for each specific skill. They can readily see how they measure up in each skill. The total score is not as important as the subscores for each skill. If a student scores below 65 percent, however, further diagnosis of his difficulties is needed. The teacher may assume that such a score indicates the need for easier material.

You can easily make a class profile as shown below:

Name of Class _____ Section _____ Teacher _____

Comments

Use of parts of books, Vocabulary, Meaning, Contextual meanings, Synonyms and antonyms, General knowledge, Word recognition, Syllabication, Accent, Prefixes and suffixes, Part of speech, Main ideas, Supporting details, Drawing conclusions, Sequence of ideas, Skimming, Speed in wpm

Name

Jones, J.

Brown, R.   (Check wherever pupil is deficient)

When reading the summary chart horizontally, the skill needs of each individual are shown. When reading vertically, class patterns are indicated. For instance, only certain students may show the need for specific instruction in getting the main idea while the entire class may show a weakness in vocabulary. A clear rationale for grouping according to need is provided and the skill instruction needed for the class becomes clear.

---

* The English, science and social studies inventories have been reproduced by the late Dr. Ruth Strang with my permission in *Diagnostic Teaching of Reading*, McGraw-Hill Book Co., 1964. The social studies and science inventories were first included respectively in *Teaching Reading in the Social Studies* and *Teaching Reading in Science*, by the author, Harper & Row Publishers, 1960.

The purpose of the inventory is to provide a basis for determining emphases in instruction. It is diagnostic—there is no other purpose. It is not intended to compare students, classes, teachers, or to assign the student a grade.

Techniques of Diagnosis Other Than Testing

Diagnosis should help fit your instruction to the student. There should not be a period of diagnosis with instruction delayed; in the classroom you continually diagnose and teach to the findings. As the student performs in class each day, you should be aware of the level and nature of his performance. You may see that you need more information. Then, you will use other techniques.

Observation. One other technique available to you is a keen observation of the student as he reads, studies, and participates in classroom activities. You will glean much general information by alert observation for specific purposes. You may watch to see
–how the student approaches an assignment,
–how he applies the techniques of study, such as survey, in reading,
–how well he is able to read to find the main idea or to note how information is organized,
–how well he is able to ascertain the meanings of new or unfamiliar words,
–whether or not he is able to use context clues,
–whether he knows how to use locational skills in a book, and
–whether he can use reference skills.
The specific purposes of your observation will largely be determined by the nature of the work in class and the students' response to it.

Observation, like many other techniques, will be more useful if you keep a systematic record of each observation. One method some teachers have used is a weekly graph showing the names of the students with spaces opposite for each day of the week.

Week of ＿＿＿＿＿＿＿＿＿＿ Mon. Tues. Wed. Thurs. Fri.

Names ＿＿＿＿＿＿＿＿＿＿

You may have such graphs dittoed as soon as class enrollment has stabilized at the beginning of the school year. By using a code of your own invention, you can note the results of observation immediately. For instance, if the student is having trouble with questions requiring noting the main idea, you may record on the chart "−MI." If the student is competent in this skill, the notation could be "+MI." In another instance, if the student does not survey before he reads, the notation might be "−survey." Or, if vocabulary is the problem, the notation may be "+voc" or more detailed "−voc—context," or "−WR:syll" (needs word recognition, syllabication help).

One of the greatest values of such a daily record is the information you have readily available for planning the next day's instruction. It is not expected that a comment would be recorded for each student each day, but only as you note signals from the student as shown by his activities in class. Some students may respond in such a manner that you record many observations. Other students may conduct themselves in ways that do not instigate your specific observation. These are the students who perform adequately but who do not stand out from the group. By keeping a chart of observations, you can see very quickly which students do not readily instigate the need for observation. You can plan to observe some performances of these students as well, thus fostering individualization of instruction.

Another value of the observation and record technique is the pattern of student development which becomes apparent over the period of a school year or semester. You can see student progress in many specific ways. Chronic and/or new needs will also be noted. Continual observations are needed to note the growth of the student and the changes which have been made in his whole being. Observations of a past performance are of interest to you only as information which may be helpful in understanding the student's present performance in class.

Observations are very subjective and there are several cautions to keep in mind when using the observation technique. Your educational philosophy and first impression of the student may color the type of observations you make. Also, the observations will occur in only one segment of the student's life. More information from other sources will be needed, and when your observations are combined with other data, strengths, weaknesses, interests, and attitudes will become apparent.

Talking with Students. During the school day you may find opportunities to talk with students individually or in small groups. Such opportunities may occur while the students are working on an assignment or project, immediately before or after a class period or the school day, or by special appointment. Since there is usually no intensive probing, these conversations cannot be considered interviews with the students. In fact, they are often very casual. But if you are attuned to opportunities for talking with students, you will find that such conversations can have diagnostic value.

Meeting with students and listening to their concerns, fears, desires, problems, and opinions can provide much insight into their behavior, attitudes, and accomplishments. You may note a student's attitude toward school, and toward reading in particular. You may uncover his concerns and fears about his school work or other problems both in and out of school. Recreational interests, study habits, voluntary reading, and vocational desires can be ascertained. Such information can be used in planning some of the emphases you may wish to make in the subject curriculum. For instance, in a history class, a student who is interested in costume design may find a project on the manner of dress during various periods of history interesting and worthwhile; this would, in turn, give him practice in the various reading-research skills.

Conversations with students can reveal little or much depending on your alertness. You must be willing to *listen*. The conversation is not a time for you to lecture or moralize. Your comments and questions should help the student to crystallize his ideas; they should be stated simply and should show respect for him.

You should try to understand his point of view, respect his opinions, and be willing to explore ideas with him.

Other observations may be combined with the conversation. You can observe much about his habits, concept of self, and relations with others by noting personal appearance (cleanliness, appropriateness of dress, posture, expressive movements of hands and face, and mannerisms), pitch, rapidity, and articulateness of speech, attitude (cooperative or hostile), and reactions to problems and situations in his everyday experience.

Cumulative School Records.   The greatest value of the cumulative school record is in the information about the previous development of the child with its resultant clues for seeing the student as a unique individual. The summary of academic progress, medical history, pertinent family background, special problems and attributes of the student over the years, and former teacher evaluations as well as accounts of past interviews with parents will enable you to gain an early knowledge of the student. This information is available before you meet the student for the first time.

There can be dangers in relying excessively on cumulative information. You must realize that the student is a developing person, and that his past needs and problems may not be his current ones. Some teachers, in order not to be conditioned by a student's record, refuse to consult it. This is not wise. You should regard the historical development of the student as a means of gaining insight into his current needs. You should also realize that the cumulative records do not preclude additional information and insights which will be obtained from daily contact.

Daily Schedule.   If a student complains about not having enough time to read or study, you may suggest that he keep a daily record of his activities to see how he spends his time. Such a record can be kept for a day, a weekend, or a week, with each day divided into half or whole hour segments. Such a schedule can be very revealing to both of you. The student is often amazed to see how he spends his time; and, you can quickly see what kind of reading he does, whether an inordinate amount of time is spent on homework, or whether the student is overloaded with outside activities and responsibilities. Once such a record is kept, both of you will be better able to formulate plans for a more efficient and productive use of his time.

Student Analysis of His Reading—The Autobiography.   The student is aware of his own reading development, and if given the opportunity, he can provide you with much information. Through an autobiography, he can give you insight into specific problems pertinent to reading by his own analysis of his skills and techniques. This autobiography should be a confidential report. It may be guided by such questions as

–What is your problem in reading as you see it?
–Can you give the history of your learning to read since you entered school?
–When did you first begin to learn to read?
–What do you think is necessary to improve your reading, or to overcome your difficulties?

–How much time outside of school do you spend reading?

–What kinds of books and materials do you like to read?

–What do you do when you find you do not know a word when you are reading?

–How do you find the main idea of a paragraph, a chapter?

As a classroom teacher, you will obtain most of your diagnostic information through the classroom. You must teach more than content. Your teaching must investigate how the student gets and relates to the content. Then you are better able to guide him in techniques of reading and study as well as to instruct toward mastery of the content. Diagnostic teaching shows concern for the student. It requires working with him as a partner in the learning process where you both work toward the common goal of his greater competence.

QUESTIONS AND PROBLEMS TO BE CONSIDERED IN REFERENCE TO YOUR OWN CLASSROOM

List A (For readers who are training to be teachers.)

1. Explain the relationship between continuous diagnosis and diagnostic teaching. Evolve ways to implement the relationship.
2. Prepare an informal inventory for your subject area.
3. Choose a topic and formulate questions which would require competence in a specific skill.
4. Determine how you would establish rapport with a student.
5. After giving an informal inventory, you note that one group of students seem to have difficulty in noting main ideas while another is weak in vocabulary. How would you plan classroom procedure to accommodate the weaknesses?
6. In your classroom diagnosis, what would be the conditions that would indicate the need for referral to (a) the reading teacher, (b) the guidance counselor, (c) the department head or supervisor, (d) the school nurse, (e) the parent, (f) the principal, or (g) a combination of persons tested?
7. If your students are reading basically and generally at the secondary school level, what should be your major concern—to increase level or to correct and develop specific skill areas? Explain reasons for your choice.

List B (For readers who are teaching.)

1. As you plan each day's lesson, note (1) how you will continue diagnosis and (2) how you will implement information attained from diagnostic teaching of previous days.
2. Prepare a chart for your class for recording observations.
3. Prepare an informal inventory for your subject area.

4. Formulate questions on the current topic you are teaching the students which would require competence in a specific skill.
5. Set up your program as a teacher for the complete diagnosis you need for your classroom teaching.
6. Work out an item analysis of the standardized achievement test given in your school. Apply your analysis to a student who shows some deficiencies.

CHAPTER THREE

Vocabulary Meaning and Word Analysis

Competence in the reading skills is basic if the student is to develop independence in obtaining information from printed matter. A skill is an acquired ability to use one's knowledge effectively. The knowledge of how to perform a skill and its effective application develop neither by instinct nor by chance. Instruction must be given and guided practice in the application must be provided. The responsibility for providing instruction and practice rests with the classroom teacher.

You, the content teacher, are traditionally concerned about the student's acquisition and understanding of information. In addition, you must be concerned about the techniques the student uses to acquire the information. Much of the effectiveness and thoroughness of a student's understanding is directly related to his level of development in using the reading skills.

In this chapter, the skills common to all of the content areas will be discussed, with suggestions for their implementation in the classroom. These basic skills include vocabulary and comprehension—literal, interpretative, critical and creative.

VOCABULARY

All content teachers will readily attest that vocabulary competence is of paramount importance in the student's mastery of content. Vocabulary consists of the language of the subject which governs the student's ability not only to communicate ideas pertinent to the subject, but also to think abstractly in it. His understanding of the concepts or ideas which the vocabulary labels—a full understanding of the words—insures a basic competence in the subject matter.

REASONS FOR POOR VOCABULARY

Many students appear to be weak in their vocabulary knowledge. They may show an overall competence in reading but, relative to the other skills, vocabulary often seems to be the weakest area. The weakness ranges from complete ignorance of words to a superficial and narrow knowledge of them. Reasons for the weakness may be several. One may be the student's association with people who use a meager collection of words, and seldom discuss ideas. Havighurst discusses the impact of social backgrounds upon disadvantaged school children:

> They lack a family conversational experience that answers their questions and encourages them to ask questions; extends their vocabulary with new words, in particular adjectives and adverbs; and gives them a right and a need to stand up for and to explain their point of view on the world.[1]

This statement could also apply to individuals other than those considered to be disadvantaged.

If such is the case, you should use words which both communicate and stretch the student's vocabulary. One teacher made it a practice to use certain key words in her speech that were basically synonymous. For instance she would say, "What factors or conditions impeded, hindered, interrupted, or caused a snag to _____?" Rephrasing questions and statements helps to attune the student's ear to the sound of less familiar words.

Another cause of insufficient vocabulary is narrow interests, often the result of a meagre background of experience. As the teacher succeeds in enriching the student's background and stimulating his interests, vocabulary will develop too, as the student is exposed to new words and uses them to think about his experiences and to communicate them to others.

Another reason for a poor vocabulary may be the lack of voluntary reading. This tends to keep the student's background narrow and to deprive him of experiencing words of differing shades of meaning. Faulty habits may result in stifling vocabulary growth; skipping over difficult words, failure to use context, sole dependence on others or on class discussion for word meanings, and the dislike of using the dictionary all are habits individual students may exhibit. Finally, of course, low intelligence may be the cause. Words are abstractions—those representing ideas are intangibles which the slow learner may find extremely difficult to fathom. Concrete representations of the word concepts are necessary for the slow learner.

Teachers who are alert to their students' backgrounds, capabilities, and habits can note any of these causes of vocabulary weakness in the individual student. But this is not enough. What can be done about the weaknesses? How can the student's vocabulary be enlarged in scope and in precision? We need now to consider the

---

[1] Robert J. Havighurst, "Social Backgrounds: Their Impact on School Children," in *Reading for the Disadvantaged,* ed. Thomas W. Horn (New York: Harcourt, Brace & World, Inc., 1970), p. 15.

bases and principles of vocabulary development, some of which have already been inferred. Then we need to consider specific classroom techniques.

THE BASES OF VOCABULARY DEVELOPMENT

In the narrow view we are concerned here about the student's reading vocabulary. In the broad view, we are concerned about his language facility, for reading is just one of the interrelated communication skills of reading, writing, speaking, and listening. Mastery in language usage requires the user not only to listen and read with discrimination and insight, but also to use language in speaking and writing with clarity and precision. The scope and depth of the student's vocabulary determine his level of articulation, and contribute greatly to his level of comprehension when reading.

Harris points out that vocabulary is one of the most significant aspects of language development. The ability to communicate with others by means of verbal symbols is the most distinct human characteristic.[2] We may also say that a distinct human characteristic is the ability to study and acquire information which can be used in adjusting to the demands of society. It is through words that we are able to communicate and to think. Words are the labels we give to thoughts, ideas, concepts, impressions. In fact, Brown maintains that word power is thought power and therefore should be given more attention throughout both formal and informal education.[3] If words play the vital role Brown says they do, then a major responsibility of all content teachers is apparent.

The effective development of vocabulary is directly related to the ability to conceptualize. Therefore, if a student is to think rather than to memorize by rote, he must understand the ideas represented by the word labels. This is not easily accomplished. The development of a concept requires an adequate experiential base by the reader, precise accurate writing by the author, and a communication between the two.

Nor is a concept easy to define. The dictionary meaning suggests that it is a thought, an idea, a mental image of an action or a thing. Marksheffel defines concept as the "systematic organization of the total meaning that one has for any idea, process, person, thing, place or word."[4] Russell adds that a concept involves discrimination, generalization and symbolization.[5] Concept development is an individual matter. Each person must discriminate, generalize and use the appropriate symbolization if he is to develop the concept for himself. A simple illustration of

---

[2] Albert J. Harris, "Development of Vocabulary—Language Development," in *Readings on Reading Instruction,* ed. Albert J. Harris (New York: David McKay Company, Inc., 1963), p. 236.

[3] James I. Brown, "Vocabulary & Key to Communication," in *Readings on Reading Instruction,* ed. Albert J. Harris (New York: David McKay Company, Inc., 1963), p. 262.

[4] Ned D. Marksheffel, *Better Reading in the Secondary School* (New York: The Ronald Press Co., 1966), p. 242.

[5] David H. Russell, *Children Learn to Read, 2nd ed.* (Boston: Ginn & Co., 1961), p. 273.

this is the concept of the term *Prime Meridian*. Basic to the idea of this term is the concept of meridian. The learner distinguishes the meridian from latitude and sees any meridian as a possible line of longitude since the meridian is an imaginary line going north and south from pole to pole. On the other hand, the meridian is the highest point of the sun during the day at whatever spot on the earth the person is. This is the noon hour meaning that the day is at its half-way mark—halfway between sunrise and sunset. The learner would need to *discriminate* between meridian and latitude and also between meridian and longitude since the meridian has a more precise and personal meaning than the general term of longitude. He would note the use of the Prime Meridian (at Greenwich, England) as the starting point for measuring degrees of longitude east and west on the earth. He would generalize as he notes the interrelationship between meridian, prime meridian, and longitude— that all are different in a precise way, but that they all have a common element— placing an imaginary line north and south through the poles to note either time of the day or distance east and west. The symbolization in this example is the word to label the appropriate and precise idea: *longitude, meridian,* or *Prime Meridian*.

We know that concepts are not static. They grow and develop as we add information and experience to our background. Suppose the student learns the differences and common elements of the terms *meridian, longitude,* and *Prime Meridian*. He may discover in a study of astronomy another application of the basic meaning—a great circle of the celestial sphere which passes through the poles and the highest point of a given place in the sphere. The concept is continually enriched and defined as the student adds meanings from many different sources. The teacher does not develop a concept totally and completely in one lesson. He merely establishes the basic meanings which then enable the student to further discriminate and generalize.

The student develops concepts both from direct activities (experiences) he has with living and nonliving aspects of the world about him, and from information he acquires through viewing, hearing, and reading. Marksheffel points out the sources of conceptual development very plainly.

> Thus we see that the child first develops his concepts from direct experiences and then as he learns the language, he has an additional aid for acquiring concepts. How do concepts and language development affect his reading? It is most important to understand that a child's success in learning to read and his growth in reading are determined to a large extent by his total background of experience, his meanings, concepts, and language. We must never forget that basic direct experiences are vital to the initial development of concepts; but once established, they need to be supplemented by a myriad of indirect experiences.
>
> Reading will provide the child with innumerable experiences that can be gained in no other way. Without vicarious, or indirect, experiences man's concepts, language, and thinking would be irrevocably restricted to his immediate environment.[6]

---

[6] Marksheffel, pp. 243–244.

Thus we see an important reason for developing student competence in reading differing types of informational material.

The sources of concepts, particularly the vicarious sources, determine the accuracy of the concepts. Concepts can be narrow, inaccurate, or completely false. Hence, the development of critical thinking and reading becomes a necessary part of learning.

A concept is the basis for vocabulary development and, as such, is basic to comprehension. It is the individual mental construct a student develops. It is labelled by a word. The word, however, is not the concept. It is merely the representation of the concept used by the student for his own thought. When meaning is understood, then only the label needs to be provided, and vocabulary development is the logical result.

PRINCIPLES OF VOCABULARY DEVELOPMENT

Vocabulary study can be dull or exciting. Much depends upon your attitude. If the student is asked to look up a list of ten to twenty words before each major reading assignment and then to write these words in sentences, it is likely that most of the students will look upon vocabulary study as a drudge. But if you introduce a few words at a time, discuss their uses and how they affect meaning, and weave them into your discussion, interest will likely increase. The students' attitude toward vocabulary development, reflecting your attitude and the nature of the assignment, can mean his success or failure in reading.

General procedural principles are inherent in any successful vocabulary program. Under these principles the specific activities can be used with a firm hope of success.

1. *Make vocabulary development an activity that permeates the entire program of study.* In class discussions, for instance, always search for the precise term such as the distinction between *round* and *spherical* when describing a shape. Discuss interesting etymologies when appropriate such as the origin of the word *chauvinism.* Help to give the students an appreciation of the functions of words in language by requiring precision as they think and communicate.

2. *Create enthusiasm for vocabulary growth.* Your enthusiasm is contagious. Play with words by adding prefixes, suffixes, inflectional endings, forming acronyms, etc.; show how specific words have emotional impact and affect meaning. Say the same idea in different ways. For instance, what different impressions are created by the following statements?

> The man is fat.
> The man is obese.
> The man is roly-poly.
> The man is robust.

There are many activities that can be used but the most important element is to enjoy and have fun with words.

3. *Attack verbosity.* High school pupils, because of their age and hence their familiarity with language patterns, verbalize very well. They may even fool us on some occasions by creating the impression that they know what they are talking about. Actually, they often have only a hazy, indistinct idea. Pin the verbalizers down. Have them explain their statements. Ask them to be more specific or to explain their idea by using other words. Discuss why their statements are too broad or too narrow to be precise.

4. *Use new words repeatedly in conversation.* As a concept is developed in class, provide the word which labels or describes it. Introducing a few words at a time enables you and the students to keep them in mind as class discussion proceeds. Then weave them into the discussion when appropriate. A student begins to feel familiar with words when they are used in language constructs of his own making.

5. *Anticipate concepts and the appropriate words in the introduction of a reading assignment.* For instance, if the students are to read a selection about ecology, *ecology* is the concept and the word which must be introduced and basically developed; it is at this point that the new concept is tied to some past experience. Enrichment of the concept will develop as the student reads and the information is discussed in class.

6. *When introducing a new concept and its label, proceed from the known to the unknown* by using familiar words; remembering appropriate past experiences; reinforcing through demonstrations, illustrations, or actual objects; and by using audio-visual aids such as films, recordings, and strip films.

7. *Introduce the dictionary as a source book of interesting information.* Provide practice in the use of the dictionary to increase the student's proficiency with it. Interest in words usually develops interest in source materials such as the dictionary and the thesaurus. The level of competence in the use of these materials governs their voluntary use.

8. *Develop within the student the idea that success in his vocabulary growth depends on his assuming responsibility for it.* Standards of precision in communication and thought plus a fascination with words will do much to develop the student's interest in his own vocabulary development. However, this interest does not develop quickly, but rather, builds slowly throughout the student's school years.

TYPES OF VOCABULARY PERTINENT TO THE CONTENT FIELDS

The vocabulary of the various content fields arranges itself into three groupings. One is the general vocabulary—words which may have application in general communication and may apply to more than one field. We associate these words with general and nontechnical writing but they may appear in technical writing as well. For instance, in a statement such as "The king of the country was an obese and arrogant monarch," *obese* and *arrogant* are examples of general words used with social studies material.

The second group includes a nonspecific and general type of word which may have a precise meaning in a given field of study. Such a word would be *court*—to court a lady (general), to be presented to the court (social studies), to play tennis on a court (physical education). Though the student may be able to call the word he may not know the specific meaning in the context in which he finds it.

The technical terms of a content field comprise the third group. These are the words usually considered when vocabulary in the content fields is studied. An example would be *photosynthesis* (biology), *integer* (mathematics), or *federalism* (social studies). Each field of study has its peculiar vocabulary.

An added dimension of the use of general words that may give students difficulty is the connotative meaning we give to many of the words in our language. The connotative use is different from its recognized dictionary (denotative) meaning. It is the use of a word for its emotional impact when another word might impart the same idea but without the emotional charge. For instance, "The speaker delivered a sincere presentation of the topic," has much less emotional impact than "The speaker harangued the audience." Words may be used that have a symbolic association for us such as *gold* or *sunrise* when we mean something other than the actual denoted meaning. Words are often used in this manner by propagandists and editorialists. The connotative use of words is one way language can be employed to influence people.

Suggested Activities for Classroom Procedure

Specific suggestions for vocabulary development which follow are activities which can be incorporated into your lesson procedure.

1. Use as many first-hand experiences as possible, particularly in teaching concrete items or situations. For example, when a new word representing a tool or a piece of equipment is introduced, show the tool or equipment. In social studies, for instance, the concept of law may be illustrated by classroom and school rules. In developing such a concept, the reasons for the rules, who made the rules, and so on would likely stimulate much discussion that may also begin to add to such concepts as forms of governance, and the responsibilities and privileges of citizens. In mathematics, actual models of shapes such as a cylinder, a polygon, etc., can be shown. To the alert teacher the opportunities in all subject areas are many for establishing the meanings of specific vocabulary concretely.

2. Use pictures, objects, dramatizations and audio-visual aids to give concrete illustrations of a word. Many textbooks contain illustrations and diagrams which explain concepts. See examples on pp. 45–46.

3. Discuss the concepts for which the words are labels. Explain them; help the students to relate them to past experiences. For example, ask the students what a word means to them. Note their definitions and/or illustrations of the word; check the meaning from the textbook or dictionary. Note the similarities or dissimilarities of the student meaning and the textbook meaning. Have the students give illustrations of the word from their own background.

4. Alert students to context by working with them in making an intelligent guess about a word's meaning by the way it is used in a sentence. Examples from three textbooks follow.

At the bottom of the zone of aeration, some water is held in tiny tube-like openings in the rock by **capillary** (kap' e ler ee) **attraction.** *A capillary is a fine, hairlike tube which is capable of holding liquids because of the attraction between molecules of a liquid and a solid.* Water is held in the small openings between rock grains in much the same way because of the attraction of the rock for the water.[7]

Two plane angles or two dihedral angles are **complementary** *if and only if the sum of their degree measures is* 90. Each is the *complement* of the other member of the pair.[8]

Some areas have voting machines which eliminate the tedious counting of paper ballots. The machine has all the choices clearly marked on it, and you vote by pulling the appropriate levers. Just as you may vote for candidates of either party on paper ballots, machines also often make it possible for you to vote for either *a straight party ticket—everyone in the same party—*or a *split ticket—some candidates from one party, some from another.* The totals for each candidate are automatically registered inside the machines. Whether you vote by ballot or by machine, you may usually write in the name of a candidate not listed on the official ballot.[9]

5.   Provide a study of antonyms and synonyms. Develop precision by noting the possible slight differences of meaning or the different application of the synonymous terms. For instance, a *dwelling* is where a person or a family lives. A *home* is also such a place, but has the additional aspect of meaning concerning interrelationship of family members. However, home and dwelling can be said to be synonymous. Other examples abound in the various subject areas: tyranny-dictatorship, section-class, cell-compartment, immunity-exemption. Antonyms tend to be less subtle as in conservation-waste, and collection-appropriation.

6.   Study prefixes and how they alter the meaning of the root word. Show the relation of suffixes to the function of a word in a sentence. For instance the words *information* and *inform* have the same root and basic meaning. Their functions in a sentence differ. Information is the knowledge or the subject matter of communication. Inform is the act of communicating knowledge. One is a noun, the other a verb. Another variation is to build words by adding suffixes: *nature, natural, naturally.* A discussion of the differences among these words which have the same root would alert students to precision of meaning by the function of the word in a sentence. The first is the phenomenon, the noun. The second "pertains to" the phenomenon of nature and is an adjective. The third indicates how and is an adverb.

7.   Encourage wide reading as a means of providing the students with various instances and variations of word usage. Though this activity is unstructured in helping students to learn words, the reader will find the use of words with multi mean-

---

[7] Margaret S. Bishop, Phyllis G. Lewis, and Richmond L. Bronaugh, Consultant, *Focus on Earth Science* (Columbus, Ohio: Charles E. Merrill Publishing Co., 1969), p. 271.

[8] Goodwin, et. al., p. 118.

[9] Miriam Roher Resnick and Lillian Herlich Nerenberg, *American Government in Action* (Columbus, Ohio: Charles E. Merrill Publishing Co., 1969), pp. 112–113.

DIHEDRAL ANGLES

Should we define angles formed by planes, or by lines and planes? Euclidean geometry evolved, in part at least, from an attempt to provide a mathematical model of our physical world. It therefore seems reasonable to develop a model in our system for the "angles" formed by two walls of a room, the roof and sidewall of a house, or the two slopes of a ridged (gable) roof. There are many other examples to illustrate why we say that intersecting planes, or lines and planes, form angles.

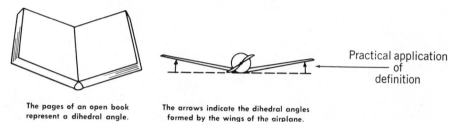

Practical application of definition

The pages of an open book represent a dihedral angle.

The arrows indicate the dihedral angles formed by the wings of the airplane.

Figure 3–3   Figure 3–4

3.01   A dihedral angle is the union of a line and two half-planes having the line as their common edge. The half-planes are called the *faces* of the angle and their common edge is called the *edge* of the angle.

Definition

A dihedral angle is denoted by naming a point in each face and two points of the edge. The two points of the edge are always the middle letters. The dihedral angle in Figure 3-5 is denoted by $\angle O\text{-}NM\text{-}L$.

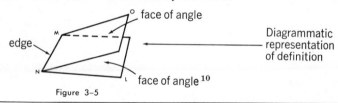

edge

face of angle

Diagrammatic representation of definition

face of angle [10]

Figure 3–5

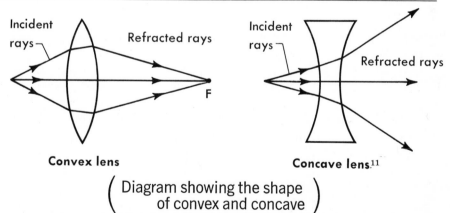

Incident rays

Refracted rays

Incident rays

Refracted rays

F

Convex lens   **Concave lens.[11]**

$\left(\begin{array}{c}\text{Diagram showing the shape}\\\text{of convex and concave}\end{array}\right)$

---

[10] A. Wilson Goodwin, Glen D. Vannatta and F. Joe Crosswhite, *Geometry* (Columbus, Ohio: Charles E. Merrill Publishing Co., 1970), p. 55.

[11] Charles H. Heimler and Jack Price, *Focus on Physical Science* (Columbus, Ohio: Charles E. Merrill Publishing Co., 1969), p. 130.

One of the finest features of frontier life was the spirit of good will and helpfulness that prevailed among most settlers. A family without friends might arrive at a piece of land only to find that within a matter of hours other settlers were helping to clear land or build their home. Below is shown a houseraising. Often groups of frontier farmers built houses in two days.[12]

ings. For example, the student may find the word *food* used as a means of nourishment, as provender, as diet, as a type—bread or meat, as board, as a ration.

8.   Encourage interest in words through the discussion of idiomatic phrases, figurative language, and interesting word origins. For example, what is meant if someone is described as "slightly touched?" What type of action is described in the sentence, "He came forward like a two ton truck"? What is the history of such words as *chauvinism* and *pasteurization*?

9.   Keep notebook records of:
   a.   new words the students meet and learn.
   b.   words relating to special subjects.
   c.   words relating to hobbies.
   d.   new uses and additional meanings of familiar words.

---

[12] Landis R. Heller, Jr. and Norris W. Potter, *One Nation Indivisible* (Columbus, Ohio: Charles E. Merrill Publishing Co., 1971), p. 231.

e.   substitutes for overworked words.

f.   words that describe or characterize particular persons, objects, or situations.

g.   words appealing to the senses—those contributing to sensory imagery while reading.

h.   idiomatic phrases.

10.   Substitute specific words for general and overworked words used by your students. The teacher may note overworked words in student compositions. For instance an overuse of the word *said* may be apparent in student short stories. In order to have students note other words which could indicate story characters speaking, referral to books they are reading might be required in which they would list all the ways authors indicate a character's conversation. From this a class listing could be compiled to which the students could refer as they write subsequent stories.

11.   Replace slang with legitimate words. Sometimes students are interested in the reverse of this activity. The class might decide to compile their own slang dictionary.

12.   Think of all the words that can be used to describe an object, a time, a person, or a situation. This is effective in a class discussion. This activity can be embellished in a number of ways. After an exhaustive listing of adjectives has been compiled, students may determine which would be best suited if they were to compose advertising copy—which words tend to have connotative or emotional overtones, which words would give a negative picture. Yet, since all could apply to the object, none of the specific descriptions would be inaccurate. Such may serve as a good introduction to the "card-stacking" technique of propaganda.

13.   Rewrite a paragraph using different words to compare with the original. Note the function of specific words which give the paragraph the desired meaning or impact. A variation of this is to rewrite the paragraph to keep the same meaning, but present a different point of view through use of connotative words. Or, in social studies, a paragraph may be rewritten to give different points of view.

14.   Point out words that denote categories such as *tree* under which many types can be listed. This idea can be used in the subject areas as a means of outlining the new vocabulary to show the organization of information. A variation could require the students to match people, places, and events—ideas from terms found at the ends of a chapter or a unit. For example:

Thomas Paine—Common Sense
minutemen   —Lexington, Concord

15.   Find substitute for pet expressions.

16.   Note words which give impressions or appeal to the emotions.

17.   Keep a classroom dictionary of new words pertinent to the subject. This can be a class project by rotating groups which can become a resource for the class. The dictionary can be a growing reference book for the class, and as elaborate as you wish to make it. It is usually a looseleaf notebook with a page for each word. The word is defined with all appropriate definitions listed. Various forms of the word can be listed showing prefixes and suffixes, and inflectional endings added.

Examples of the word used in different sentences to show changes in contextual meaning can be shown. It may be graphically illustrated when appropriate. A history of the word may also be included.

18.   Have the students keep a vocabulary file of new words on index cards. Determine the type of information to be recorded on each card—meanings, form of the word, etymology, pronunciation, examples of usage, etc. Use one card for each word. The cards may be organized in various ways: alphabetically or according to subject unit or categories.

19.   Match words with pictures to show the meaning of the word. Students may be directed to find pictures which would show the meanings of such words as ruin, destruction, variation, reflection, balance, tetrahedron, excruciating pain, ecstacy, and so on.

20.   Rewrite slanted headlines and articles taking out the words appealing to the emotions. Material for this activity will be found in newspapers, magazines, and trade books about various current topics. In the social studies, such material can be located by using original sources or writings contemporary with periods of history.

21.   Note differences in connotation of words which are basically synonymous—*wise, smart, shrewd, adroit, clever, astute, devious, sly.*

22.   Write advertising copy for some product, choosing words to give different impressions of the products.

23.   Have the students note jargon and determine a more succinct statement; for instance, changing "met with the approval of the principal" to the more succinct "the principal approved."

24.   Note euphemisms such as *funeral director* for *undertaker.*

25.   Note words which may imply a symbolic meaning different from their denotations; e.g., *sunrise:* hope, beginning, new, freshness.

26.   Note acronyms. Many acronymic words are being devised, particularly in science and the social studies. Such words as *radar, sonar, laser, Nato,* and *Vista* are examples.

27.   Devise vocabulary "bees," crossword puzzles, dictionary races, vocabulary games where knowledge of words is the skill of the game.

28.   Use questioning to elicit student understanding of words:
   a.   What is the key word in this heading? Why?
   b.   What does _____ mean as used in this sentence?
   c.   What other meanings do you already know for _____?
   d.   What does the glossary in your book say about _____?
   e.   How many meanings does your dictionary give for _____?
   f.   Which meaning is appropriate in this selection?
   g.   What other words may be substituted for this word?

29.   Discuss indefinite words such as *few, many, any, large, small, little, much, some, several, most.* Students should realize that these words do not convey precise meanings.

30.   Discuss definite words such as *all, always, certain, every, sure, never, right, true, whole.* Alert students to their effect on the meaning of a sentence.

31.   Investigate and discuss the history of the English language, its changing form and its various levels of usage—slang, informal English, formal English, technical language. Investigate obsolete but still legitimate words such as *flivver, galluses, celluloid.*

There are several methods of vocabulary study which can help vocabulary development: memorization of word lists, wide reading, study of word histories, use of context, use of the dictionary, and prefix-root analysis. But no one of these methods is adequate when used alone without consideration of the student's needs and interests. McDonald summarizes the key aspects and benefits of a viable vocabulary program:

> Thus, a functional vocabulary program will provide each student with words he needs in such a way that he can master the conceptual categories they represent. The program will be multi-dimensional, drawing on all of the traditional methods *where appropriate* and in ways consonant with the principles of learning. As an outcome, the student will be able to guess at meanings of unfamiliar words, using one or more methods as appropriate. He will check the guess with the meaning of the whole and (where necessary) with the dictionary. He will look for familiar words used in unfamiliar ways and so gradually extend the range of referent attributes symbolized by each word.[13]

WORD ANALYSIS AT THE HIGH SCHOOL LEVEL

The skills of word analysis comprise the methods which a reader uses to recognize and pronounce a word. Word analysis is also intrinsically interwoven with word meaning. Indeed, it would be difficult to teach the meaning of a word without investigating the root, its affixes and the sentence use. Many teachers have commented, "They (the students) just can't read the word." For the students who are deficient in such a basic skill, all of the skills of understanding the printed materials are affected. It is quite evident that the competence of the student in his analysis of words determines in large measure the size of his vocabulary, and hence his ability to understand what he reads and to exchange ideas.

Options Readers Can Use for Recognition of Words

There are several methods of word analysis a high school student can use either singly or in combination. They are:
contextual clues—how the word is used in a sentence.
phonic analysis—how the word is broken into its sound components.
structural analysis—how the word is built from units of meaning—root, prefix, suffix, inflectional endings.

---

[13] Arthur S. McDonald, "Vocabulary Development: Facts, Fallacies and Programs," in *Teaching Reading in High School: Selected Articles,* ed. Robert Karlin (New York: The Bobbs-Merrill Company, Inc., 1969), p. 166.

dictionary—the reference which is the key to both pronunciation and meaning when other methods do not help.

combination of methods—these methods are listed somewhat in the order of use by the reader.

The reader will, at first, attempt to recognize the word in question by its contextual use. If he knows how to pronounce it and is successful with the contextual method, he need go no further. However, if he is not sure of the pronunciation and/or is not sure about the meaning, he will resort to phonic and structural analysis. He will attempt to divide the word into syllables, give appropriate letter-symbol relationship to each syllable, and use his knowledge of where the accent usually falls. He may also analyze the word to note the root and the affixes to it, determining the meaning as he is able for each part. If he is successful, he will see if the word, as he has analyzed it, fits contextually. If it does, he will go no further. If not, he will consult the dictionary. Again, he will need to fit the appropriate meaning into the sentence. The reader in actual practice uses all of the methods, checking one against the other.

In the primary grades other means of word analysis would also be included, such as the sight method and configuration. The sight method, commonly called "look and say," is a rote memorization of the printed symbol of the word that is in the pupil's speaking vocabulary. The other method, configuration, is the peculiar shape of the word which seems to be of some help to the beginning reader. Neither of these methods is used to any great extent at the high school level.

However, we must recognize that the high school student does use the sight method. Once he has analyzed a word and knows its pronunciation and meaning, the word becomes a sight word. Effective readers do not analyze every word anew each time they meet it. Consequently as the reader increases his knowledge of words and his scope of reading, he will find fewer and fewer words he must analyze.

When a mature reader analyzes a word, he does it quickly, using the various options open to him in combination simultaneously, not stopping to label for himself the method(s) being employed. To get the student to this point of expertise continual review and reteaching must be interwoven into the presentation of vocabulary in each subject area. It is well to remember that the various methods of word analysis are taught in the elementary grades, but they are applied only to the simpler words the student needs at the time. The more complex and polysyllabic words from the subject areas at the high school level are not taught. The high school student will often need help with the words he is expected to recognize.

Contextual Analysis

Contextual analysis has often been characterized as "intelligent guessing" by the reader. It is a quick and valid technique but not adequate as the only method. The student's ability to use this method is dependent upon his background in the subject—that is, his degree of general knowledge of the subject determines how well he is able to supply the unknown word. Also, his general knowledge of language usage such as the function of the word in the sentence helps him to determine the proper pronunciation and function of a word. For instance,

"The king will present a land grant to the explorer."
(verb)

"The land grant was a present from the king to the explorer."
(noun)

One application of contextual analysis is the student's noting the meanings of technical words in his textbooks. Most new words are defined in the material when they are first used. The student will have to note a clue to expect the meaning when the word first appears in the printed material in italics or boldface print. For example, *"Oxides* (ahk′ sieds) are also important minerals, but much less common than either silicates or carbonates. **Oxides** are combinations of oxygen and some other element."[14] In two sentences the student finds a basic definition of oxides. The word is highlighted by both italics and boldface print. The context here is a direct explanatory clue which is the most common one as technical terms are introduced.

Besides the direct explanation the word may be one used as a synonym to one the student may already know. For example: "The pirates started firing when their ship was *alongside* or *abeam* of ours." It may be explained also by an example as in the sentence, *"Strip farming* and *terracing* to keep land from washing away are techniques of *land conservation."* It may be used as a summary of a description or action. Such a sentence as the following might be found in a social studies textbook, "Theodore Roosevelt was successful as a *statesman, soldier, sportsman, explorer* and *author;* he was a *versatile* man."

Needed Phonic Skills

Though the English language has been characterized as an irregular one, it is generally stated that 85% of English words are phonetic and therefore can be analyzed in accordance with specific principles.

The high school student has a familiarity with his language which is a vital asset. He may not know specific rules or generalizations but his use of language over the years will have familiarized him with certain usages. However, he may not know he has this general knowledge which the teacher must help him to realize and implement. He is familiar with the basic sounds of the language and the letter combinations which represent them. For example, he would likely know the sounds of the letters of the alphabet, the basic vowel sounds as well as the consonants, consonant blends, diagraphs and dipthongs. He may not, however, know the "rules" governing their pronunciation—the letter-sound relationships.

In order to make use of the phonic principles the student should realize some basic conclusions about the letters of which words are comprised.

1. We have 26 letters in our alphabet which are used to spell all of the words in English.
2. There are 43 different sounds called phonemes in English which are represented by numerous and various combinations of letters.

---

[14] Margaret S. Bishop, Phyllis G. Lewis, and Richmond L. Bronaugh, *Focus on Earth Science* (Columbus Ohio: Charles E. Merrill Publishing Company, 1969), p. 66.

3. The letters of the alphabet are basically classified as vowels and consonants. The vowel letters are *a, e, i, o, u,* and sometimes *y.* The remaining letters are consonants.

4. In many English words the same vowel may represent different sounds. This is true also for some consonants, e.g., *c, f,* and *s,* though some consonants may be silent and not produce any sound for the word.

5. In many English words some vowels and consonants may be silent and not produce any sound for the word.

6. There are combinations of vowels and of consonants which produce unique sounds.

The more important phonic principles which would help the high school student are:

1. The vowel in a syllable which ends with one or more consonants (a closed syllable) has a short sound. Examples: *a*sh, c*e*ll, f*i*fth, t*o*n, b*u*d

2. A vowel which is the final letter of a syllable (an open syllable) is usually long. Examples: vill*i,* z*e*ro, rat*i*o

3. A syllable having two vowels, one of which is a final *e,* usually has the long sound of the first vowel with the final *e* silent. Examples: nitr*a*te, sec*e*de, l*i*me, n*o*de, c*u*be, dy*e*

4. The sound of a vowel followed by the letter *r* is controlled by the sound of the *r.* Specifically, *a* or *o* followed by *r* is neither long nor short. The vowels *i, e,* and *u* followed by *r* sound the same. Examples: *a*rbitrate, v*e*rmin, int*e*rnal, f*o*rce, n*u*rture

5. In words that contain two vowels together (digraph) such as *ai, ay, oa, ee, ea,* usually the first is long and the sound is silent. Example: imp*ea*ch, br*ai*n, st*ea*m, r*ay,* st*ee*l

6. In words that contain two vowels together such as *au, aw, eu, ew, oo,* the vowel letters (digraphs) have a special sound unlike either of the vowels. Examples: c*au*stic, past*eu*rize, f*oo*d, s*ew*erage

7. In words that contain two consonants together such as *sh, * wh, th, ch,* the consonant letters (digraphs) produce a single and new sound. Examples: *sh*ip, *wh*eat, *th*is, *th*ird, *ch*ange, *ch*orus, *ch*ef
   * The w is silent when followed by *o;* example: *who*

8. Some words have a blend of two or more consonants each of which retains its own sound. Examples: *bl*ood, *st*omach, *gl*and, *pr*onounce, *tr*ade, *dr*aft, *st*raw

9. Some words have a blend of two vowels (diphthongs) which produces a blended sound. Examples: c*oi*l, b*oy*cott, m*ou*th, fl*ow*ery

10. When *c* or *g* is followed by *e, i,* or *y,* each is usually soft. Examples: *ci*ty, *ce*ntury, *cy*st, *ge*ometric, *gy*roscope

11. The unaccented syllable of a word may cause the vowel to have the schwa sound (the schwa sound designated by the inverted *e* (ə) is indistinct and does not give the vowel a distinctive sound). Examples: resp*i*ration, c*o*rolla, ventr*a*l, quadr*u*ped

Whenever and wherever the student needs assistance in analyzing words, the appropriate principle should be cited. The teacher may ask the student to bring it to mind by asking what sound the vowel combination *oi* represents, or what is the function of the silent *e* at the end of a word. Many times the student will remember his former teaching. And, such a quick review will serve to restore former teaching to his active memory as well as to illustrate further an application of it. If the student does not know or remember, the teacher can tell him and then ask him or the class for other examples.

Irregular Symbol-sound Relationships

In any discussion of phonic principles, the students will likely remind the teacher of exceptions. If so, build on the interest and cite exceptions. Review with them various possible explanations for the exceptions. For instance, help them to understand how the English language has developed. It evolved through usage rather than by a set of rules. Hence, the language is not uniform. Also, review with them the influences of other languages on English, where we have adopted certain spellings though the pronunciations have been "anglicized" through usage. The ending "-tion" is an example. It is a French ending but slurred to "shun" through English usage. Students are often intrigued by such discussions of their language, and some may wish to delve more deeply into the evolution of English.

The Need for Increasing Sight Word Vocabulary

As the high school student reads widely in many subject areas, his need for an ever-widening sight vocabulary increases. Fortunately, each word the student learns becomes a sight word. Thus, he is able to place his attention upon meaning. His skill in word analysis must develop to the point where his attention remains on understanding. The word analysis skills are a means to this end. In addition, the speed of the student's reading increases with a widening sight vocabulary and when he does not have to analyze a disproportionate number of words.

Another reason for increasing the student's sight word vocabulary is that around 15% of English words cannot be analyzed by phonic principles. These do not have letter-sound relationships which have the sound expected of the letter(s) used in the word. Some of the letters are silent and other combinations have variations of sound that are not usually attributable to the letters.

There are numerous examples of such letter combinations. They include:

1. *gn*   In words beginning with *gn,* the *g* is silent before *n*
   Examples: *gn*eiss, *gn*ostic
2. *gh*   In words beginning with *gh,* the *h* is silent following *g.*
   Example: *Gh*ent
   Within a word when preceded by an *i* it is usually silent.
   Example: li*gh*t
3. *kh*   In words beginning with *kh,* the *h* is silent following *k.*
   Examples: *kh*aki, *Kh*an
4. *rh*   In words beginning with *rh,* the *h* is silent following *r.*
   Example: *rh*ombus

5. *kn* In words beginning with *kn,* the *k* is silent before *n.*
    Example: *k*nown
6. *lm* *l* is usually silent before *m.*
    Example: pa*l*m
    mb *b* preceded by *m* is silent at end of syllable.
    Example: com*b*
8. *pn, ps* In words beginning with *pn* or *ps,* the *p* is silent before *n* or *s.*
    Examples: *p*neumonia; *p*salm.
9. *tch* *t* is usually silent before *ch.*
    Example: wa*t*ch
10. *wr* In words beginning with *wr,* the *w* is silent.
    Example: *w*rought
11. *Double consonants* Only one is sounded.
    Example: com*m*on
12. *t* When *t* follows *s* or *f,* the *t* is sometimes silent.
    Example: of*t*en
13. *ck* The *c* is silent when followed by a *k* at the end of a word.
    Example: hac*k*neyed
14. *qu* Since *q* has no sound of its own, it usually takes the sound of *kw.*
    In English *q* is always followed by *u.*
    Example: e*qu*ivalent
15. *ph* Neither consonant is sounded. Instead, the sound of *f* is used.
    Examples: *p*hotosynthesis; gra*ph*
16. *que* At the end of a word, the *que* has the sound of *k.*
    Example: opa*que.*
17. There is also variability with the sounds of some consonants. Note:

S	u*s*	s
	fu*s*e	z
G	*g*et	g
	*g*iant	j
C	*c*at	k
	re*c*eive	s

Suggestions for Classroom Activities

1. *Words Borrowed From Other Languages.*

Since some words in English have been borrowed from other languages and incorporated into the English language, have the students in your class keep a continuing file of such words. These words are generally among the 15% of words in English that are exceptions to phonetic principles.

French: bur*eau* (bū rō̄)   a chest of drawers, usually with a mirror
                            a government department

Spanish: m*e*sa (mā̄ sa)   a flat topped hill with steeply sloping sides

Italian: concerto* (con *cher* tō)   a musical composition in symphonic form for one instrument

Hawaiian: ukul*e*le (ū kə la′ le)   a small four stringed instrument

(*The *c* sound in concerto has neither the s or k sound.)

2.   *Noting the Silent Letters of Words.**

As you say the following words LISTEN to the sound of the word. What letter or letters are not sounded?

Say the words in Column A. Under B draw a line through the letters which are not sounded. Under C write the word as the dictionary would show how it is sounded.

A	B	C
know	know	no
wrap	wrap	rap
island	island	
comb	comb	
hour	hour	
sight	sight	

3.   *Noting the Schwa Sound in Words.*

fed*e*ral	chrom*a*tin
col*o*ny	alternate
dem*o*cratic	ep*i*dermus
del*e*gate	imm*a*ture
competition	sep*a*l

4.   *Almost Sound-Alike Words.**

Such an experience can be used to give practice in precision of sound.

quit–quick	for–four–fur–fore	bunny–bully
and–an	clothes–close	python–piston
where–were	since–sense–cents	cinder–cider–flinder
weather–whether	panted–painted	immerse–immense
been–bin	recipe–receipt	defiant–definite
where–wear	gem–gym	reverse–revere
very–vary	gorge–gouge	interview–intervene
hair–heir	plumes–plums	sanity–sanitary

* Unpublished exercise devised by Dr. Arthur Heilman.

pitcher–picture	jaunt–joint	fiend–friend
singing–sinking	sheaves–shelves	construct–constrict
series–serious	organ–orphan	imprudent–impudent
strip–stripe	slab–slat	cavalry–calvary
from–form	poacher–preacher	rouge–rogue
couch–crouch	far–fir–fur	revenue–retinue
descent–decent	bury–berry	chief–sheaf
coffee–coffer	wasp–wisp–whisk	blight–bleach
canon–cannon	kit–kite	veterinarian–vegetarian
cornet–coronet	trout–troll	turban–turbine
censer–censor	cub–cud	croquet–croquettes
corps–corpse	duke–duck	salve–suave
bawl–brawl	spooks–spools	budge–bulge–bilge
solder–soldier	necklace–negative	otter–artist
desert–dessert	macaroni–marconi	horde–hurdle
whither–whether	village–villain	obvious–oblivious
baggage–barrage	steak–stake	concentrate–consecrate
dairy–diary	bray–pray	invert–invent
gem–Jim	fluffy–flabby	insolent–insolvent

5. Words Often Confused—"Look-Alike" Words.*

There are a great number of words which are often confused because they are very similar either in spelling or pronunciation. These words can slow your reading unless you develop the ability to recognize them *instantly*. You probably will not have much difficulty with the *meaning* of the following words. The point of the exercise is to give practice in reading each series of three words as rapidly as possible. You may wish to come back to the exercise several times—until you can pronounce each word without hesitation.

decent	descent	descend	ballot	ballet	ballast
though	thorough	throw	severe	several	sever
tired	tried	trial	farther	father	further
cease	crease	crash	crayon	canyon	cannon
mouth	month	moth	quiet	quite	guilt
allow	alloy	allure	with	which	width
rogue	rouge	rough	depot	deport	despot
board	broad	broth	except	accept	expect

* Unpublished exercise devised by Dr. Arthur Heilman.

adopt	adapt	adept	reflect	respect	relate
bother	brother	bather	revere	reverse	revise
desert	dessert	deserve	mental	metal	medial
daily	dairy	diary	easiest	earliest	earnest
easiest	earliest	easterly	brother	bather	bother
began	begin	begun	device	devise	demise
vary	very	every	scared	sacred	scarred
advice	advise	adverse	whether	weather	whither
crash	cash	clash	thing	think	thank
hoarse	hearse	horse	broad	board	brood
chance	changes	chants	flash	flesh	flush
lymph	lynch	lynx	basal	basic	basis
devote	devout	devour	patent	patient	patience
amass	amaze	amiss	censor	censer	censure
malice	malady	malign	discourse	discord	discuss

6.   *Instant Recognition of "Look Alike" Words.**

There are approximately 600,000 words in the English language, all of which are spelled with the same 26 letters. The following material will provide practice on rapid recognition of words often confused. Read each series of words as rapidly as you can.

amass	amaze	amuse	immoral	immortal
manage	manger	mangle	prosecute	persecute
nature	native	natural	imminent	eminent
statue	stature	statute	turban	turbine
imitate	intimate	initiate	obvious	oblivious
adopt	adapt	adept	insolent	insolvent
meditate	mediate	medicate	sheaves	shelves
descent	descend	decent	jaunt	joint
deport	depot	despot	cavalry	calvary
malice	malady	malign	imprudent	impudent
alloy	allure	allow	construct	constrict
patent	patient	patience	immerse	immense
discourse	discord	discuss	veterinarian	vegetarian
devote	devout	devour	defiant	definite

* Unpublished exercise devised by Dr. Arthur Heilman.

scared	sacred	scarred	revenue	retinue
reverse	revise	reserve	croquet	croquette
illumine	illusion	illuminate	salve	sauve
devise	device	demise	reverse	revere
sable	sacred	saber	concentrate	consecrate
generalize	generally	generous	sever	severe
through	throw	thorough	assert	asset
dispense	disperse	dispose	carton	cartoon
parlor	parley	parole	discard	discord
couch	crouch	crunch	adept	except

7. *Test of Phonic Ability (Nonsense Words).* *

Try your students with these nonsense words. Discuss their pronunciations of the words and have them explain the principles they used for syllabication and pronunciation.

besmoray	cokakin
abtenfab	bamboobum
calrastion	rasmotex
fasnobile	tufgoboy
gebsotel	obsebong
fabraytion	fammosab
hegleetol	septosab
telohock	woptogtion
abransed	boledoray
wilseego	ashtabula
motsemflo	amberglo
lipranfas	pinitup
debloman	cupoffjam
extahbop	howgoboy
gemraysob	concuncan
hapnosod	boombamby
jeptinod	dispension
memlopac	dungarees
kedsoro	interlate
absolo	intoxacab

---

* Unpublished exercise devised by Dr. Arthur Heilman.

camtobim	jibjabzentive
dafmosil	mantoman
jaymohak	texderbar
hohetob	semibarbe
teeheho	pumsaltic
rasmaytay	gunseebok

8.   *Frequently Mispronounced Words.**

This exercise deals with words that are quite frequently mispronounced. Often these lapses are the result of lazy speech habits. However, after you mispronounce a word many times you tend to spell it like you pronounce it—thus, even though you may know the meaning of these words you may have developed the habit of mispronouncing or misspelling them each time you use them in speaking or writing. For example, the words *clothes, arctic, probably* and *February* are frequently "slurred" in pronunciation. In the following sentence these words are misspelled in such a way as to parallel the most common mispronunciation.

"His clo*se* are pro*bly* not warm enough for the *ar*tic blasts we expect in Feb*u*ary."

Be sure you can correctly pronounce (and spell) each of the following words. The *italics* indicate where mistakes usually are made.

	Syllabication	*Common Mispronunciation*
ar*c*tic	arc tic	artic
gro*c*ery	gro cery	groc ry
hist*o*ry	his to ry	his try
gover*n*ment	gov ern ment	gov er ment
thousan*d*	thous and	thous ann
Feb*r*uary	Feb ru ary	Feb u ary
pi*c*ture	pic ture	pit chur
lib*r*ary	li' brar y	li barry
sep*a*rate	sep' a rate	sep per ate
han*d*kerchief	hand' ker chief	han ker chief
di*a*monds	di' a monds	di' monds
nat*u*ral	nat' u ral	nat churl
umb*r*ella	um brel la	um brul la
El*e*anor	El ea nor	El ner
hydr*o*gen	hy' dro gen	hy der gen

---

* Unpublished exercise devised by Dr. Arthur Heilman.

coroner	cor' o ner	corr ner
emperor	em' per or	em per er
century	cen' tu ry	centh ry
Dorothy	Dor o thy	Dor thy
caramel	car' a mel	car mel

Using Structural Analysis

Analyzing words in accordance with the meaning units is called *structural analysis*. In this method the student uses his knowledge of word-form changes through the analysis of prefixes, suffixes, roots, grammatical inflectional endings and his recognition of compound words. Each of these contributes to the meaning of a whole word. Both teachers and students think of this method as a very logical one of word analysis. It relates closely to the meaning of words and the function of a word in a sentence.

Inflectional endings are those which denote tense, number, and degree.

			inflectional ending
tense:	ask	asked	ed
	ask	asking	ing
number:	boy	boys	s
	speech	speeches	es
degree:	green	greener	er
	green	greenest	est

The high school student likely has been taught that the meaning of the word is altered, and the principles of adding inflectional endings to words serve as guides for spelling, as well as for correct usage in the precision of meaning. Though these are included in the curricula of most English classes, they should be carried over when appropriate to all classes. The principles are:

1. When the root word ends in a final *e*, the *e* is usually dropped before an ending that begins with a vowel as in the case of *produce—produced* (*ed* added), *raise—raised*. However, when the root words end in *ce* or *ge*, the *e* is retained when the ending begins with *a* or *o*, as in the case of *change—changeable, notice—noticeable*.
2. If a syllable or root word ends in a single consonant preceded by a vowel, the consonant is usually doubled when a consonant is added. Example: *ship—shipped, shipping*
   map—mapped, mapping.
3. Words ending in *f* or *fe* usually form their plurals by changing the *f* to *v* and adding the plural ending as in the case of *half—halves*.
4. When a word ends with *y* preceded by a consonant, the *y* is usually changed to an *i* before an ending is added in such cases as *century—centuries, cavity—cavities*.

Prefixes and suffixes are added to the root of a word to condition the meaning of the root. The meaning of the root is not altered, but modified. For example, *trace, retrace*—to trace again; *possible, impossible*—not possible. In addition, many suffixes indicate the function the word has in a sentence. For example, *govern* is a verb and denotes an action. *Government* is a noun and is the means or instrument for governing.

Many of the most common prefixes and suffixes are listed below with meanings and examples given. Wherever possible, in all of the subject areas the appropriate prefixes, roots and suffixes should be reviewed when they are used in the words the students are expected to learn.

1. Negative prefixes

	Meanings	*Example*
in- im- ir- il-	not, non-, un-	*in*sensitive *im*possible *ir*responsible *il*legal
un-	not, in-, non-, contrary, removal or privation of	*un*necessary
non-	not, un-, in-	*non*sense
dis	separation, reversal, depriving, negation	*dis*suade
mis-	amiss, wrong, ill	*mis*spell
anti-	opposite, against, instead, counter	*anti*toxin

2. Direction, Time, Occurrence

ex-	out of, off, from beyond, away from, without, thoroughly, formerly—but not now	*ex*it
in-	in, within, into, toward, on	*in*fuse
per-	throughout in space or time, away or over, completely, perfectly, extremely, very; largest or relatively large, highest, or relatively high (chem.)	*per*mit
re-	back, backwards, back from advancing, again	*re*trace
de-	down; separation, off; away; out of; intensification, completely; reversing, undoing, depriving, freeing from	*de*face

	Meanings	*Example*
circum-	round, about, on all sides, revolving about, surrounding	*circum*spect
sub-	under, below, beneath, lower; next lower than, subordinate to; forming a further division, a repetition, continuation of below the category of but above the category which follows (biol.); situation on ventral side or under (anat.); having less than normal amount (chem.); near base of, bordering upon (geog., geol.); inversely (math.)	*sub*terranean
syn-, sy-, sym-	with, along with, at the same time	*syn*chronize
trans-	over, across, beyond, through, transcending	*trans*port
retro-	backward, back, situated behind	*retro*active

3. Indicating Relationship

auto-	self	*auto*mobile
co-	with, together, in conjunction, jointly; corresponding function of the complement of an arc or angle (math.); complement of the delination, latitude (astron.)	*co*operate
com-	with, together, in conjunction, very	*com*mit
con-	equal to *com-* before consonants except b, h, l, m, p, r, w	*con*form
col-	assimilated form of *com-*	*col*lude
cor-	assimilated form of *com-*	*cor*respond
counter-	opposite or contrary, reciprocal, retaliatory, complementary	*counter*act
contra-	against, contrary, in opposition	*contra*dict
hyper-	over, above, beyond, beyond the norm; super; extra; denoting position above (anat., zool.); equal to *per-* (chem.)	*hyper*active
super-	above, over; on or at the top of, over and above, more than; that surpasses all or most others of its	*super*cilious

Meanings	*Example*
kind; exceeding, in excess; in addition, extra; secondarily; situated over, on upper part or dorsal side (biol.); having the ingredient in large proportion (chem.)	

4. Time and Number

pro-	priority in place, or time, or order; before	*pro*ceed
pre-	before in time, previously, previous, in advance, in front of, ahead of, prior to	*pre*cede
post-	after, subsequent, later; behind or posterior (biol.)	*post*pone
uni-	one, single, have but one	*uni*form
bi-	two, twice, double; relation to each of two symmetrically paired parts (biol.)	*bi*ennial
tri-	having three, into three, thrice, every third; denoting presence of three atoms, groups, or equivalents of that signified by the term to which it is attached (chem.)	*tri*ennial
quadr-	four	*quadr*ilateral
tetra-	four	*tetro*meter
penta-	five	*penta*gon
quin-	five	*quin*tet
sex-	six	*sex*tet
hexa-	six	*hexa*gonal
sept-	seven	*sept*ennial
oct-	eight	*oct*agon
dec-	ten	*dec*ade
centi-	one hundred	*centi*meter
milli-	one thousand	*milli*gram
kilo-	one thousand	*kilo*gram
hemi-	half	*hemi*sphere
semi-	half; approximately half, partly; precisely half; halved	*semi*circle

	Meanings	*Example*
	or bissected; coming twice; in one half, in some particular; in low degree, no more than half; little more than, little better than	
multi-	many, much; having many; many times over; more than two	*multi*ply

5. Additional (Misc.)

ante-	before, preceding, in front of, prior, anticipatory, anterior, fore	*ante*dote
inter-	among, between, together; mutual, mutually, reciprocal, intervening	*inter*cede
intra-	within, inside, into	*intra*mural
intro-	to, into, within, inward	*intro*duce
fore-	in front, as forerunner, beforehand, preceding, before	*fore*cast

Suffixes indicate the function of the word in the sentence which indicates its "part of speech." As the student becomes familiar with the various suffixes he should be able to give the correct form of the word as determined by its function in the sentence. There is also a categorization of suffixes in accordance with the usage of the word.

Noun Suffixes	*Meanings*	*Example*
-ion	result of	fus*ion*
-sion	the act, quality, condition of result of	explo*sion*
-ation	the act of	form*ation*
-ity -ty	state or condition	dens*ity* plen*ty*
-ance	quality or state of being	disturb*ance*
-ence	quality or state of being	pres*ence*
-ment	result of or a means, agency, or instrument	govern*ment*
-ness	condition, state of being	good*ness*
-hood	condition, state of being	neighbor*hood*
-ship	condition, state of being or ability as in penmanship, friendship; or rank as in lordship	partner*ship*

	Meanings	*Example*
-dom	rank of, position of, state of being one who has to do with; one of a size, capacity, value, date; resident of; agent	free*dom*
-or	state, quality, agent, doer	elect*or*
-ant	person or thing acting as agent	attend*ant*
-less	lacking or without	worth*less*
-most	the most	fore*most*
-able	able to, able to be	formid*able*
-like	similar	life*like*
-ward	in the direction of	for*ward*
-itis	inflammation	appendic*itis*
-ize	to subject to, to render; to impregnate, treat, or combine with (chem); practice or carry on	minim*ize*
-fy	to make, to form into	rati*fy*
-ate	combine, impregate, treat with (chem.)	agit*ate*

Adjective Suffixes

-able(-ible)	implication of capacity, fitness, worthiness to be acted upon; tending to, given to, favoring, causing, able to, liable to	service*able*
-ive	having the nature or quality of, given or tending to	dece*ive*
-al or -ial	belonging to, pertaining to, indicating the presence of the aldehyde group (-al, chem.)	natur*al* remed*ial*
-ful	full of, abounding in, characterized by; able to or tending to	master*ful*
-ish	of the nature of, belonging to;	mann*ish*
-less	without, destitute of, not having, free from; beyond the range of; unable or without power	self*less*
-ary	pertaining to, connected with; a person or thing belonging to or connected with; a place for	residu*ary*

	Meanings	*Example*
-ous (-ious)	full of, abounding in, having, possessing the qualities of, like; denotes valence lower than that denoted by -ic (chem.); used to form adjectives corresponding to nouns of classification (biol.)	grac*ious*

The words which comprise the English language come from many different languages. Of these, Latin and Greek are considered to be the primary sources. Many technical words in the subject areas have one or more roots belonging to Latin and Greek. When specific words are being studied, the teacher may call attention to the root, its origin, and its meaning. Students may find that a growing knowledge of roots will gradually develop their skill in recognizing and defining new words. They will also note how many words can develop from a single root. In fact, upon learning a root, they will be able to list a number of related words. For example: if the student is learning the word *photometer* and discovers that the root *photo* is of Greek origin and means light, and *meter* is of Greek origin and means measure, the meaning of the word can be determined: a device to measure the intensity of light. They will also be able to think of other words using the same roots.

Photo:		*Meter:*	
	photoelectric		thermometer
	photogenic		hydrometer
	photographic		ammeter
	photosynthesis		metric
	photolens		barometer
			centimeter

The following listing of Latin and Greek roots is highly selective and will give some indication of the extensiveness of this aid.

COMMON ROOTS (Latin)

Root	*Meaning*	*Derivatives*
-aud-, audit-	hear	auditorium
-avi-,	bird	aviation
-caput-	head	capital
-ced-, -cess-	move, yield	recede
-clar-	clear	clarify
-clin-	lean	incline
-clud-, -claud-, -clus	shut	seclude
-cord-	heart	cordial

COMMON ROOTS (Latin)

Root	Meaning	Derivatives
-corp-	body	corporal
-cred-	to believe	credible
-curr-, -curs-	run	current
-dic-, -dict-	say	predict
-domin-	master	dominate
-duc-, -duct-	lead	conduct
-fac-, -fic-, -fact-, -fect-	to make, do	factory
-fer-	bear, carry	transfer
-fin-	end	finish
-fort-	strong	fortitude
-jun-, junct-	join	junction
-laud-, -laudat-	praise	applause
-let-, -lect-	gather, choose, read	collect
-legis-, -lex-	law	legislature
-lux-, -luc-	light	elucidate
-magn-	great	magnificent
-mal-	bad	malevolent
-man-	hand	manual
-mit-, -miss-	send	missile
-mov-, -mot-	set in motion	motor
-nov-, -novus-	new	renovation
-pac-	peace	pacific
-pel-, -puls-	urge, drive	propel
-pend-, -pens-	hang, weigh	pensive
-plic-, -plex-	bend, fold	plexiglas
-pon-, -pos-	place, put	postpone
-sci-	know	science
-scrib-, -script-	write	describe
-solv-, -solut-	loosen	solution
-sepec-, -spect-	look	spectator
-sta-	stand firm	stable
-stru-, -struct-	build	construct
-tend-, -tens-	stretch	tendency
-tort-	to twist	distort

COMMON ROOTS (Latin)

Root	Meaning	Derivatives
-ven-, -vent-	come	convention
-ver-	true	veritable
-vert-, -vers-	turn	reverse
-viv-, -vit-	live, life	vitality
-vid-, -vis-	see	evident
-voc-	call	vocation

COMMON ROOTS (Greek)

Root	Meaning	Derivatives
-anthrop-	man	anthropology
-arch-	first, chief	monarch
-aster-	star	astronomy
-bibl-	book	bibliography
-bio-	life	biology
-chrom-	color	chromatic
-chron-	time	chronological
-crypt-	secret	cryptic
-dem-	people	democracy
-derm-	skin	epidermis
-dox-	opinion	paradox
-dynam-	power	dynamic
-gam-	marriage	polygamy
-gen-	birth	eugenics
-geo-	earth	geography
-gyn-	woman	gynecology
-graph-, -gram-	write, written	photograph
-hetero-	different	heterogeneous
-homo-	same	homogeneous
-hydr-	water	hydrometer
-lith-	stone	monolith
-log-, -logy-	speech, word, study	astrology
-metr-	measure	thermometer
-micro-	small	microscope
-path-	feeling, suffering	sympathy
-phil-	love	philosopher
-phon-	sound	dictaphone
-photo-	light	photogenic

COMMON ROOTS (Latin)

Root	Meaning	Derivatives
-physio-	nature	physics
-pod-	foot	tripod
-polis-	city	metropolis
-psych-	mind	psychology
-scop-	see	microscope
-tele-	far	telescope
-the-	god	atheist
-tom-	cut	anatomy
-zo-	animal	zoology

Many compound words in English are formed by combining two words. These words are pronounced the same as each of the combining forms except for accent, and the student will need to use appropriately all of the various means of word analysis. The meaning of a compound word is the combined meaning of the individual word components.

Examples:	highflown	high'flown	fly high; elevated proud inflated language
	rainfall	rain'fall	the fall of rain in amount
	earthquake	earth'quake	quaking (trembling) of the earth.

Syllabication relates to aspects of both structural analysis and phonetic analysis. Prefixes, suffixes, and many inflectional endings add one or more syllables to a root. A basic general understanding that each syllable must contain at least one vowel letter and that each syllable has one vowel sound must be part of each student's knowledge. Then he can easily determine the number of syllables a word contains if he says it carefully noting the number of different vowel sounds. Further, he can determine the accent by listening for the syllable(s) that receive stress. Many of the new and long words a student meets in his reading would be recognizable to him if he could break the words into pronounceable one-syllable units. It is at this point that his general knowledge of language sounds could be used. Through continual application in class, the student should become familiar with the following principles of syllabication and accent:

1. The number of vowel sounds that is heard in a word tells how many syllables the word contains. There is one vowel sound for every syllable: *u*m-br*e*l-l*a*, r*e*-c*ei*ve, r*ai*n.
2. If a vowel is followed by two consonants, the first syllable usually ends with the first of the two consonants: le*t*-*t*er, e*x*-*c*ept, ca*n*-*d*y.

3. If a vowel is followed by a single consonant, that consonant usually begins the second syllable. Examples: ba-*con*, pa-*per*, ti-*ger*.
4. If a word ends in *le* and a consonant comes before the *l,* this consonant usually begins the last syllable. Example: tum-*ble*, ma-*ple*, ta-*ble*.
5. Generally, consonant digraphs (ch, th, sh, and wh) and consonant blends are not divided. Examples: ma-*chine*, wea-*ther*.
6. Prefixes and suffixes usually form separate syllables. Examples: *com*-promise, *un*-constitutional, *a*-septic, termin-*al*, hydraul-*ic*.
7. When the suffix (inflectional ending) *ed* is added to a word ending in *t* or *d,* a separate syllable is formed. Examples: weight-*ed,* expand-*ed*.
8. Words of two or three syllables are usually accented on the first syllable. Examples: *ster*-i-lize, *in*-su-late, *sul*-fur.
9. Words ending with the suffix -sion or -tion are usually accented on the syllable preceding the suffix. Examples: in-*fec*-tion, plan-*ta*-tion, di-*men*-sion.
10. Some words are accented differently in accordance with their function in a sentence. Examples: *con*-tract (noun)—con-*tract* (verb); *re*-cord (noun)—re-*cord* (verb).
11. When the last syllable of a word ends in *le,* the syllable is usually unaccented. Examples: *tum*-ble, *ma*-ple, *ta*-ble.
12. When one or more prefix(es) or suffix(es) is added to a root word, the accent is usually on the root word. The root and the prefix are generally not in the same syllable. Examples: dis-*prove,* re-*count,* un-*clean,* a-*bout,* *great*-ly, *deal*-ing, *mile*-age, *rest*-ful.

Suggested Activities for Classroom Use

1. *Using endings to determine word function.*

    Change the following verbs to nouns.

verb	noun
pay	pay*ment*
transpose	transposi*tion*
diffuse	diffu*sion*
elevate	eleva*tion*
direct	direc*tion*

    The same type of exercise can be constructed to change words to verbs, adjectives, and adverbs.

2. *Building words.*

    Have the students select a word and make as many new words as possible by adding various prefixes and suffixes. Then, (1) determine the basic thread of meaning to all, (2) the way each alters this meaning, and (3) the function of each word as it is used. For example:

	Function	Meaning
construct	verb	to build (the basic thread of meaning)
construc*tion*	noun	the state or act of building
construc*ting*	verb-participle	process of building
construc*ted*	verb-past tense	was built
*re*construct	verb	same as above except for the addition of the prefix *re* which adds to the meaning— building again
*re*construc*tion*	noun	
*re*construc*ting*	verb	

3. *Noting words with the same root.*

Have the students select a root and determine all of the words they can which use the root. Have them, (1) give the meaning of the root, (2) give the meaning of each word showing how the change in word function and/or use of affix alters the basic meaning. For example: *graph, graphy*—write (meaning of root). Samples of the use of the root follows:

photography-	writing with light-producing images on a sensitized surface by the action of light
photographer-	one who writes with light
photograph-	the product of writing with light
autograph-	self *written:* a person's written account of his life experiences
phonograph-	the instrument used to *write* with sound
dictograph-	instrument used to write speech
biography-	a written account of life
bibliography-	the written listing of books
biographer-	one who writes an account of a life
paragraph-	a written subdivision of a discourse (para-aside from: refers to the line or character drawn in margin that indicates the paragraph subdivision)
orthography-	correct writing
cartography-	written maps or charts

cartographer-   one who draws (writes) maps or charts
geography-   earth writing—description of the earth or
    region therein—of its features and life
stenography-   small writing—shorthand
stenographer-   one who writes small

Each of these can be expanded further by grammatical inflections. (See suggestion #2)

For Example:

photograph   noun
photograph*ing*   verb-particle
photograph*ed*   verb-past tense

A variation of this exercise is to present to the students an outline of word forms which the students are to fill in with words of a single root. One is worked out as an example.

Verb: (to) photograph   Adjective: photographic
Noun: photograph   Adverb: photographically
    Person: photographer
    Action: photography
    Thing: photograph

Sometimes the noun and verb form will be the same. Also, sometimes there may be several forms for a single part of speech.

4.   A similar exercise is a listing of words by the student with the use of a single prefix. For example:

in means not,
*in*clusive means not conclusive

Also alert the student to assimilated forms of the prefix.

For example: ir   *ir*responsible
    il   *il*logical
    im   *im*possible
    ig   *ig*noble

5.   *Dividing words by their structural components.*

Have the students divide words from their textbooks into prefixes, roots, and suffixes.

Prefix	Root	Suffix
multi –	plic –	ation
inter –	nat –	ion al
in	– sol –	uble
ex	– pos –	ition

An extension of this type of exercise is to have each part of the word defined in order to note its basic meaning.

multi-   many
plic-   fold   } condition of folding many times
-ation-   state, condition

inter-   between
-nat-   nation   } pertaining to the condition between nations
-ion, al   condition, pertaining

in-   not
-sol-   dissolve   } not capable of being dissolved
-uble-   capable of

ex-   out of   } the act of placing out ("putting out")
-pos-   place, put   } (writing designed to convey information)
-ition-   action

6. *Acronyms:* Some modern words in the English language are formed by using the first letter(s) of each word in a name. For example, NATO comes from *North Atlantic Treaty Organization.* Have the students form lists and define acronyms such as:

CORE   *Congress of Racial Equality*
SNAFU   *Situation Normal, all fouled up*
LORAN   *Long range navigation*
LASER   *Light Amplication by Stimulated Emission of Radiation*
AWOL   *Absent Without Leave*
NOW   *National Organization of Women*

7. Similar to acronyms are abbreviations of terms which do not form acronyms, but are used in place of the full title. Have the student evolve a listing of such abbreviations as:

PTA   *Parent Teachers Association*
NBC   *National Broadcasting Company*
TV   *Television*
AD   *Anno Domini*
CPA   *Certified Public Accountant*

8. *Pronunciation Exercise with prefixes and suffixes.**

Note the underlined parts of the first word in each column. Every word in a given column begins and ends with the same prefix and suffix. In every case these

---

* Unpublished exercise devised by Dr. Arthur Heilman.

are pronounced exactly the same. Reading down the columns, pronounce these words as rapidly as you can. This practice should help you to "sound out" such words when you meet them in your reading assignments.

con*duction*	re*fillable*	*dis*appoint*ment*	*preven*tive
conformation	remarkable	disagreement	predictive
condensation	reclaimable	disarmament	preservative
conservation	recoverable	disarrangement	presumptive
concentration	redeemable	displacement	preparative
conscription	recallable	disfigurement	prerogative
contraction	respectable	discouragement	prescriptive
contribution	reliable	disenchantment	preservative
conviction	renewable	dislodgment	presumptive
consolidation	restrainable	discontentment	precipitative

(Part B)

The following words contain prefixes and suffixes, but the words are in mixed order. Also, some prefixes—suffixes not found in *Part A* are introduced. Practice pronuncing the words as rapidly as you can.

dishonorable	resentment	discernment	remorseless
relentless	preoccupation	resistant	presumably
premeditate	consolidation	distractable	configuration
reconstruction	distributive	preparatory	reelection
protective	recollection	consignment	disqualification
confederation	presumably	prohibitive	constructive
unseasonable	imperfection	automotive	protectorate
implication	discoloration	concealment	unwholesome

Dictionary Usage

Though the dictionary skills will have been taught prior to high school, high school teachers must be aware that these skills may need further refinement in application.

There are three basic clusters of skills needed in the efficient and effective use of the dictionary. The first group are the locational skills. These involve knowledge of alphabetical sequence, the use of guide words, knowledge that words appear according to the sequence of their letters, and a knowledge of structural analysis since the word in the context may not be in the same form as the dictionary entry. For example, *excite* will be a dictionary entry, but *exciting* probably will not; *necessary* will be, but *unnecessary* may not.

The second cluster of skills includes the pronunciation skills. This involves an understanding of the phonetic spellings, the use of diacritical marks, and the use of the pronunciation key. Also, knowledge of the accent mark is important. Usually, students are not required to memorize a diacritical marking system since slight differences occur in dictionaries of different publishers. The understanding and use of the phonetic spelling is abetted if the student's phonetic knowledge is applied.

The final cluster of skills helps the student to get the definition he desires. Here he must be able to discriminate between meanings and select the one appropriate in a given context—the one the author means. Also, he needs to adapt the meaning to the grammatical, inflectional form of the word in the context. For example, the past tense of a verb in context would require the present tense of the meaning found in the dictionary to be adapted. This leads to an important responsibility of the dictionary user. He must "tune in" to the defined meaning proper for the context. This may be simple or complex; "tuning in" may require only the substitution of a definition for the unknown word. Or it may become increasingly complex as the student needs to transpose the order of words in the context or to completely para-phrase the context in order to have the meaning fit. For example, if the student did not know the word *authorize* in the sentence, "The Congress authorized the space program," he would find that the meaning—approved by authority—cannot be sub-stituted directly. He must transpose the words of the original context and of the definition to read, "The Congress approved the space program by its authority."

Suggested Activities

1. *Alphabetizing*—In each series below, number the words in the order in which you would find them in the dictionary.

Sample

4 gouge	___ placate	___ mansion	___ realist
1 fabulous	___ piston	___ needle	___ scribe
3 gossip	___ pitiful	___ pedestal	___ tension
7 haggard	___ place	___ lava	___ tentacle
6 habitat	___ pitch	___ organic	___ union
2 faculty	___ plane	___ quill	___ wave
5 governor	___ pivot	___ jaguar	___ vacuum

2. *Using Guide Words*—The top of each dictionary page contains two "guide words" (these are the first and last entries on that page). Guide words are to help you to rapidly determine if the word you are looking up is found on a par-ticular page. You must decide if alphabetically your word falls between the two guide words. Underline the word(s) in Column B which would be on the page indi-cated by the guide words in Column A.

Column A	Column B
1. come—command	comedy companion comfort
2. frank—free	fret freckle fraud
3. spread—sputnik	sprout squat sport
4. hinder—historic	Hindu hoist hitch
5. plan—plaster	plasma plantation plane

6. minute—mischief

7. ranger—raspberry

8. trace—transit

9. weave—weight

10. average—awkward

miserable miracle miner

rascal rather rally

transport trademark traitor

weekly welcome weapon

autumn avoid aware

3. Determine the derivation of each of the following words by reading the information between the brackets in the dictionary entry for that word.

radius	indent	erg
perimeter	parenthesis	laser
quadratic	prefix	colloid
factor	conversation	equilibrium
trapezoid	antecedent	galvanometer

4. Use the dictionary to note the syllable(s) accented in the following words. Note that some may have two accented syllables—a heavier or primary accent and the lighter or secondary accent.

investment	interrogatory	streptococcus	reclamation
binomial	correspondence	insoluble	unconstitutional
factorable	homily	protoplasm	indemnity
vertices	personification	vertebrate	execution
equilateral	antithesis	atmosphere	strategic

5. Extensions of the above exercise may include:
   a. Using the dictionary to divide the words into syllables.
   b. Noting vowel sound of each accented syllable as shown by dictionary.
   c. Noting which, if any, of the syllables contain the schwa sound.

6. Write the form of each of the following words which would be the form used to find it in the dictionary.

rectangles	arguing	fumigating	savageness
retailed	modifier	sterilizing	wharves
companies	synopses	exhalation	oases
radii	delineated	chlorinated	annulled
algebraic	sagas	liquefier	strategically

7. Determine the appropriate meaning from the dictionary that fits the context in which the word is used in a textbook. Direct the student to use his textbook to see how the word is used, or give him sentences with the word included.

8. Have the students use the dictionary to see if the word has a usage other than in the subject you are teaching. Alert them to such labels as *Slang, Colloq.*

(colloquial), *Obs.* (obsolete), *Law, Math.* and so on. For example the word *company* can be used in a general sense, in business, colloquially, militarily, and nautically.

    9.   Discuss with the students the meanings of the abbreviations *n., v., adj., adv., pron., prep., conj., interj.* Note the usage of a new word from the context in order to select the appropriate meaning. Also have your students study words in your subject noting the form and meaning when more than one of the abbreviations are used.

Teachers at the high school level should be familiar with various methods of word analysis in order to apply the principles of the methods in their subject areas as the need arises. Though the student has been taught and ostensibly is using the methods of word analysis in the elementary grades, he must be given guidance as necessary with the more complex words usually found in the high school subjects.

    The teacher's goal is to develop student independence in reading to the point at which the student does not need to puzzle over word analysis, but rather can concentrate on the information and ideas. The word analysis methods should become natural and commonplace to the student. This requires extensive practice and application. As each subject teacher guides the student in the use of the word analysis methods, one of the prerequisites of maturity in reading will be met.

SUGGESTED QUESTIONS AND PROBLEMS TO BE CONSIDERED IN REFERENCE TO YOUR OWN CLASSROOM

List A (For readers who are training to be teachers.)

1.   Select a passage from a textbook and note the number of concepts the student must know. Note how many should be known from previous instruction. Note the new concepts.
2.   Select a concept and plan how you will develop its meaning with the students.
3.   Make a listing of general words used with specialized meanings in your subject.
4.   Review some textbooks in your area and determine the roots of the technical words the student will need to know.

List B (For readers who are teaching.)

1.   For your class, plan specific on-going vocabulary procedures. Invite your students to suggest ideas.
2.   Have your students: (1) note the new words in an assignment and (2) note the contextual meaning given for the word.
3.   Have your students divide the new words of an assignment into syllables. Also have them note the use of prefixes and suffixes. Discuss with them the influence of the prefixes and suffixes upon the root.
4.   Organize a committee of students who will investigate the etymology of new vocabulary words.

CHAPTER FOUR

Comprehension
of Reading Material

Comprehension is complex. It is very difficult to teach and yet it is the essence of all instruction. A synonym for comprehension is understanding. Sochor states that we must think if we are to understand.[1] Thinking is the process which involves the student's usage of language. Indeed, the goal of each content teacher is to help his students to think, to understand, and therefore to comprehend.

Reading comprehension is the ability of the student to think about the information presented by the author. The student must understand the author's language usage and strive to obtain the intended meaning. In reading, the student uses the graphic form of the language; we find the word recognition skills and the study and research skills aimed toward the ultimate goal—understanding. But these skills do not in themselves secure understanding. It is dependent upon two major prerequisites. One is the student's own facility with language—his level of language acquisition as well as his knowledge of the language used by the author. The second is the student's background of experiences which can bear upon and help to elucidate, organize, and evaluate the data and ideas of the author. The level of language usage and the scope of experiences are two determinants of the student's successful comprehension.

LEVELS OF COMPREHENSION

The comprehension of information requires many skills, some quite simple, others more complex. They range from getting the facts to drawing inferences

---

[1] E. Elona Sochor, "Comprehension in the Reading Program," in *Reading in the Secondary Schools,* ed. M. Jerry Weiss (New York: The Odyssey Press, Inc., 1961), p. 214.

and synthesizing ideas. Smith and others have categorized the comprehension skills into four levels—the literal, the interpretative, the critical, and the creative.[2,3]

The literal level is the simplest level since all the student needs to do is to reproduce the facts as they are related by the author. The skills needed for this level of understanding include noting factual data, sequence, chronology, and enumeration. It is assumed that the student understands the facts, but this is not always the case. Some students are quite glib and can state in a parrot-like manner what the author has written with little or no understanding. At this level, questions are factual and detailed such as:

> List the steps of the photosynthetic process.
> What was the reaction of the colonists to the Stamp Act?
> What materials and equipment do you need for the experiment?
> Where did the robber hide the stolen money?

The interpretative level, requiring the student to go beyond the information given by the author, depends upon competence at the literal level. The student is now required to see the significance of the data: to note various relationships such as cause and effect and relation of the part to the whole, to make comparisons, to draw conclusions and inferences, and to make generalizations. Class discussion is vital for the development of competence at this level. The comments and ideas of the students help develop each other's interpretation. The teacher can help the students see how facts are interrelated by such questions as:

> Explain why the photosynthetic process is essential to life on earth.
> Why was the Stamp Act an unwise law?
> Why do you need to have exactly two grams of sodium sulfate for the experiment?
> Explain how the hiding place for the stolen money showed the robber's ingenuity.

The critical level depends upon the first two. At this level the student learns to evaluate and judge the information and the author's presentation of it. Skills at this level are aimed toward evaluating the author's use of language for guiding the reader's interpretation; noting evidence of the author's fairness or bias, his qualifications, his point of view, intent, and truthfulness; and determining adequacy of information coverage. Recognizing the techniques of the propagandists are also included among the skills of critical reading. Class discussion is again valuable since students will need help in making evaluations and judgments, and in realizing that critical reading requires a standard against which to make judgments. This standard may come from factual evidence, or from society's and their own scale of values. For example, whether or not an author is truthful could be determined

---

[2] Nila Banton Smith, "Levels of Discussion in Reading," in *Readings on Reading Instruction,* ed. Albert J. Harris (New York: David McKay Company, Inc., 1963), pp. 285–289.

[3] Constance McCullough, "Creative Reading," in *Readings on Reading Instruction,* ed. Albert J. Harris (New York: David McKay Company, Inc., 1963), pp. 289–294.

against factual evidence, but whether or not an author is biased must be determined against not only factual evidence, but also against the student's or society's sense of fairness. Questioning at this level may take the form of:

> Explain scientist X's point of view about the photosynthetic process when he stated that forest cutting must be highly controlled and kept to a minimum.
> How might an author favorable to the British cause have viewed the colonists' reaction to the Stamp Act?
> What would be the result of your experiment if you used three grams of sodium sulfate?
> Judge the validity of the young man's arguments for leaving his job.

The creative level requires the student's involvement with the information presented as he uses it to formulate or to rethink ideas of his own. Obviously, the reader is best able to think creatively about the information he has read when he knows what the author has written, has made interpretations basic to his purpose, and has evaluated the pertinence of the information. This level is viewed as the culminating one. Questioning at this level might consist of open-ended queries which require the student to include his own knowledge, views, and values:

> Give your views about the importance of the photosynthetic process. Support your answer with factual evidence.
> How would you have reacted if you were a colonist at the time of the Stamp Act? And, if you were a member of the British Commonwealth?
> What is the most crucial part of the experiment? Why?
> What would you do if you found yourself face to face with the robber in the story?

QUESTIONING

Pertinent to each level of comprehension are appropriate questions. These are not difficult to formulate, but do require some preparation:

1. Read the material prior to class.
2. Ascertain the level of comprehension the students should employ with the material, which is determined by the importance you place on the information.
3. Formulate the key questions *before* class for the levels of comprehension required.

Among her list of skills of comprehension, Niles has included "the ability to read with adjustment to conscious purpose."[4] Questions signal to the student what his purpose should be as he reads—what he is to look for. He can then adjust his reading to the level of comprehension required. For example, "Read to find out what the old man did when he lost his fortune," does not require the same careful reading that the question, "How did the old man feel when he lost his fortune?"

---

[4] Olive S. Niles, "Comprehension Skills," in *Reading Instruction,* ed. William K. Durr (New York: Houghton Mifflin Company, 1967), p. 132.

requires. In the first, the action of the story will reveal the answer. In the latter question the reader will be searching for clues such as specific words and descriptive action to formulate the answer.

FREQUENT DIFFICULTIES STUDENTS HAVE IN COMPREHENSION

The different school subjects require different types of thinking. Whereas we know that the general reading skills apply to all subject areas, each area has its own organization. The organization may range from narrative, descriptive, or fictional material to the detailed explanation of a process. Science and math usually require intensive reading for details and the interrelationship of the many details to each other. Social studies and English materials require large quantities of reading and may be comprised of much anecdotal material. The connotative uses of words, the author's intent and relationships such as cause and effect are important in these areas.

When faced with the different demands of each subject area, the student may become confused. He may not know how to adjust his reading to the demands of each subject. The teacher will need to give instruction in appropriate techniques of reading and study for his subject area.

In addition to the specific demands of each subject area upon the student, there are difficulties in comprehension common to all subjects.

The Student May Regard "Word Calling" as Synonymous With Reading

This student places his emphasis upon recognizing the words and on reading fluently. He is the glib student who can say the correct words but who is unclear about the author's ideas. This student must be taught to look for specific information while reading, thus refocusing attention from word calling to the information contained in the words. Try to develop within the student the habit of anticipating what the author will write. Most textbooks have headings within chapters which give a clue to the reader about the type of information which follows. For example, if the heading is "The Three Main Advantages of the St. Lawrence Seaway," the student can anticipate the information that will follow. (To the mature reader it is obvious that the ensuing text will discuss the three advantages. However, there are many students who fail to use the topical headings in this fashion.)

The Student Does Not Read for a Well-Defined Purpose

Many students read an assignment because they were told to. When questioned, these students have at best only a fuzzy idea of what they are to learn except "the information in this chapter or on these pages." As part of your teaching procedure you must make the purpose—what to find while reading—very clear. This must become standard procedure whenever a reading assignment is made. Leading students to evolve their own guide questions for reading is also a wise procedure. This study technique must become a habit and the reasons for its use made apparent if they are to learn to apply the SQ3R (SURVEY, QUESTION, READ, RECITE, REVIEW) study formula independently. (See pages 102–103.)

The Student May Not Distinguish the Central Idea From Details

Such a student may read all of the factual data and even understand it, but only as isolated and unique bits of information. Very little of the interrelationship of ideas is noted. This student needs help in noting the chapter organization and the paragraph structures used by the author. Again, the topical headings in a textbook are of value. The topical headings are the author's outline of the information. It must be made apparent to the student that as the Table of Contents can show the organization of a book, so the topical heads in a chapter can show the organization of the chapter.

Anticipating what an author may write about a subject is a means of suggesting the main topics. For example, if the students are to read about photosynthesis, have them list prior to their reading what type of information the author is likely to present. They should include a definition of photosynthesis, a description of the process, the importance of the process, and the way the process affects man and other living organisms.

You may also find that this student has difficulty sorting the information given in a paragraph. He may not know how to spot sequence, chronology, steps of a process, or sort important from unimportant details, and anecdotal material from factual information. James McCallister points out the importance of having the student learn to recognize different paragraph patterns, and lists several roles paragraphs play as determined by their purpose:[5]

1. *The central thought supported by details.* Though this may be the commonest form of paragraph structure, it is by no means the only one. In this structure, often the central idea statement is expressed in the first sentence, or the last. The other sentences of the paragraph include the details which may give additional information about the central thought, conditioning information which qualifies in some way the central thought, or examples of application of the central thought. A typical example is shown below:

<u>Television and radio reporting of election returns is a new problem in this country.</u> Some people object to the networks' recent practice of forecasting national election results by means of computers on the basis of meager early returns from eastern states. They claim that such premature predictions could influence voters in western areas where polls are still open due to the time difference. This type of forecast could distort election results if the voters are influenced to vote for the apparent winner or if they fail to vote because	Central thought Information— Explanation supporting the central thought

[5] "Using Paragraph Clues as Aids to Understandings," *Journal Of Reading* VIII, No. 1 (1964): 11–16.

they think their candidate has won or
lost already. <u>Therefore,</u> laws are being
proposed to keep the television pre-
dictors and their computers silent until
after the polls have closed all over the
country.[6]

Conclusion—solution to central
thought

2. *Introductory statements.*   This type of paragraph is often found at the
beginning of selections or units and chapters in textbooks. These are a great help
to the student because they can give him a mental set that aids greatly in comprehension. In the introductory paragraph usually the purpose of the author is
stated, a preview of a selection is given, a plan of organization is indicated and
sometimes definite questions are cited to guide the reader. Thus, the reader is
prepared for the information he will find. For example:

Cultural and Social Change

*We have seen how the American people conquered the frontier, tilled
the rich earth, dug treasure from the mines, threaded the country with railroads, and built great factories. But such material progress must be accom-
panied by advances in <u>education, art,</u> and <u>literature.</u> How has the United
States progressed in these important fields?*

3 major areas of chapter

1. More Students Attend More Schools

The last three decades in the nine-
teenth century and the first two in the
twentieth saw many <u>changes</u> in American life. This was <u>especially</u> true in
<u>public education.</u> People were begin-
ning to accept the principle of free
public education for all, realizing that
without such education a free democracy cannot exist. Even so, there was
still much room for improvement in the
educational system as the new century
opened.[7]

Clues to content of
first section

Introduction to
first chapter section

[6] Miriam R. Resnick and Lillian H. Nerenberg, *American Government in Action* (Columbus, Ohio: Charles E. Merrill Publishing Co., 1969), p. 113.

[7] Landis R. Heller, Jr., and Norris W. Potter, *One Nation Indivisible* (Columbus, Ohio:
Charles E. Merrill Publishing Co., 1971), p. 382.

3.   *Paragraphs of definition.*   These paragraphs are often found in textbooks. They develop concepts or define technical terms pertinent to the information. Usually the new term or word is written in italics the first time it appears. Competent readers give special attention to paragraphs of definition because they recognize that such paragraphs furnish background for further information and understanding. Two examples are:

All moving bodies have kinetic energy. A swinging pendulum, a soaring rocket, your beating heart, running water, and moving air are examples of moving bodies which have kinetic energy. <u>Kinetic energy is energy of motion.</u> Name five other examples of bodies that have kinetic energy.[8]

Practical illustrations

Most of our <u>conclusions</u> in previous chapters were <u>based upon experimental observation and measurement.</u> This process is called *<u>inductive reasoning</u>* and leads only to <u>tentative or probable conclusions</u> called *<u>conjectures.</u>*

To avoid confusion and to enable us to think more precisely, we had to define the words we used. During this process we described some undefined terms and developed the criteria for a good definition.

As we studied the basic building blocks of geometry (points, lines, and planes) and their relationships, we assumed the truth of certain statements. <u>Such statements, called assumptions, with the definitions and undefined terms led to necessary conclusions concerning geometric figures.</u> These conclusions are called <u>theorems.</u>[9]

A series of paragraphs of definition

4.   *Principle explained by illustration.*   Sometimes the author attempts to make a principle or process which is abstract easier to understand by giving illustrations or examples of practical applications of the principle. He tries to make the principle more concrete and more easily understood by providing examples which may be similar to situations the reader has experienced. Sometimes the reader may confuse the illustration with the principle that the author is explaining. This confusion stems from the fact that often the language of the illustration is more readable, and as a result the illustration attracts more attention or is more interesting to the reader. However, competent readers differentiate carefully between the author's thought and the illustrations.

When the teen-ager's parents paid damages to the owner of the car he

Illustration relates to student's experiential knowledge

---

[8] Heimler and Price, p. 82.

[9] Goodwin, et al., p. 87.

struck, they were following a _precedent—accepted idea_—established under the English system of *common law,* which governs many of the dealings of one man with another. This kind of law grew out of custom and common practice in early England when people brought their disputes to judges who issued rulings based on their interpretation of what was both usual and right. By deciding in many similar cases that such-and-such a rule was just, the judges built up a considerable body of law which was understood and respected by all. These common laws are written down in judges' decisions and are called precedents.[10]

Meaning in context

Meaning, explanation of common law

(This paragraph uses illustration, but is mainly a paragraph of definition.)

5. *Comparison and contrast.*   An author may use this pattern to clarify specific points he wishes to make. Two questions should be kept in mind by the reader. One, "What main point does the author intend to convey?" and two, "What likenesses or differences does he utilize to reinforce the point?"

Among the colonies of the North, Middle, and South there were many similarities as well as differences.① The colonists' right to worship as they pleased was an important reason for the settlement of the Plymouth Colony as well as for the settlement of Rhode Island and Connecticut. The first Southern colonies were inspired more by a search for② new opportunity than by a search for religious freedom, although later Southern Colonies, especially Maryland, were settled by colonists seeking religious freedom. In the Middle Colonies, Pennsylvania was settled by Quakers, although New Netherland

Evidence of comparison and contrast which follows:

Paragraph shows the similarities and the differences of the reasons for the settlement of each colony.

Three reasons given for settlement:

Differences

Religious freedom: Plymouth
                    Connecticut
                    Rhode Island

New opportunity: Southern
                    colonies
                    (Maryland)

Commercial gain: Middle colonies
                    (Pennsylvania)

Similarities

---

10 Resnick and Nerenberg, p. 165.

(later New York and New
Jersey) was③ settled for
commercial gain.[11]

6. *Cause and effect.*   Interpretation in reading is often dependent upon seeing certain relationships among the facts. The reader must be alert to these relationships and his thinking guided to make them. An author may cite causes and
he may cite effects. He does not often label them as such.

The Grange

As a means of bettering their hard lot, the farmers
at last decided to organize themselves into a group that
could force the state and national government to pass   ____Cause
laws that would help them.. The leading spirit in this   ____Effect
movement was Oliver H. Kelley, a government clerk in
the Department of Agriculture in Washington. Since he
had been a farmer himself, he understood the problems
of rural life. In 1867 he started the National Grange of
the Patrons of Husbandry—more widely known as the
Grange.[12]

7. *Problem solution.*   Some paragraphs are designed to present problems
and then offer solutions. The reader will engage his attention first upon the problem, then the evidence presented, and finally the solution proposed by the author.
Sometimes the reader may draw his own conclusions or make his own solution
from the evidence presented by the author. Such paragraph patterns are often found
in scientific selections and some social studies materials. An example from a social
studies textbook is:

Do you blame the government when you can't get   Problem
a decent program on television? Many people do. Carry-
ing not people or goods but pictures and voices in inter-   Discussion,
state commerce, television is another modern miracle   "evidence"
which the Founding Fathers could hardly have foreseen
in 1789. The interstate commerce clause of the Consti-   However,
tution provides the basis for the federal government's   Solution
power to regulate today's methods of communications.[13]

8. *Events in chronological order.*   Obviously this pattern is a sequential
time order of events. It helps the reader to place an event in time and to know
when it occurred in relation to other events.

---

[11] Hollis and Potter, p. 43.

[12] *Ibid.*, p. 359.

[13] Resnik and Nerenberg, p. 398.

In^①1215, the <u>Magna Carta</u>, wrung from King John of England at Runnymede by rebellious English barons, laid down the important principle that the power of a king or any government must be exercised within limits laid down by law. More than four centuries later, the <u>Petition of Right</u> of^②<u>1628</u> and after it the <u>Bill of Rights of 1689</u>^③spelled out basic freedoms on which the monarch or government was forbidden to trespass. Taxes could not be imposed without the consent of the people's representatives. No one ought to be jailed without a trial. In peacetime, armed force might not be used against the people. The people could freely elect representatives who would meet regularly to make laws which would be binding on those who governed as well as on those who were governed. Also included were other rights which were ^④<u>later translated into the American Bill of Rights.</u>[14]

Paragraph showing the chronology of the rights of people

9. *Enumeration or Summary.* These paragraphs are often found at the end of chapters or sections within a chapter. They are usually a compilation of the main ideas presented throughout the selection or chapter. In that they are so highly concentrated, the reader may find that he needs to read these paragraphs slowly and intensively. At other times, an enumeration paragraph is used for a listing of details. If the reader needs to remember the details, slow and intensive reading again is required.

EXAMPLE 1. ENUMERATION OF PRINCIPLES:
In 1905, Albert Einstein (1879–1955), an American physicist, proposed a theory to explain the photoelectric effect of light. He based the new theory on an idea suggested earlier by Max Planck (1858–1947), a German physicist. The theory includes the following principles:
1. Light consists of tiny "bundles" of energy called photons.
2. Light energy is gained or lost as photons.
3. The energy of a photon varies directly with the frequency of the light. For example, a photon of violet light has more energy than a photon of red light because violet light has a higher frequency than red light.
4. One photon may liberate one or two electrons in the photoelectric effect. Two photons cannot combine to liberate one electron.
5. The intensity or brightness of a light is a measure of the number of photons liberated by the light-producing source. Intensity varies directly with the number of photons.[15]

EXAMPLE 2. AN ITEMIZED LISTING OF MAIN IDEAS:
1. The many attempts to classify the elements in a systematic manner include Dobereiner's triads, Newland's law of octaves, and Mendeleev's and Meyer's tables.

---

[14] *Ibid.,* pp. 18–19.
[15] Heimler and Price, p. 141.

2.   The modern periodic law states: The properties of the elements are a periodic function of their atomic numbers.

3.   Today's periodic table is based on the electron configurations of the atoms.

4.   All elements in a horizontal line of the table are called a period; all elements in a vertical line are called a group.

5.   The most stable atoms have eight electrons in the outer level. Helium atoms are stable with two electrons in the outer level.

6.   The periodic table may be used to predict electron configurations.

7.   Full and half-full sublevels represent states of special stability.

8.   Elements with one, two, or three electrons in the outer level tend to be metals; those with five, six, or seven outer electrons tend to be nonmetals.

9.   The periodic table, together with the octet rule, may be used to predict oxidation numbers.

10.   The most active metals are listed toward the lower left-hand corner of the table; the most active nonmetals are listed toward the upper right-hand corner.[16]

10.   *Transitional paragraphs.*   Their function is to shift the reader's attention from one aspect of a topic to another, or a variation in an argument or a shift in time. Many times, simple transition is done by just a sentence at the beginning or the end of a paragraph.

Now it is possible to discuss the mass of an individual atom. Because of the extremely small size of the particles in the atom, however, chemists have continued to use masses of large groups of atoms, rather than using the masses of the individual atoms. You can imagine the difficulty in working with the mass of an individual atom. For example, the relatively simple helium atom has two protons, two neutrons, and two electrons. Since the mass of the electrons is negligible, we need to consider only the two protons at 1.673×10^{-24} g each and the two neutrons at 1.675×10^{-24} g each for the mass of the helium atom. From these masses, you can calculate that there

} Transitional sentence—Reader's attention is specifically directed.

} Central thought

The remaining paragraph has a central thought supported by details, illustrated by an example.

---

[16] Robert C. Smoot, Jack Price and Richard L. Barrett, *Chemistry* (Columbus, Ohio: Charles E. Merrill Publishing Co., 1971), p. 185.

are approximately 1.5×10^{23} atoms in *one* gram of helium. Such a large number of atoms could not be handled individually. Thus, you can see that masses of large aggregates of atoms are more useful. As discussed in Chapter 5, chemists have chosen 1 mole, or Avogadro's number, of atoms as a standard unit for large numbers of atoms. This number of atoms was chosen so that N atoms weigh in grams what one atom weighs in atomic mass units. We know that the unit gram was originally defined as $\frac{1}{1000}$ the mass of the international prototype kilogram, but what about the atomic mass unit?[17]

The question-problem—at the end, leads the reader to the next paragraph.

11. *Descriptive paragraphs.*   These occur in literature and sometimes in social studies materials. Their purpose is to help the reader see a mental picture and indirectly to note the mood or tone which the author wishes to convey. Many times they do not have a central idea sentence but merely one that labels the object, person, place, or event being described.

A Hard and Lonely Life

The farmer's resentment against the railroads and the "moneymasters" of the East was made sharper by the fact that his daily life was often <u>bare</u> and <u>comfortless.</u> In the early days, at least, the Western dirt farmer lived in a small house built of sod dug from the prairie, or of logs from the trees that he had cleared away. He had few schools, churches, or libraries. Weather conditions and poor roads often prevented him from visiting neighbors or journeying to the country store to buy supplies. It was a <u>lonely</u> life, particularly <u>hard</u> on women and children. As time went on these conditions improved, but still the farmer felt that he should be better rewarded for his efforts to feed the nation. He believed that his situation was not understood by the public.[18]

Information to support the adjectives: hard, bare, comfortless, lonely

12. *Narrative paragraphs.*   These are story-type materials which relate an anecdote or tell of a sequence within a story. There may not be a central idea

---

[17] *Ibid.,* p. 119.
[18] Hollis and Potter, p. 358.

statement. Sequence of events is often part of this type of paragraph. The paragraph following, though from a chemistry textbook, is narrative.

The Neutron

A third particle remained undetected for a long time. Its existence had been predicted by Lord Rutherford, an English physicist, in 1920, but the first evidence of the particle was observed by Walter Bothe in 1930, ten years later. Bothe was conducting some experiments in *radioactivity,* and, one of his tests failed to produce the expected results. He expected the material with which he was working to emit protons. Instead, he obained high energy rays which he thought were *gamma rays,* a form of *X ray.* We will discuss gamma rays in greater detail in Chapter 19.[19]

The Student Does Not Sense the Author's Purpose

This is the student who misses the significance of the material. He may understand the facts which are presented, but he does not understand why they are important or what the relationship to other ideas may be. He is unable to draw conclusions or to infer adequately. As we have noted before, his awareness of introductory paragraphs will assist him in detecting the author's purpose. Also, the Preface of a book or the "Foreword to the Student" found in many textbooks will alert him to the author's purpose. In editorials, newspaper columns and essays, background about the author may give the basic frame of reference from which the author writes.

The Student Does Not Follow the Author's Organization

Unless the student can see the author's organization of ideas, many bits of information and ideas seem unrelated and isolated from each other. Such a student finds himself reduced to the rote memorization of a myriad of facts in order to master the content.

There are a number of techniques the student can employ to help himself follow the author's organization.

a. The Table of Contents of a textbook will help him to see the scope of the material included as well as the order of the specific topics. Depending upon the detail of the Table of Contents, major sub-topics related to each of the major chapter or unit headings may be listed.
b. The topical headings within a chapter clearly show the author's outline of the information. He should read first the topical headings in a chapter, then read the chapter in detail.
c. The student may read a chapter title or a section heading and think before reading about the type of information that will be included. He might jot down his listings, and see if the author includes the same type of information.

[19] Smoot, et al., p. 116.

    d. Basic knowledge of composition can be applied to a reading selection. Have the student note the basic structure in a unit or chapter—introduction, body, and summarizing statement.

    e. The student should note structure words in the material to discover how the author thinks and the interrelationships he wishes to give to ideas.

Commonly used structure words are listed:

I.   Structure words indicating additional ideas

    A. Words pointing to coordinate ideas, adding to the total thought

AND	FURTHERMORE	BESIDES	LIKEWISE
ALSO	PLUS	TOO	SIMILARLY
ANOTHER	OTHERWISE	AFTER THAT	AGAIN
IN ADDITION	MOREOVER	AS WELL AS	SINCE
SINCE THEN	NOT ONLY BUT ALSO		

    B. Words pointing to final or concluding ideas

CONSEQUENTLY	IN CONCLUSION	THEN
THUS	IN SUMMATION	TO SUM UP
HENCE	AT LAST	IN BRIEF
THEREFORE	FINALLY	IN THE END

II. Structure words indicating a change in ideas by reversing, qualifying, or modifying ideas already presented

IN CONTRAST	ON THE OTHER HAND	FOR ALL THAT
TO THE CONTRARY		NEVERTHELESS
OPPOSED TO	BUT	YET
CONVERSELY	IN SPITE OF	STILL
HOWEVER	ALTHOUGH	EVEN IF
EVEN THOUGH	EITHER-OR	

III. Structure words indicating concrete application of a thought

BECAUSE	SPECIFICALLY	PROVIDED
FOR EXAMPLE	FOR INSTANCE	LIKE, AS

IV. Structure words pointing to relationships among and between ideas

    A. Time relationships

IN THE FIRST PLACE	LAST	PREVIOUSLY
AT THE SAME TIME	NOW	HEREAFTER
THEREAFTER	LATER	AT LAST
IN RESTROSPECT	AFTER	AT LENGTH
MEANWHILE	BEFORE	FOLLOWING
FINALLY	IMMEDIATELY	

B. Space relationships

HERE	CLOSE	BY	FURTHER ON	TO THE EAST
THERE	FAR	AWAY	ABOVE	WESTWARD
YONDER	NEAR	UNDER	ACROSS	BENEATH
EVERYWHERE				

C. Related in degree

MANY	LITTLE	SOME	BEST	FEWER	GREATER
MORE	LESS	ALL	WORST	FEWEST	GREATEST
MOST	LEAST				ABOVE ALL

D. Pointing to show emphasis

THIS	THAT	ONE	SOME	FEW
THESE	THOSE	SEVERAL		

The Student Encounters So Many Strange Words That the Passage Means Little to Him

In this situation, the obvious and best solution is to replace the material with more easily written material. In instructional material, new concepts and the words which label them are expected. The usual ratio is the maximum of one strange word out of every twenty. When this ratio increases, the material begins to be frustrating to the student even with teacher instruction and guidance.

However, should this situation present itself when there is no other material available, you can help the student though the difficulty of the material may still preclude student success. Techniques the teacher can use include:

a. Spend as much time as needed developing a background and a knowledge of the vocabulary prior to the student reading.
b. Use audio-visual aids to develop a background of information.
c. Explain the information included in the reading selection thoroughly before the student reads. As each point is explained, direct the student to that section or paragraph in the material which makes the same point.
d. Call the student's attention to the graphic aids (pictures, maps, graphs, tables) which help to illustrate and give concreteness to the information.
e. Be sure the student has well-defined and specific purposes before he reads.

Ideas Are Introduced Which Are Entirely Outside the Student's Experience

In this instance you have a clear-cut responsibility—increase the background of the student so that the information and ideas will have some meaning. You may use any of many appropriate aids—films, filmstrips, recordings, pictures, models, field trips, anecdotes, explanations, experiments. These means of increasing background are presented prior to the student's reading and again during the ensuing discussion.

The Student Fails to Relate What He Reads to the Experiences Which He Has Had

Many times, the student does not realize the background of information he does have. At first glance he says to himself, "I don't know anything about this at all." Often the student does have related information in his background which he does not recall or to which he does not see any relationship in the material to be read. In the introductory discussion prior to reading, you can help him recall his background information by previewing the material with him, by probing through questioning ("What do you know about____?"), and by relating similar experiences you know the student has had. In probing, the student must have time to think. Do not always expect immediate recall.

The Student Has Difficulty With the Complexity of Sentences

Goodman states that reading involves an interaction between thought and language.[20] The student must have an understanding of how his language is structured in order to formulate ideas. He must know the meanings of words and how these meanings interact when in various sentence patterns. By the time a student comes to high school he has some knowledge of sentence structure because he uses it in his oral communication. He knows various sentence patterns which he has heard and used. However, he may not be able to identify the parts of sentences nor know principles governing the function of the parts. Allen points out that a grammar is needed which will help students to recognize the sentence units in the more complicated sentences they will meet in their reading. He goes on to say, "Above all, such a grammar must *not* be a grammar that emphasizes words. It must be a grammar that teaches students to regard a sentence as a hierarchy of constructions within constructions, on different levels, rather than as a string of words in linear sequence."[21] Ives follows the same theme. He says, "occasionally pointing out syntactic distinctions in . . . class can, it seems likely, help comprehension and serve as preparation for more systematic teaching of the grammatical system." Grammar, says Ives, should be the means contributing to the expression of meaning and therefore should be introduced as an aid to comprehension rather than as fragments of a structural system.[22]

Deighton elaborates, "The reader's structural problem is to determine the word groups and then to see how these groups relate to one another. Until he has done this distinguishing, he must hold the meaning of the sentence in abeyance."[23]

---

[20] Kenneth S. Goodman, "Reading: A Psycholinguistic Guessing Game," in *Theoretical Models and Processes of Reading,* ed. Harry Singer and Robert Ruddell (Newark, Delaware: International Reading Association, 1970), p. 260.

[21] Robert L. Allen, "Better Reading Through the Recognition of Grammar Relationships," *The Reading Teacher* XVIII, No. 3 (December 1964): 194–196.

[22] Sumner Ives, "Some Notes on Syntax and Meaning," *The Reading Teacher* XVIII, No. 3 (December 1964): 179–183, 222.

[23] Lee C. Deighton, "The Flow of Thought Through an English Sentence," in *Vistas in Reading,* ed. J. Allen Figurel. Vol. II, Part I, Proceedings of the Eleventh Annual Convention (Newark, Delaware: International Reading Association, 1967), p. 323.

Subject area teachers may need, on occasion, to help their students in the analysis of sentences with the view in mind of attaining better comprehension. For example:

The <u>nineteenth century</u> in the United States <u>was an age of invention</u>.[24]

    Subject   Predicate: gives a characteristic
                                              about the nineteenth century.

A <u>plane mirror</u> <u>is a mirror with a flat surface</u>.[25]

    Subject   Predicate: identifies the plane mirror.

A <u>circular region</u> <u>is the union of a circle and its interior</u>.[26]

    Subject   Predicate: identifies the circular region.

Deighton further maintains that there are two types of sentences: one denotes action and the other is attributive. For example, "Light rays travel from you to the mirror" denotes action, whereas "An image is an apparent reproduction of an object" is attributive.[27] The image is identified. The verb is a form of *be* which is called a linking verb. Deighton notes that the words following the verb refer to the words preceding the verb. This occurs with all linking verbs such as *look, remain, stay, sound*. The meaning in such sentences is that of identification, characterization or description. The verb *have* is also used in descriptive sentences.[28] For example:

In 1865 the nation *had* about 40,000 miles of railroad track, but by 1900 the railroads *had laid* almost 200,000 miles of track, more than that of all the European Countries put together.[29]

When the student reads complicated sentences such as those of two independent clauses joined by a conjunction (compound), those with independent and subordinate clauses (complex), and the long sentences which are both compound and complex, he has a more involved job of understanding. Not only must he understand the interrelationship of the parts of each clause as in a simple sentence, but he must also see the interrelationship of the clauses to each other. The student can note the interrelationship of large units of complicated sentences by the use of specific structure words called connectives, such as: *although, and, because, but,*

---

[24] Heller and Potter, p. 335.

[25] Heimler and Price, p. 123.

[26] Goodwin, et al., p. 315.

[27] Heimler and Price, p. 123.

[28] Deighton, p. 325.

[29] Heller and Potter, p. 342.

for, however, if, so, that, thus, when, where, which, who, and *yet.* In a study of student knowledge of the function of connectives in comprehension, Robertson summarized by saying

> although children acquire language structures using connectives early in life, they gain mature understanding of them gradually throughout their school years. Children use clauses in speech before they go to school but they do not develop a sufficient understanding of the meanings of connectives in print for a number of years after that. Therefore, children should be given systematic training through the reading program so they may develop more facility at an earlier age in understanding increasingly complex communications from the printed page.[30]

For example, the subject teacher may help his students by alerting them to the use of structure words as they read complicated sentences. A passage taken from a social studies text shows the use of structure words.

The Threshing Machine. <u>As a result</u> → indication of application of thought
of better plowing and harvesting methods,
the grain grower's crops were greatly in-
creased. He could <u>now</u> grow and harvest → time relation
large amounts of wheat, oats, or barley
with relatively little help. <u>However,</u> he → condition qualification
still needed a more efficient way to sep-
arate the grain from the stalk. The threshing machine was the best answer to this
problem.[31]

A sentence from a geometry text shows also a qualification of thought:

indicates condition, qualification
A point is in the exterior of a circle *if the distance from the point to the center of the circle is greater than the measure of the radius.*[32]

The teaching of sentence comprehension, traditionally considered the premise of the English teacher, is actually the responsibility of each content teacher as he helps his students read the language of his subject. Indeed, this knowledge is as much a part of professional preparation as the acquisition of the subject matter of the discipline to be taught.

---

[30] Jean E. Robertson, "Pupil Understanding of Connectives in Reading," *Reading Research Quarterly* III, No. 3 (Spring 1968): 416.

[31] Heller and Potter, p. 335.

[32] Goodwin, et al., p. 315.

**The Student Does Not Visualize the Situations Described
With Word Pictures**

Whether or not a student can construct mental pictures from the reading material is evidence not only of his comprehension but is also a basis for developing interest. Ability to visualize is particularly noted in story-type reading with its descriptive and narrative paragraphs. The student's reactions to the words and his sensory images of them enable him to sense the mood and tone of a selection. Visual imagery is also employed in the content subjects when there are descriptions: sequential development of processes in science; political and social events in history, particularly in sensing the feelings of a people; as one of the first steps in solving a mathematics problem; and in visualizing the end product in home economics or industrial arts.

To help students use sensory imagery you can:

a. Discuss the meanings of words. Ask students to state quickly the mental picture or the sensory feeling a word indicates to them.

b. Investigate the connotative uses of specific words and alert the students to the emotional impact of the words.

c. Guide the student's reading by purposes which require sensory imagery. ("How would you feel if_____?", "What is the situation taking place in this math problem?", "Describe your feelings if you lived in the cramped quarters of a whaling ship for two years before reaching home port", "Show by simple sketches the various techniques of land conservation", etc.)

d. Dramatize situations from literature and social studies.

e. Ask students to draw pictures to show how they visualize a descriptive passage.

**The Student Does Not Understand Figurative Expressions and Subtle
Meanings Used by the Author**

Student deficiencies in this area are largely due to a lack of background experiences and an unfamiliarity with idiomatic expressions in language. Many of our idiomatic expressions originated when people lived in a less technological and urban society. Hence, many are outside the experiential base of the students. They must learn that idiomatic expressions and figures of speech are not translated literally but are symbolic—inferences which are based on the literal meanings. Direct instruction in figures of speech is important to sensitize the students to them. Certainly instruction in those figures of speech used in the reading material of a subject should be taught as they occur. Students will also enjoy attempting to create their own figures of speech. They will note that figures of speech can add to the flavor of a selection and thereby make it more interesting.

**The Student Cannot Locate, Master, and Apply to Any Given Topic or Problem
the Pertinent Information Contained in a Selection**

His ability to do this is a measure of his independence in reading and study. This is considered a reading-study skill (see pages 102–123, 143–145).

The Student Cannot Weigh Evidence and Draw Valid Inferences and Conclusions

If there is deficiency in this area, two prerequisites to weighing evidence and drawing conclusions must be considered. One is the student's background of information. Valid inferences and logical conclusions cannot be made in a vacuum. The reader needs some information against which to gauge his inference or conclusion. Secondly, he needs depth and precision of vocabulary to catch subtle meanings and connotative usage. Once these prerequisites are met, you can guide the student in obtaining the literal comprehension so that he knows what the author has written. Then, help him to apply various skills of critical reading to note the author's point of view, bias, and intent. Questions that might be helpful in this area are:

"What is the author attempting to do in this selection and how does he try to accomplish it?"

"What evidence does the author give? Show whether or not the author's arguments are logical."

"What is the significance of the information the author has presented?"

"What conclusions can you draw?"

Finder points out that skills of comprehension may be identified by showing that the reader is able to (1) identify the effects intended by a reading selection and (2) to explain the elements within the selection which produced the effects.[33]

The Student Cannot Interpret Special Materials Such as Graphs, Tables, Maps, and Diagrams

Most high school teachers would expect that students would know the techniques of using the graphic aids in a reading selection. Probably they have been taught, but many high school students either cannot or do not use them. It is possible that these aids are not emphasized and to teach them or to use them extensively would be considered tantamount to returning to primary reading levels. However, they are valuable aids for any student at any level. The use of these aids is considered to be a reading-study skill. Techniques for assisting the students in their use are found on pages 106–120.

SUGGESTED QUESTIONS AND PROBLEMS TO BE CONSIDERED IN REFERENCE TO YOUR OWN CLASSROOM

List A (For readers who are training to be teachers.)

1. Select a passage and identify the paragraph patterns.
2. Select a passage and note the structure words. Determine how they affect the meaning, import and relationship of the ideas.

---

[33] Morris Finder, "Comprehension: An Analysis of a Task," *Journal of Reading* XIII, No. 3 (December 1969): 199–202, 237–240.

3. Determine how you would relate a topic to the students' experiential background. What would you do to enlarge their background?
4. Select a passage which you would consider as a typical assignment and plan how you would teach a comprehension skill such as noting the main idea and the content at the same time.

List B (For readers who are teaching.)

1. Before your next reading selection in class, formulate comprehension questions for each of the literal, interpretative, critical and creative levels.
2. In your lesson procedures, identify questions of purpose to guide the students' reading. Evolve some questions from them. Determine with them the rate and intensity of reading required.
3. Investigate a reading assignment for your students and do the following:
   a. make a listing of the general words used with a specialized meaning.
   b. identify the paragraph patterns.
   c. note the structure words and determine how they affect the meaning import and relationship of the ideas.
4. Select a comprehension skill such as noting the main idea, drawing conclusions, evaluating the signficance, and so on, and plan instruction in it to accompany your coverage of subject matter.

CHAPTER FIVE

Reading Study Skills
for the Student

The reading-study skills are aimed at helping the student develop independence in gaining information from printed materials. These skills are ones the student will need to use when he is on his own and must direct his own study efforts. Obviously, the student must have instruction and guidance from his teachers in ways to become independent. He will need guided practice in completing a textbook assignment, in reading to do research on a topic, in seeing the author's method of organization, and in techniques of organizing the information he obtains.

STUDY SKILLS

McKay states a functional definition of the study skills when he says they include any technique students use in learning school assignments.[1] The study skills, sometimes called reading-study skills, are those used by students when they need to understand and remember information from a reference book such as a textbook. Harris calls this assimilative reading[2]

Obviously, the student needs many specific skills to master the information contained in his reading-study assignments. In fact, nearly all the skills of reading, ranging from word recognition (decoding) skills to the various comprehension

---

[1] William McKay, "The Nature and Extent of Work-Study Skills," in *Teaching Reading Skills in Secondary Schools: Readings,* ed. Arthur V. Olson and Wilbur S. Ames (Scranton, Pa.: International Textbook Company, 1970), p. 160.

[2] Albert J. Harris, "Research on Some Aspects of Comprehension: Rate, Flexibility, and Study Skills," *Journal of Reading* XII, No. 3 (Dec. 1968): 205–210, 258–260.

(encoding) skills will at some point be used. As might be expected, different scholars in the literature of reading have different lists of skills to be included as reading-study skills. Yet, each uses as a core the techniques of independent assignment study. In fact, the goal of the study skills is the student's total independence to gain information for himself.

For the student who is able to decode words, knows the vocabulary, and understands basic sentence syntax, there are reading-study skills which will help him to be more productive in his efforts. Those to be discussed in this chapter will include:

1. The SQ3R study procedure
2. Organizing information
3. Following directions
4. Using graphic aids
5. Research reading

The teaching of study skills along with content does not detract from or hinder the coverage of the content. Rather, the acquisition of content increases. McKay fosters this position when he says, "[Study skill instruction in the various content fields] is preferred because the skills are taught and practiced where they are needed and in proper combination for the particular subject area, rather than in isolation. In addition, the actual materials of the course are used for the teaching and practice so that students can see the usefulness of the skills."[3]

The SQ3R procedure

Francis Robinson's procedure for individual and independent study is probably the best known for use at the secondary and college levels.[4] Though there are variations of the formula, all follow the same basic steps as the original. Thomas and Robinson have adapted the formula PQ4R (Preview, Question, Read, Reflect, Recite, Review) in their book, *Improving Reading in Every Class* (Boston: Allyn and Bacon, Inc., 1972). Students have been instructed, exhorted, coaxed, and advised to use this procedure, but many still seem neither to be aware of it nor to see the efficiency of the method. I have asked college freshmen over a period of several years if they know the method. In no class (eighteen students each) have more than two known it except by name. In one instance I taught the method only to have a student say, "Look, you're lucky if I even read the material once, much less survey, question, recite and review! I'd never get my homework done!" This student, of course, failed to see the efficiency of the method. He saw it only as taking more time for no greater return. Teachers have found that students need not only to be instructed in the method, but also shown its value. If they read two comparable selections, one by their usual method and the other using he SQ3R method, and are quizzed for recall, they will usually see that they have greater recall and understanding with the SQ3R.

---

[3] McKay, p. 161.

[4] Francis P. Robinson, *Effective Study*, Rev. ed. (New York: Harper & Row, Inc., 1961), pp. 13–48.

The steps of the procedure are:

Survey—Surveying the introductory statement, the headings, and summaries quickly to get the general idea and scope of the assignment. Readers may also give general attention to the graphic aids and the questions at the end of the chapter.

Question—The student formulates his own purpose questions. He may use the headings or a question which the survey of the material may have prompted. Teacher-directed questions (the assignment questions) may serve as purpose questions, though it is wise for the student to become independent in formulating his own.

Read—The material is read to answer the purpose question(s).

Recite—The student pauses to relate to himself the answer to his question. He may also recall to himself the main ideas of the author and the author's organization of information.

Review—The student looks through the selection to perceive again the organization and basic ideas and to make whatever notes he deems important.

Organizing Information

Efficient and effective study requires that the student be able to organize the data into a structure which shows the logical interrelationships. There are two aspects of organizing information, both of which are needed for student competence. In one the student must note, as he reads, the organization used by the author. The other, closely related, is the ability of the student to produce his own organization, relative to his purpose, through his note taking and outlining. Essentially the general points for assisting the student in organizing information are: (1) The student needs to be able to note patterns of thought in paragraphs and larger segments of written material (See pages 83–91 for discussion of paragraph patterns). (2) The student needs to acquire and apply his skills of outlining, summarizing, and note-taking. (3) The student needs a continuous motivation to apply the skills of noting and producing organized information. The high school student needs to see vividly how the skills of organization can benefit him personally.

You are the key person to develop the organization skills as they apply in your content area. McKay underscores this position and suggests ways the teacher can help the student.

1. By being aware of its values and patterns himself.
2. By asking the kinds of questions which encourage students to observe the structure of what they have read.
3. By surveying the next lesson with his class, calling attention to the organization they are about to study.
4. By alerting them to headings which almost outline the material.
5. By reading materials to his class and asking anticipatory questions with a focus on structure.
6. By using visual aids such as colored overlays on an overhead projector.
7. By showing students *how* to take notes and *how* to outline.[5]

---

[5] McKay, p. 160.

Teaching Notetaking

One teacher told her class they should never do any study-type reading unless they had a pencil in hand to take notes. Two reasons were given for taking notes. One, notetaking makes study active. It compels the student to think about what he is reading when he writes in his own language the information from the textbook. Two, reviewing becomes easier, particularly if the student has developed the ability to make his notes brief. They then become memory joggers rather than a restatement of the textbook. Obviously the student's note-taking ability depends upon his ability to note the author's structure by the use of introductions and summaries, boldface headings, paragraph analysis and alertness to structure words which signal direction in the author's thought. Certainly the students will need systematic instruction in the skills of notetaking.

Notes may take several forms. The student may outline the information, write a précis, or devise a chart of the material. Whatever form is used, specific principles must be observed. (1) The notes should be in the student's own words. Often phrases and sentence fragments are sufficient unless the notes are in the form of a précis. Quotes should be kept to a minimum. Most often the quote, if used, would include the author's specific definition of a word, or formulas. (2) The notes should be brief. One way for a student to do this is to select only the outstanding points—the major ideas. Brevity in notetaking also helps the student to see in almost a graphic form the total structure of the information. (3) The student should note hints to structure—such words as *first, more important, finally,* etc. In summaries the student should be alert to the main ideas by such clues as "remember," "the essential difference in," etc. (4) The student should be urged to invent a code of abbreviations. These are uniquely his own, particularly since the notes are for his use solely. Abbreviations and symbols can be used as he sees fit to reduce the length of his notes and save time. (5) The notes should be consistent in form and orderly. If an outline is used its form should be consistent throughout. Caution students on this point since one of the purposes of notetaking is to be able to use notes after a lapse of time and still have them make sense. (6) The notes should be filed in consecutive order and dated.

When the student takes notes from various references in preparation for a research report additional considerations and practices must be implemented. Usually such notes are from books and materials which will be read only once. Additional principles for the student to keep in mind would be: (1) keep the notes as brief as possible but realize that their length and detail will depend on the amount of material and the purpose; (2) use cards so that the notes from several references can be reorganized into proper sequence for the report; (3) record on each card the complete bibliographical reference and the main ideas and details relevant to the purpose.

As you teach you can incorporate instruction in notetaking into regular class procedures. (1) Read a chapter or section with the students and suggest the ideas which should be recorded in the notes. (2) Discuss specific material with the students and evolve with them the most efficient form for their notes. Notes can take the form of an outline, a list, a chart, a time line, parallel columns, comparing two or more entities, or any other form which the student finds helpful. (3) Guide the students to take notes in class by writing the main points on the blackboard as the lesson progresses. Help the student to note the items to be included under each heading. (4) With a newspaper article instruct students to take notes to answer questions of Who? When? What? Where? Why? and How? (5) Outlining is the form of notetaking that is particularly effective in helping the student to sort out information in order to see the interrelationships of main ideas and related details. Students will need guidance in correct outline form which is not difficult if they are able to note the main idea and the factual detail relating to it. Therefore, you have a dual process to teach. The first and most basic is the student's ability to see the structure of information which may involve paragraph analysis and chapter or unit organization in the textbook. The other is the more mechanical skill of outline form. Students may learn the basic form through direct instruction followed by guidance in applying it to selected passages. Once they have mastered this, more latitude can be granted to develop their own personal form. However, clarity and the proper relationships of ideas must still be apparent, or the outline will be of little value to them.

Most textbooks in the subject areas are organized to facilitate the student's ability to note the organization of the subject matter. The relationship of the main ideas and sub ideas can be noted through:

Title of the Book
    Unit title
        Chapter title
            Chapter section
                Topical headings
                Paragraphs.

The title of the textbook presents the overall area of study. The unit and chapter titles, and often the chapter sections, can be investigated in the Table of Contents. For example one typical science textbook is organized in this manner:

Focus on Physical Science
    Unit I—Motion
        Chapter 1—Forces
            Force and Resistance
            Speed
            Acceleration
            Deceleration
            Units of Force
            Vectors
            Velocity
        Chapters 2, 3, 4, and so on
    Units II, III, IV, and so on.[6]

---

[6] Heimler and Price, pp. v–xii.

The students may be stimulated to think about the subject matter organization by conjecturing the kinds of data that would be included. Also, as the Table of Contents is investigated, the beginning of knowledge about and familiarity with some concepts can take place. For instance, concepts of resistance, acceleration, and deceleration can be initially and casually clarified.

The unit, chapter, and chapter section organization in the textbook is helpful to the student's comprehension if he is aware of such textbook aids. If we assume that the students have been assigned to read about the classification of matter, they should be guided to see the overview of the topic. It is in Unit Three entitled, "Matter." The first chapter is Chapter 10, "Classification of Matter," which is broken up into the following sections:

> Matter
> Elements
> Compounds
> Mixtures
> Physical Properties
> Physical Change
> Chemical Change

As the students read the assigned chapter, their purpose-for-reading question would probably be, "How is Matter classified?" By noting section headings and supporting details within the sections as they read, they will then obtain a clear outline of the answer to their purpose question.

Graphic Aids

The graphic aids of a textbook include maps, diagrams, charts, tables, graphs, pictures, cartoons, and time lines. They are intended to aid the student in understanding the expository information. Yet students often do not use these materials to full advantage. There may be several reasons for this. Little emphasis on use of them may be fostered in the classroom. Some teachers consider these aids to be a type of reading assistance needed only by beginning readers and feel that the high school student is far superior to this material. It may be that the use of this material seems so obvious that anyone should be able to obtain pictorial information. This can be an incorrect assumption. High school students often do not know how to use these materials effectively; they do not know what purposes to keep in mind when using them; or they do not wish to take the time. Yet, often the expository materials are interwoven with references to the graphic materials as a means of making the exposition more concrete. This is their major purpose.

It is impossible for the student to experience at first hand all of the data to be learned in his various subjects. In many subjects he is confronted with concepts which are abstractions. The graphic material aids his comprehension by giving some concreteness to these abstractions. Summers notes the purpose of graphic aids very succinctly.

> Audio-visual aids play an important role in developing understandings of abstract concepts at all levels of learning. Often a simple picture, model, or

film adds measurably to the interpretation of the verbal message of printed material. In particular, the visual aids in the reading materials of a subject such as maps, charts, tables, graphs, diagrams, pictures and cartoons add to interpretation and understanding. If students can profit from such aids, their achievement in a subject is enhanced. However, visual aids are a means to an end and not an end in themselves. The only rationale for the inclusion of visual aids in reading is the contribution they make to creating interest and adding to the understanding of content.[7]

Maps. Much of the world's information has been recorded on maps of various types. Usually the subject where map reading skills are most consistently used is social studies. However, map study may pervade aspects of the entire school curriculum. They are an essential tool of modern life.

The types of information gained from maps depends upon the type of map used. They may be listed as follows:

street maps which show the streets of a city and may show information leading to a study of local problems such as the placement of redevelopment or urban renewal plans, location of cables, telephone lines, power lines, or railways.

road maps which show distances between cities, types of roads, natural park areas.

relief maps which show the physical features of the terrain, usually represented by a scale of color and lines to note elevation above sea level. These maps can also indicate information about the location of cities, roads, industries and crops.

physical maps are closely related to relief maps, and indicate land use and type, potential boundaries and population centers.

vegetation maps show the types of vegetation of a region and may often be superimposed upon a physical map.

political maps show political divisions of cities, counties, states and countries, and may show shifts of political control over areas.

product maps show the principal products, crops, resources, and goods of a region.

pictorial maps use pictures or cartoon figures to show historical and natural features, natural wild life, dress of the people.

population maps show the centers of population of a region.

historical maps show explorers' interpretation of the world's land forms in centuries past, the boundaries of ancient countries, lines of explorations, battle arrangements.

war maps are used to show where battles took place and the strategy used.

weather maps use a specific set of symbols to give information about current and future weather conditions—high and low pressure centers, type of precipitation, air movement.

blank outline maps are mostly used in schools for helping students become competent in map usage.

Just as with types of paragraphs, a map may be a combination of two or more types. For example, a historical map may use pictorial symbols and may also give

---

[7] Edward G. Summers, "Utilizing Visual Aids in Reading Materials for Effective Learning," in *Developing Study Skills in Secondary Schools* ed. Harold E. Herber (Newark, Delaware: International Reading Association, 1965), pp. 98–99.

political information. Basically the types of information that can be obtained from maps are land and water forms, relief features, direction and distance, social, political, and scientific data and evidences of human habitation.

The map reading skills are very similar to the skills needed to read language. Both use symbols and abstract representations. As with the usual skills of reading, the map reading skills should be taught in a consistent and systematic manner. It may be expected that secondary school students will have some competence in them. However, you cannot rely on this. Therefore you need to review elemental map reading skills (telling direction, understanding longitude and latitude, using map scales, locating places and making inferences about the correlative patterns as well as the association of people and things in particular areas), and to teach the more advanced secondary skills. Thralls presents the major map skills, understandings, and appreciations which junior and senior high school students should know.[8] Essentially they are:

Junior high school:

1. Read information from weather maps and understand their value to the individual and to industry.
2. Interpret world pattern maps that show different types of distribution (i.e., products, resources).
3. Understand that parallels and meridians on some maps may be curved lines.
4. Understand that the map scale depends on what is to be shown.
5. Know map vocabulary such as *world pattern, isoline, isotherm, isobar, cold front, warm front, wind direction, wind velocity, ocean current, warm ocean current* and *cold ocean current.*

Senior high school:

1. Read all commonly used map symbols.
2. Read descriptive facts from regional and world distribution maps.
3. Draw inferences or raise questions from information shown on two or more maps.
4. Use longitude and latitude for location.
5. Make inferences about the climatic conditions of a country or region.
6. Use large scale maps of cities and special areas and be able to relate these to small scale maps showing a large area.
7. An understanding that a map may be distorted deliberately.
8. Understanding of a polar map and how it is used.
9. Know the advantages and disadvantages of different types of projections.
10. Know how maps may aid in understanding some current event.

The skills of map usage are similar to the comprehension skills. The basic level is the ability to use the features of the map to gain specific information. This level

---

[8] Zoe A. Thralls, *The Teaching of Geography* (New York: Appleton-Century-Crofts, Inc., 1958), pp. 59, 62–63.

corresponds to the literal comprehension level in reading. The student may then need to make interpretations depending upon his purposes, make inferences, and draw conclusions from the data. He may need to make comparisons of one area with another; to note facts as well as distortions; to think critically of the relationships between facts on maps, and between maps and current events. Map reading is essentially the same as reading language.

For example, some maps taken from a social studies textbook can be found on pp. 111–115. In the following list, each is identified as to the type of knowledge needed to read the map. Questions pertinent to each map are also included. Some questions may require further research and inferential thought.

Historical map (p. 111).

In order to read the map students must know where to locate:
    North-South directions
    East-West directions
    Atlantic Ocean
    Great Lakes
    Gulf of Mexico
    Mississippi River

Questions:
1. In what part of the continent of North America were the 13 colonies located?
2. Why were they located in this area?
3. Why are the Western boundaries not shown for some of the colonies?

Historical map (p. 112).

Students must know how to read the key.
In order to read the map, students must know where to locate:
    States
    States in which cities noted on the map are found
    Physcial features such as rivers and mountains
    Great Lakes
    East-West, North-South

Questions:
1. Explain why most of the roads went west from the northeastern part of the United States.
2. To what river did most of the railroads and roads extend? Explain why.

Political-historical map (p. 113).

Students must be able to read the key.
In order to read the map, students must know where to locate:
    Area of the 13 original colonies
    The Northwest Territory

Cities: New York, New Orleans, Washington, Chicago
States included in the Louisiana Purchase
The Great Lakes
North-South, East-West

Questions:

1. Compare the land area of the Louisiana Purchase to the United States.
2. To what mountain range did the Louisiana Purchase extend?
3. What principal seaport did the Louisiana Purchase make available to the United States? Explain the importance of its location.

Historical-political map (p. 114).

In order to read the map, students must know location of:

The states
Cities: Washington, New York, Chicago, New Orleans, San Francisco
Principal rivers, Great Lakes
North-south, East-west directions
Countries: Canada, Mexico
Relation of Alaska to the other continental United States
Physical features: mountains, prairie

Questions:

1. What is the advantage of the United States begin bound by the Atlantic and Pacific Oceans?
2. By consulting other maps, determine the climatic regions of the United States.

Political map (p. 115).

Students must be able to read the key.
In order to read the map, students must be able to locate:

East-West
North-South
Hemispheres
Equator
Climatic zones
Major countries of each continent
Areas of current interest

Questions:

1. Why is the United States interested in both Asia and Europe? Explain.
2. Why is the position of the United States beneficial for world trade?

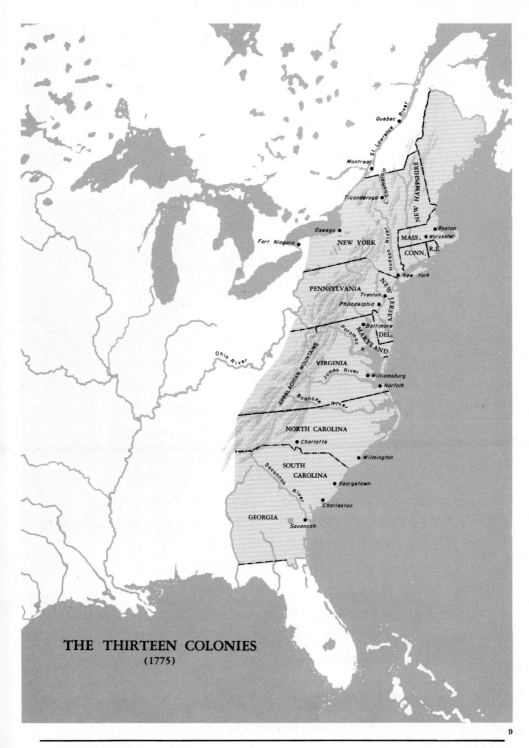

THE THIRTEEN COLONIES
(1775)

[9] Heller and Potter, p. 106.

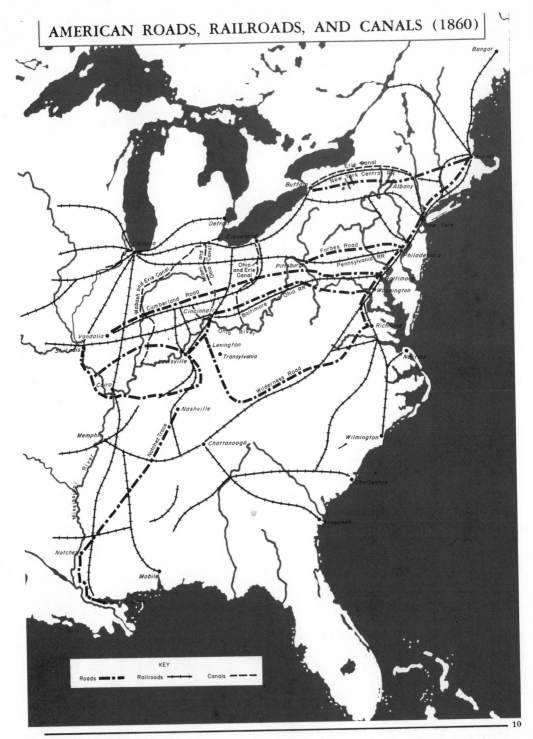

[10] *Ibid.*, p. 202.

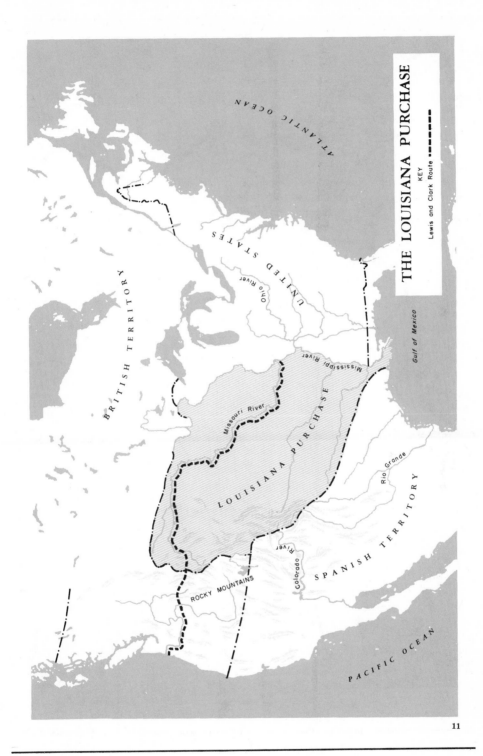

THE LOUISIANA PURCHASE

KEY

Lewis and Clark Route ▬▬▬▬▬▬

11

11 Ibid., p. 176.

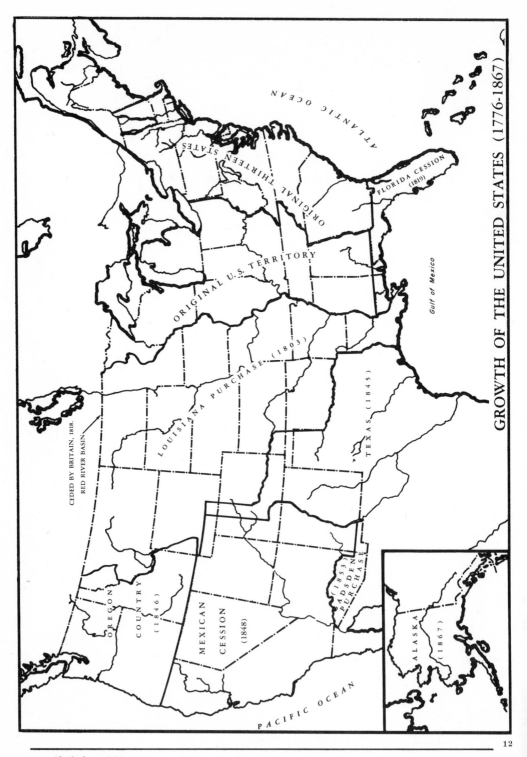

GROWTH OF THE UNITED STATES (1776-1867)

ATLANTIC OCEAN

ORIGINAL THIRTEEN STATES

FLORIDA CESSION
(1819)

ORIGINAL U.S. TERRITORY

Gulf of Mexico

LOUISIANA PURCHASE (1803)

TEXAS (1845)

CEDED BY BRITAIN, 1818.
RED RIVER BASIN.

GADSDEN
PURCHASE
(1853)

OREGON COUNTRY (1846)

MEXICAN CESSION (1848)

ALASKA (1867)

PACIFIC OCEAN

12

12 *Ibid.*, p. 255.

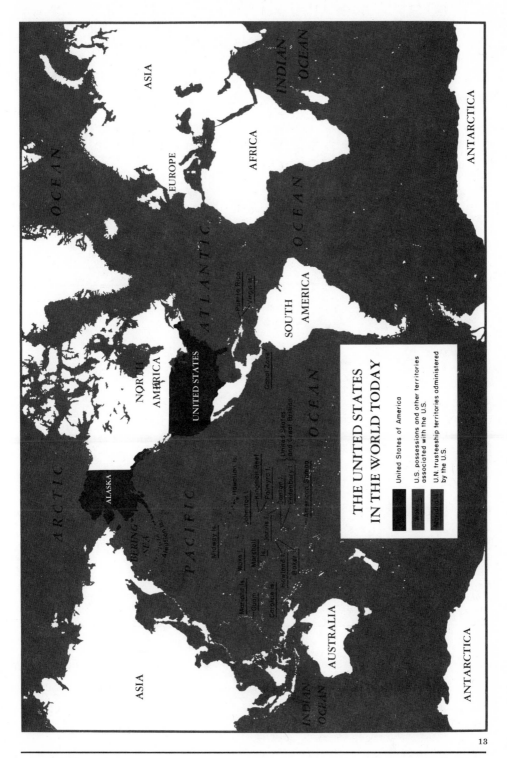

THE UNITED STATES
IN THE WORLD TODAY

United States of America

U.S. possessions and other territories
associated with the U.S.

U.N. trusteeship territories administered
by the U.S.

[13] *Ibid.*, p. 628.

Charts.   Textbooks in the subject areas use many different types of charts, such as time lines, diagrams, and charts showing sequence, organization, process, comparison, development, and the flow of types of information. They are used to supplement the text by making the data more visual. Sometimes charts and dia-

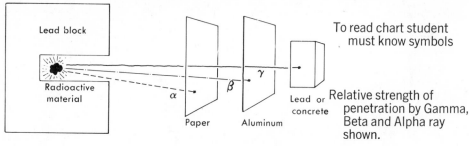

FIGURE 19-1.   Gamma rays are the most penetrating rays; alpha rays are the least penetrating. 14

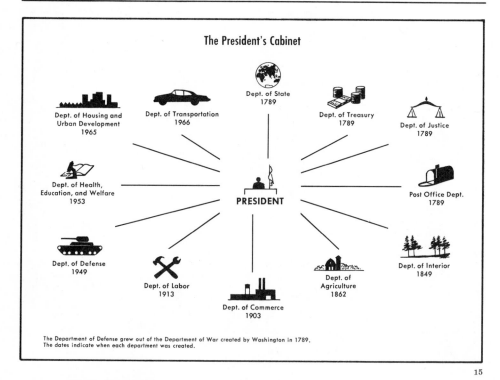

Students must:
1. read charts, and
2. know areas of responsibility of each cabinet member. Pictographic symbol serves to give clue.

---

14 Smoot, et al., p. 461.
15 *The Great Law of Our Land* (Columbus Ohio: Charles E. Merrill Publishing Co., 1970), p. 23.

grams summarize information that has been presented in the text. One reason that some high school students fail to make use of charts is that they are not aware of the purpose of this type of visual aid. The student must be able to extract the information contained in the chart, and then to draw generalizations or conclusions from the data. When using charts and diagrams the student needs to ask himself: What type of chart is it? How is the information presented? What symbols are being used? For example, note the information and relationships that can be derived from the charts on p. 116.

Tables. Tables are usually used to present statistical data which supplements the descriptive passages in the text by adding concrete detail. To read tables adequately the students need to answer:

What is the title—what does the table represent?

What units of measurement are used?

What do the columns and rows represent?

What special explanations (footnotes) are used?

What is the significance of the data of the table?

Ask students to study table to see what patterns appear and what angles have easily remembered ratios. (Sine and tangent increase as angle measure increases. Cosine decreases as angle measure increases. Sine of an angle equals cosine of its complement. Sine and cosine always less than or equal to 1.)

Direction in Teacher's Edition to help students note:

1. organization of table

2. relationship of sine, tangent and cosine to angle.

Before the table can be understood, students must know the concepts of:

Angle

Sine

Cosine

Tangent

Trigonometric ratios

Purpose of functional use of table should be made clear to students as appropriate content is studied.

Table of Trigonometric Ratios

Angle	sin	cos	tan	Angle	sin	cos	tan
0°	.0000	1.0000	.0000	45°	.7071	.7071	1.0000
1°	.0175	.9998	.0175	46°	.7193	.6947	1.0355
2°	.0349	.9994	.0349	47°	.7314	.6820	1.0724
3°	.0523	.9986	.0524	48°	.7431	.6691	1.1106
4°	.0698	.9976	.0699	49°	.7547	.6561	1.1504
5°	.0872	.9962	.0875	50°	.7660	.6428	1.1918
6°	.1045	.9945	.1051	51°	.7771	.6293	1.2349
7°	.1219	.9925	.1228	52°	.7880	.6157	1.2799
8°	.1392	.9903	.1405	53°	.7986	.6018	1.3270
9°	.1564	.9877	.1584	54°	.8090	.5878	1.3764
10°	.1736	.9848	.1763	55°	.8192	.5736	1.4281
11°	.1908	.9816	.1944	56°	.8290	.5592	1.4826
12°	.2079	.9781	.2126	57°	.8387	.5446	1.5399
13°	.2250	.9744	.2309	58°	.8480	.5299	1.6003
14°	.2419	.9703	.2493	59°	.8572	.5150	1.6643
15°	.2588	.9659	.2679	60°	.8660	.5000	1.7321
16°	.2756	.9613	.2867	61°	.8746	.4848	1.8040
17°	.2924	.9563	.3057	62°	.8829	.4695	1.8807
18°	.3090	.9511	.3249	63°	.8910	.4540	1.9626
19°	.3256	.9455	.3443	64°	.8988	.4384	2.0503
20°	.3420	.9397	.3640	65°	.9063	.4226	2.1445
21°	.3584	.9336	.3839	66°	.9135	.4067	2.2460
22°	.3746	.9272	.4040	67°	.9205	.3907	2.3559
23°	.3907	.9205	.4245	68°	.9272	.3746	2.4751
24°	.4067	.9135	.4452	69°	.9336	.3584	2.6051
25°	.4226	.9063	.4663	70°	.9397	.3420	2.7475
26°	.4384	.8988	.4877	71°	.9455	.3256	2.9042
27°	.4540	.8910	.5095	72°	.9511	.3090	3.0777
28°	.4695	.8829	.5317	73°	.9563	.2924	3.2709
29°	.4848	.8746	.5543	74°	.9613	.2756	3.4874
30°	.5000	.8660	.5774	75°	.9659	.2588	3.7321
31°	.5150	.8572	.6009	76°	.9703	.2419	4.0108
32°	.5299	.8480	.6249	77°	.9744	.2250	4.3315
33°	.5446	.8387	.6494	78°	.9781	.2079	4.7046
34°	.5592	.8290	.6745	79°	.9816	.1908	5.1446
35°	.5736	.8192	.7002	80°	.9848	.1736	5.6713
36°	.5878	.8090	.7265	81°	.9877	.1564	6.3138
37°	.6018	.7986	.7536	82°	.9903	.1392	7.1154
38°	.6157	.7880	.7813	83°	.9925	.1219	8.1443
39°	.6293	.7771	.8098	84°	.9945	.1045	9.5144
40°	.6428	.7660	.8391	85°	.9962	.0872	11.4301
41°	.6561	.7547	.8693	86°	.9976	.0698	14.3007
42°	.6691	.7431	.9004	87°	.9986	.0523	19.0811
43°	.6820	.7314	.9325	88°	.9994	.0349	28.6363
44°	.6947	.7193	.9657	89°	.9998	.0175	57.2900
45°	.7071	.7071	1.0000	90°	1.0000	.0000	∞

16

[16] Eugene P. Smith, et al., *Discoveries in Modern Mathematics Book 2* (Columbus, Ohio: Charles E. Merrill Publishing Co., 1968), p. 288.

Graphs.   Much the same type of information as is shown in tabular form can be shown by graphs. However, graphs are more dramatic in showing quantities, growth or decline, or the size of relative parts. Usually, direct instruction in graph usage is extended in the mathematics classes, but textbooks in all subjects use them. Therefore, teachers in all subjects must help students to gain pertinent information from graphs and to apply the knowledge they have learned in their mathematics classes. Graphs include several different types: line or profile, bar, circle or pie, and picto-graphs.

Since graphs are a visual representation, the size and shape may present an impression which is inaccurate. In a line or bar graph the one which is basically horizontal will give the impression of a slower growth than one that is vertically shown, thus:

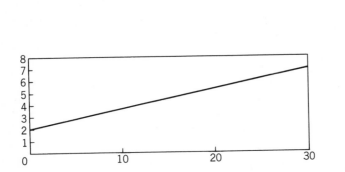
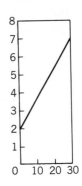

In the circle graph shown at an angle, *A* looks larger than *B* even though they are the same as when shown straight:

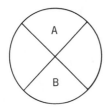
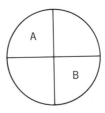

In a line graph the mean of a line can preclude important details:

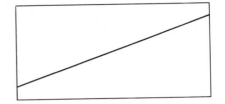

Finally, the scale may not show the true representation unless it is started from zero:

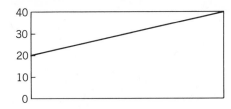   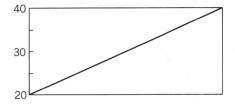

The latter looks as if the increase started from zero, unless it is carefully read.

The student needs to keep the following considerations in mind as he interprets graphs:

The type of graph.
The kind of data presented.
The unit of measurement.
The arrangement of the data.
The numerical guides of the horizontal and vertical axes.
The significance of the information.

Pictures.   These are probably the most widely used of all the graphic aids. They can supplement the information while adding interest and motivation. They do much to make a textbook look manageable to the student rather than formidable. Summers points out that "with pictures the learner gets more and clearer ideas than he does with the text material alone. Pictures, through realism, can expand experience and help to avoid misunderstanding. Pictures are particularly effective in showing step by step developments, contrasts and comparisons, and the status of things, processes, scenes, and events."[17]

Students often do not get as much information from a picture as they might if they had purpose in mind when they look at it. Even a picture may not show much unless the reader looks for something and takes the time to study it. He will need to recognize the objects shown, describe details and draw inferences from what he sees, and make generalizations about the question and problem at hand.

Cartoons are a special type of picture which are symbolic. They are used widely in the social studies. The cartoon presents a message or a point of view through symbolism and broad exaggeration. Herein lies the difficulty some students have. They are not cognizant of the symbolism used or they do not have a broad enough background about the topic of the cartoon to note the broad exaggeration. Students must first recognize the technique used in the cartoon—humor, an appeal to emotion, satire, symbolism, caricature. Next, the student needs to identify and analyze the symbolism to get the message the artist is attempting to show. Students may need to have the symbols identified and explained. Finally, an interpretation is made—a generalization drawn from the cartoon. The students should also learn to

---

[17] Summers, p. 146.

evaluate the cartoon for its bias, emotional tone, and prejudices. Discussion in the classroom about the content of the cartoon, the techniques used and the message intended is advisable in increasing student competence with this form of representation. Students also enjoy drawing their own cartoons.

Following Directions

This is a specific type of reading which all students need to be able to do and which requires an intensity and precision not required by most other reading. You can help your students in this area in two ways. One is to make your directions to the students as clear and unambiguous as possible. The other is to alert them to techniques of reading directions correctly. The usual procedure is to have the students read the directions in their entirety to get a general picture of what is to be done, read each step, do what is directed, reread the step to check, and go on to the next step, until the activity is completed. Then reread the entire set of directions as a final check. Such intense reading is usually not within the ken of the student unless he is taught how. You will need also to check with the students for accuracy of meaning. For example, *compare, superimpose, match, select* and other such words are general ones and the student may have a general idea of what they mean. The specific meaning as applied to a particular set of directions, however, may elude him.

Study the set of directions on p. 121 and note what would make it clearer, the words the student must know precisely, and the purpose of the diagram.

Research Reading

Research reading requires that the student use a variety of references to find information supplementary to the textbook. It is also his application of the skills of comprehension involving the location, selection and evaluation of information. Reference reading, usually to prepare reports, is the student's opportunity to develop independence in gaining information. All of the reading skills—word recognition, vocabulary and comprehension—are required, as well as locational skills. Though the student is given the opportunity to show his independence by applying the skills, the skills do have to be taught prior to his embarking on a research project or report.

Perhaps one of the first prerequisites is that you understand the nature and content of the reference materials pertinent to your discipline, and be interested in teaching your students the use of these materials. You must also see that the reference materials are available. One source for both you and the students is the school librarian. He can be invaluable in assisting in the location of information. However, no librarian has the time to guide students step by step through a project requiring reference reading. Therefore, in addition to the skills of comprehension and notetaking, you need to be aware of and to teach the locational skills. They are:

1. the ability to use the alphabet
2. the ability to locate materials using the Dewey Decimal Classification or the Library of Congress System
3. the ability to use the card catalog

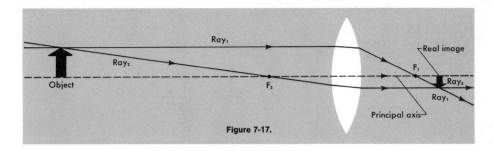

Figure 7-17.

EXPERIMENT.   The location of a real image produced by a convex lens can be predicted. You can diagram the location of a real image. On the left side of a piece of paper, draw an upright ½-in. arrow representing the object. Seven inches to the right of the arrow, draw a side view of a convex lens 2 in. high. With a ruler, draw a dotted line across the paper through the center of the lens to show its axis. Then measure two 2-in. focal lengths, one to the right of the lens and one to the left of the lens. Mark the principal focus to the left of the lens F_2, and mark the principal focus to the right of the lens F_1.

Now draw a line parallel to the axis from the top of the arrow to the lens. This line represents a light ray. Continue the line from the lens to the principal focus F_1. Draw a second line from the top of the arrow through the principal focus F_2. Continue the line until it meets the lens. As the ray leaves the lens on the opposite side, continue the ray parallel to the principal axis. The point at which the two lines cross, or intersect, is the location of the top of the real image of the object. (Figure 7–17.)[18]

This set of directions is simply stated, but would be easier to follow if each step were itemized in a listing. (Steps are numbered. In the original form each step was signalled by a separate clause or sentence.) There are ten steps in all.

One direction is not clear except that the diagram the student is to draw is represented above the set of directions. There is no indication that the arrow should rest on the dotted axis line.

Words the student must understand:

Direction words:		Content words:
left side	axis	real image
draw	mark	focal lengths
upright	parallel	principal focus
representing	top	principal axis
represents	continue	
right	meets	
dotted line	opposite side	

4.　the ability to use such indexes as *The Reader's Guide to Periodical Literature*
5.　the ability to use specific reference materials
6.　the ability to use guide words
7.　the ability to determine the best source(s) of information
8.　the ability to differentiate between factual sources and fictional sources
9.　the ability to list a source of information properly in a research paper
10.　the ability to skim.[19]

The general steps of a research project requiring reference reading are: (1) select a topic or problem—determine what is to be found; (2) discuss resource material—type and how used; (3) teach and review with students the techniques of note-taking; (4) guide the students in techniques of organizing their information into a report; (5) discuss ways of presenting the information to the class.

If committees are organized for group reports, standards for committee work must be evolved with the class and the responsibilities of the committee chairman specifically stated. This would be done before instruction in the types and uses of resource material.

I have suggested a general plan for getting the students started on their reference reading.

The teacher plans the research assignments with the students. Usually, problems for research are evolved after the students have a basic knowledge of the topic. Through the basic understandings obtained from the textbook and other required readings, the students develop a background which enables them to identify with the teacher topics or problems for research. The problems, in many classes, are determined through class discussion as both the teacher and class see the need for more information.

When research problems are assigned, the teacher will then need to insure the students' competence to execute their projects. For example, students may need help in analyzing problems to determine the key words or "entry words." Sample problems should be analyzed in class, with the students determining the key words and then checking to see if they lead to the appropriate information.

During this preliminary instructional period, appropriate sources of information are determined. For instance, the problem determines whether a biography, an encyclopedia, an atlas, periodical source, *The World Almanac,* or some other source is to be used. If the problem is about the life history of some famous person, an encyclopedia or a biography may be used. *Who's Who in America* would be used for currently well-known persons. One of the skills of using sources of information is selecting the appropriate ones.

The teacher must also be sure that his students know how to use important sources of information before they engage in research problems. If the topic requires the use of periodical sources, students will need to know how to find

---

[19] David L. Shepherd, "Using Sources of Information," in *Developing Study Skills in Secondary Schools,* ed. Harold E. Herber (Newark, Delaware: International Reading Association, 1965), p. 46.

the specific issues they need in the *Reader's Guide to Periodical Literature.* If they are to use general information books in the library, they must know how to use the card catalog and how to find the appropriate volumes.

When the student is able to note his key words, identify the sources he needs and use them properly, he is then ready to conduct his research with competence and success. His actual research is then an application of the instruction he has received. At the time the student is doing the research, the teacher will be able to individualize instruction by giving further help when it is needed.[20]

In addition, you will need to teach the students the techniques of proper bibliographical form, use of quotations, and use of footnotes.

RATE OF COMPREHENSION

As many high school students become aware or interested in reading improvement, one of their first concerns is their reading speed—the number of words they read each minute. They wish to complete their assignments with dispatch. To a degree their concern with speed is valid. Smith and Dechant point out that "no one actually reads faster than he comprehends, but many read much more slowly than their comprehension would permit. Generally the limiting factor to rate improvement is the mind rather than the vision."[21]

Perhaps a better term than speed is the term *rate of comprehension* since the reader's quickness of understanding in large measure regulates the speed of coverage. Also, a distinction must be made between reading nontechnical and/or story-type information, and study reading. The latter takes much slower and more analytical reading. In assignments for the content areas, as he applies the SQ3R formula, the student needs to skim for the overview, read intensively for the purposes of the assignment and then read slowly (review) as the demands of the material require. The student's rate of comprehension is dependent upon (1) the difficulty of the material, (2) the experiential background with the topic, and (3) the purpose of reading.

One mark of a mature reader is that he is able to select and adjust his rate of reading to the demands of the material and the assignment. He is flexible in his rate, not only with different types of material, but also within a single selection. He reads faster when he is familiar with the information, and when the author is giving illustrations of an anecdotal nature. He slows up when the author is presenting and developing concepts and arguments. He may read slowly also when he wishes to savor the beauty of a literary passage.

One technique related to rate in which students should grow in competence is scanning to find a specific fact or material related to the specific topic or skimming to get a general overview or point of view. Skill in both is needed in reference read-

---

[20] *Ibid.,* pp. 46–47.

[21] Henry P. Smith and Emerald Dechant, *Psychology in Teaching Reading* (Englewood Cliffs, New Jersey: Prentice-Hall, Inc., 1961), p. 222.

ing. Students know that scanning and skimming require faster reading than usual, but they often do not know how. All content teachers can give students practice in these skills prior to their engagement in reference reading.

To help students scan:

(1)   Determine clearly the specific information desired by identifying specific key word or figure to look for.

(2)   Look down the page for the key word or figures (use finger as guide).

(3)   Read carefully as soon as the key word is spotted to determine whether the desired information is included.

To help students skim:

(1)   Use introductory paragraphs including Table of Contents and the Preface.

(2)   Use topical headings.

(3)   Read first and/or last sentences of major paragraphs.

(4)   Note italicized words.

(5)   Note graphic aids.

(6)   Read summaries.

As you will note, skimming is essentially the same as previewing or doing an overview which is advised before careful slower reading is undertaken.

Flexibility in rate of reading is the goal for the students. They need to realize that it is permissible as well as desirable to know when and how to skim, scan, read at a cruising speed or to read with intensive slowness.

The major premise of this chapter is that the skills of reading are best taught and practiced when the student will use them. Therefore, as the student reads in each of his content areas, he needs to be taught how to apply the reading skills in the appropriate manner to each area when the skill is required for understanding. It is essentially the sequence of need, instruction, and application.

SUGGESTED QUESTIONS AND PROBLEMS TO BE CONSIDERED IN REFERENCE TO YOUR OWN CLASSROOM

List A (For readers who are training to be teachers.)

1.   Plan to guide your students in the steps of the SQ3R formula.

2.   Plan a research project and note the skills or tasks the students will need to do in order to complete the project successfully. Then plan to incorporate appropriate teaching into your unit plan.

3.   Plan questions which students are to answer by using only graphic aids such as maps, pictures, charts.

4.   Investigate the topics included in your subject area and determine the reference materials you would consider important for students.

5.   Investigate the printed material pertinent to your subject area and determine the various ways you might teach them to organize their notes, i.e., outline, comparative columns, diagram, chart.

List B (For readers who are teaching.)

1. Use a group of research topics and through class discussion evolve the subtopics, the most appropriate sequence, and interrelationships.
2. Analyze a set of directions with the students to note the equipment needed, the number and order of steps, and important specific details.
3. After giving an assignment, ask the students how they intend to plan their study.
4. In various assignments, evolve with the students an appropriate organization of notes, i.e. outline, comparative columns, diagram, charts.
5. Discuss with your students appropriate reference materials pertinent to your subject.

CHAPTER SIX

Basic Procedures

The goal of every classroom teacher is probably that each student become independent in his ability to think about and use the understandings of the subject. Some teachers put specific emphasis upon content, with the hope that as the student absorbs information he will become competent in thinking and reasoning. Mastery of information is necessary, but it is not enough for independence. Specific habits and attitudes are also important. Inculcated into the student's thinking should be the habit of inquiry. The mature student wishes to know and strives to find out. Independence in the study of a discipline means that the student discovers much for himself. He does not need to be told all that he needs to know—he inquires and discovers. The teacher can encourage the development of the habit of inquiry by insuring that the student has the tools of study and understanding he needs for inquiry and self-discovery.

Related to discovery is the problem-solving procedure since it is a means of discovery. The student formulates his question—inquiry—and uses the steps of problem-solving to discover the answer. The student will need to be guided to use the elementary steps of problem solving in his attempt to find answers and to plot action from his concerns with the subject. The steps of problem solving indicate that the student needs to be able to:

1. Realize what he needs to know.
2. Identify specifically the area or problem.
3. Collect and organize pertinent information.
4. Consider hypotheses and choose the most likely one.
5. Draw conclusions and make generalizations.
6. Implement the conclusion in thinking about subsequent information.

The habits of inquiry, discovery, and problem solving have in common the fact that each requires the student to think. Thinking means effort, activity, and involvement on the part of the student. Yet, many teachers lament the lack of active involvement which their students display. They seem to read like a sponge—to soak up information from the page without any activity on their part other than looking over the line of print in a somewhat systematic left to right pattern. Such students do not have a purpose for reading other than, "Mr. Smith said to read this chapter," or "We have to be able to discuss the material in class." Such reading results in little comprehension other than a hodgepodge of facts. There is no inquiry, discovery or problem solving. There is no active thinking. When you note this type of attack on a reading assignment, you will need to implement classroom procedures which require active learning.

Guilford describes three major types of thinking. One type he labels as *convergent thinking,* in which the student gathers together from numerous sources various aspects of information about a topic in order to arrive at carefully thought out conclusions, the most comprehensive generalization, the most appropriate answer in view of the evidence given. Another type is *divergent thinking,* which involves elaboration upon given information which may go in many directions. The third type of thinking, according to Guilford, is *evaluation,* which encompasses knowing whether two units are identical or not identical, whether there is a logical consistency in relationships, whether the information is workable. The sensitivity of the reader to problems, and the implications he sees, are also part of evaluative thinking. The type and level of thinking used, Guilford maintains, is determined by two factors. One is the material—whether it stimulates the imagination of the reader, leads him in sequence toward a specific conclusion, gives alternatives, calls for checking and listing facts and arguments. The other factor is the creative teacher who will use the material in provocative ways, largely through skillful questioning.[1]

PRINCIPLES OF LEARNING APPLIED TO PROCEDURE

The formulation of classroom procedure is guided by the teacher's educational philosophy as well as by specific goals of skill instruction and information to be taught. The teacher whose goals include the student's ability to study and learn independently will keep in mind the following principles of learning.

Purpose and Motivation—Prerequisites to Learning

Hildreth points out that teachers cannot teach a child anything that the child does not want to learn.[2] Purpose and motivation go hand in hand. The students' motivation is heightened if they know specifically what they are to find from their

---

[1] J. P. Guilford, "Frontiers in Thinking That Teachers Should Know About," *The Reading Teacher* XIII, No. 3 (February 1960): 176–182.

[2] Gertrude Hildreth, "Some Principles of Learning Applied to Reading," in *Readings on Reading Instruction,* ed. Albert J. Harris (New York: David McKay Company, Inc., 1963), p. 32.

reading. This establishment of purpose occurs in the beginning of the study of a topic. The purpose should be related to things the students wish to know about the topic. It should be related to their concerns. Effective classroom procedure will elicit purposes for reading from the students as you preview the material together, discuss their background knowledge and as the students air their opinions and impressions about the topic.

Students Need Experiential Base to Understand New Information

Sometimes students will find a subject difficult to understand because they bring little information to it. Students often do not realize the background of under- standing that they do have, either because they do not readily remember or because they do not relate the information in their background to the topic. In such cases the teacher's task is to help them remember and relate what they know to supply infor- mation which can be used as background. Various audio-visual materials can be used for this purpose; previewing the material to point out significant facts and concepts as well as organization can also help.

Concepts and Information Must have Meaning and Significance

The personal satisfaction a student gets from the material and the relevance of it to his life increases his interest and motivation. Students often comment, "I don't see why I have to study this, I'll never use it." Unless the student is the rare one who will study because he wishes to do well no matter what the subject matter, he needs to be shown how and why it is important that he learn it. In order to assist the students in seeing relevance, the teacher must know his students' past school records, their reading proficiency, their interests, and their goals. He must know them as individuals. Unless he does, the class is nothing more than a period for the dissemination of information.

Effective Procedure Considers Individual Differences of Students

This principle is obvious because no two people are alike. There are similarities of feature, interest, desire, and personality, but each individual is unique. There- fore, for classroom procedure to be effective for all students it must apply to each individual. This is where much classroom procedure breaks down in practice. Many teachers give up in frustration and resort to mass instruction, aiming toward the median of the group. Getting to know and planning for each individual in a class is difficult, especially at the secondary school level where you meet a new class group each hour comprising a daily total of approximately one hundred twenty-five students. But there are techniques you can use. See Chapter 7 on indi- vidual differences, pages 147–168.

The Student Must Be Actively Involved to Learn

That learning in the classroom takes place as a result of the student's own effort is an established fact. The teacher's procedures and techniques cannot do the learning for the student but rather give the student explanations and guidelines. In- struction should enable the student to learn effectively by helping him to organize his information and to indicate to him the significance of it to real life. The teacher is in actuality a resource person to the student.

Learning a Skill Requires Practice

Reading is a skill and requires practice. As in any other skill such as playing some sport or a musical instrument, the student's level of execution is dependent upon the amount of productive practice he does. One way he can practice reading is to read widely from a variety of sources. Students should be encouraged to do wide supplementary reading, both for research and for recreation. Each classroom should have a library of supplementary books, and assignments should foster their use. Time in class will need to be devoted to reading supplementary materials and discussing their contents; the textbook alone is often not enough.

The Student's Emotional Attitudes Determine How Well He Learns to Read

Emotional attitudes can affect a student's understanding in two ways. One instance is the student who has a history of reading deficiency. Such a student is "turned off" by reading. It is too much work to be an activity in which he engages voluntarily. He tends to perpetuate his deficiencies because of his lack of practice through voluntary reading. In this case there needs to be a wide range of materials available so that there will be some material the student can read with mastery. Success on the part of the student is a cardinal necessity. Instruction in the basic skills pertinent to his need must be given as it applies.

The other instance is the student's predisposed feelings toward a topic or an issue. The student may find that the information presented by an author differs widely from his own preconceived ideas and beliefs. That can be disturbing and he may turn away because of his own disparate views. Betts maintains that attitudes affect the student's interpretation and recall of information. His conclusions are:

1. How a reader interprets a selection depends upon what he takes to it of information, of techniques, of inquiry, and of attitudes.
   a. Unfavorable attitudes tend to contribute to inaccurate interpretations, to interfere with comprehension.
   b. Ideas in harmony with the learner's attitude are more easily learned.
   c. Ideas contrary to attitudes contribute to confusion and irritation.
   d. The stronger the attitude, the more it influences interpretation.
2. Attitudes influence recall of ideas.
   a. Ideas in harmony with the learner's attitudes are more likely to be recalled than those in conflict.
   b. Vividness of recall depends upon the strength of the attitude.
3. The tendency to rationalize is increased to the degree that an idea conflicts with attitudes.
4. A disinclination to read on a topic is increased to the degree that attitudes toward the idea are unfavorable.
5. The older the child the more his interpretation is influenced by attitudes.[3]

---

[3] Emmett A. Betts, "Reading as a Thinking Process," *The National Elementary Principal* XXXV, No. 1 (Sept. 1955): 90–91.

The teacher's role in this case is to develop the student's abilities to read for inquiry and to read critically. The problem-solving approach with conclusions drawn from evidence is helpful because the student must rely more on his rational judgment than on his attitude.

Learning to Read Should be Integrated with the Study of How Language is Used in Many Different Situations

Reading, being one of the aspects of the language arts, should not be isolated, but taught in relation to its position as a way language is used. Effective subject-matter teaching is dependent upon the student's facility with language as it is used in all forms of oral communication in the classroom.

PLANNING THE LESSON

The principles cited above can serve as guidelines for planning instructional procedure. Beyond the guidelines is the specific planning which must be done for each lesson, which may encompass one to several class periods. Whatever steps of procedure are followed, the strengths and weaknesses of the students in reading will affect the emphases on reading skill instruction made as well as the content of the subject. The fusion of these two aspects of teaching is accomplished largely through adjusting the content instruction to the student's background and skill proficiencies. For example, if the students are weak in noting the main idea, your instruction will focus largely on the main ideas of the subject matter and how they are discerned.

As you review, for the purpose of planning instruction, the needs of the students and the requirements of the subject, behavioral objectives will help you define specific goals. Behavioral objectives are statements which describe what students are to be able to do after completing the instruction pertaining to a body of content. Considerations of the degree of student achievement expected and in what form and under what conditions the student will exhibit this achievement will be conditions of the total objective. For example, "Without the use of class notes or other references the students will be able to describe the cycle of the photosynthetic process showing how each part leads to the next." When considering a specific reading skill, "The student will note the main ideas and details of the material describing the photosynthetic process and record them in the form of an outline."

Reading instruction applied to the different content fields will use behavioral objectives in two domains. One is *cognitive* and the other is *affective*. The *cognitive domain* involves the student's performance in learning and using the knowledge of each subject. Essentially, cognitive objectives mean (1) that he is able to recall the important ideas, methods, processes, structure, classification and categories; (2) that he has a knowledge of the vocabulary; (3) that he understands the structure of thought by being able to study, organize and evaluate it; (4) that he is able to communicate by conventional forms of language, both oral and written; (5) that he is able to judge facts, opinions, hypotheses, and principles; (6) that he is able to use the problem-solving procedure as a pattern of inquiry and (7) that he has knowledge of and is able to apply principles and generalizations. The reading skills are instruments used by the students to accomplish objectives. The *affective domain* involves attitudes, values and beliefs that determine how a student responds to his environment. The student's interest and attitude toward reading as well as the value he places upon it would be in the affective area.

The Reading Lesson Applied to the Content Fields

Stauffer points out that scholars of the reading process are basically in agreement on the matter of reading as a thinking process and on the basic plan of classroom procedure for teaching the reading-thinking process. The plan has been developed for direction in teaching the story-type material in basal readers. Though there are minor variations from one basal series to another in the reading-thinking procedure, the fundamental steps remain the same. The emphasis has been to lead students to use elements of the thinking process as they read material. Students are guided to read for purposes, to relate the information to their background of experience and knowledge, and to evaluate the information by making judgments about the significance, accuracy, and pertinence of what they read. Stauffer goes on to say that declaring purposes, reasoning, and judging are three aspects of the reading-thinking process and are fundamental to the reading-to-learn process. He adds a fourth step which is refining and extending ideas from the reading material.[4]

A careful study of the reading-thinking process as outlined by Stauffer shows that this plan is as applicable to the content areas as it is to the basal reader of the elementary school.

The Basic Plan:
Directed Reading-Thinking Applied to Content Fields

I. Preparation for reading
   A. Investigating and expanding the background of student experience.
      1. Finding out what the students know.
      2. Noting misconceptions of the students.
      3. Filling in with information to give the students an adequate background for understanding.
      4. Arousing student interest.
      5. Giving them an awareness of the significance of the information.
   B. Previewing the reading material
      1. Noting the basic structure of the information—the introduction, summary, specific sections.
      2. Discussing the title and subtitles.
      3. Directing attention to the graphic aids: maps, pictures, diagrams, etc.
      4. Noting study aids: specific summaries, questions, vocabulary lists.
      5. Noting new vocabulary which is usually italicized in a textbook.

---

[4] Russell G. Stauffer, *Teaching Reading as a Thinking Process* (New York: Harper and Row, Inc., 1969), pp. 14–15.

   C.   Introduce the vocabulary pertinent to the fundamental concepts
1. Clarifying basically the fundamental conceptual terms, usually one to five in number.
2. Analyzing the structure of the words, if necessary, to aid word recognition.
3. Assisting students to bring their experiences to bear on the meanings of words.
4. Alerting students to the specific meaning as the word is used in the text.
   D.   Evolve purposes for reading
1. Evolving purposes in terms of the student's own background and needs, those of the group, and in terms of the understandings desired from materials.
2. Helping students to think of purposes as well.

II.   Reading the material silently
   A.   Noting the students' ability to adjust their reading to the purposes set up, and to the material.
   B.   Observing students to note specific areas of need.
1. Vocabulary: recognition of the word, specific meaning as applied to the content.
2. Comprehension: organization of data, finding answers to purposes, noting relationships within data.

III.   Developing Comprehension
   A.   Discussing answers to purpose questions.
   B.   Clarifying and guiding further development of the concepts and vocabulary, introducing new vocabulary if needed.
   C.   Assisting the students in noting organization of information and in recall of pertinent facts.
   D.   Noting need for further information from both the text and other source materials.
   E.   Redefining purposes; setting new purposes for reading.

IV.   Re-reading (silent and/or oral, in part or in entirety)
   A.   Clarifying further the essential pertinent information and concepts.
   B.   Giving specific skill training in comprehension as indicated by needs of individuals and the group.
1. Seeing organization of data.
2. Interpreting data: drawing conclusions, making inferences, making generalizations, seeing interrelationships of data.
3. Evaluating: making judgments, noting author's intent, seeing the significance of the material, noting the use of language.
4. Applying information to real life situations, formulating new ideas, reorganizing old ideas.

5. Noting use of words: emotive, new meanings, contextual usage, technical terms, indefinite and general terms.
6. Setting up areas for further reading and research.

V. Following up the information
    A. Setting up problems requiring further information
        1. Using problem-solving; delineating the problem.
        2. Locating additional information.
        3. Reading to get additional information.
        4. Selecting and organizing pertinent ideas related to problem.
        5. Concluding and generalizing from data.
        6. Preparing the presentation of the report.
    B. Choosing supplementary recreational reading related to topic to develop and extend interests, attitudes, and appreciations.
    C. Extending further understandings and clarifying further concepts as necessary.
    D. Analyzing the information and helping students to relate it to their own lives.

It is apparent that the teacher must serve as a guide to the students in the reading-thinking plan. Students are not merely assigned a specified number of pages to read which will be the basis of a class recitation. Instead, students are *guided* through the reading material three times for different reasons: to establish background and concepts, to increase clarification of the information, and to apply the reading skills needed for understanding. The reading-thinking plan goes beyond rote learning and mere memorization of data. Students are guided to seek information, to evaluate it, and to apply it. Needed skills at each stage should be incorporated into the plan to give the students the tools they need. A discussion of each step follows to show further how the reading-thinking plan operates.

    I. Preparation for reading is probably the most vital step of a reading lesson. It sets the stage for the lesson. Your preplanning to relate the information to the student's background and your selection of objectives to be accomplished insure the student's reading success. Sometimes this step is equated to the assignment, but it is a great deal more than merely telling the students what they are to read for and how.

    In the four aspects of this step—establishing background, previewing the material, clarifying basic concepts and evolving purposes—the teacher must perform a delicate balancing act. On one hand he needs to insure student knowledge of the topic while on the other allowing enough information to be discovered so that the student can have the satisfaction of inquiring and discovering for himself. The goal should be to provide just enough background and guidance to enable the student to continue learning with success and competence.

    An important precept in learning is that the student's ease in learning new information is affected by his background of information. Sometimes this has been expressed as "the more a student knows about a topic, the more he can get from other specific information." Judging the amount of background information needed by the student is part of preplanning.

Experienced teachers know the value of graphic materials, models, diagrams, and various other audio-visual aids. Reading selected information from sources outside the textbook can be valuable on occasion. Questions to probe the student's fund of knowledge will help the student remember related information and ideas. Yet another means of providing background information is by previewing the content material to be studied.

Previewing the material is a "warm-up" for the student. He can note the scope and depth of the information. He can note the form of organization used by the author—the topics included and their interrelationship. It serves both to build additional pre-reading background and to alert the student to the nature of the information. Through the preview he may note new vocabulary and gain a first acquaintance with the terms before he reads. He may note questions posed by the author which can serve as purposes for reading. With your help he may acquire the skill of restating topical headings in question form as another means of formulating specific questions of purpose. You direct the preview for two principal reasons. One is to establish background about the subject and the manner in which it is presented. The other is to assist the student in the technique of previewing so that he will learn how to do it when he is reading independently.

During the preview new terms can be clarified. These must be kept to a minimum. Whereas the nature of the material will determine the number of new terms or words, the number clarified at this time should be no more than five. Other words can be clarified subsequently in the discussion of the lesson. For example, as the student is reading about ecology the basic terms might be *ecology, pollution* and *conservation.* These would be basic, and ones the students should understand prior to reading. Subsequent terms such as the various types of land conservation will be developed later. Two reasons for introducing only a few at a time are (1) the terms can be kept in mind and woven into the discussion by both the teacher and the students, perhaps used in sentences of original composition; and (2) terms less basic to the understanding of the information are left for the student to learn by using the various techniques of context and the knowledge of word and sentence structure which he has been taught.

The fourth aspect of establishing readiness is evolving purposes for reading. The student needs to know what to look for as he reads. Purposes stimulate both his curiosity and thinking. They serve as motivators. Stauffer states:

> When pupils have become involved in the dynamics of a purpose-setting lesson, the self-commitment on an intellectual as well as an emotional level has tremendous motivating force . . .
>
> The reader, having helped to create the reading climate, will strive to maintain it. Its tempo is geared to the finding of answers and to the proving or disproving of conjectures. He will want to move forward to test his ideas, to seek, to reconstruct, to reflect, and to prove. What is most astonishing about all this is the integrity with which the reader operates. He is out to seek the truth, and this is his dedication.[5]

These four aspects of the readiness for reading step are not handled separately. They are interwoven. As you preview the material with the students, background

---

[5] Stauffer, p. 25.

will be enriched and expanded, new vocabulary will be clarified and purposes will evolve. How long you spend on this step can not be predetermined. It depends on (1) the extent of the student's background (if the background is meager, obviously more time will be needed), (2) the length and difficulty of the material, (3) the purpose for using the material—the importance of the information to the purposes of the subject. Some preparation for reading would take only five minutes of class time. Other selections may require a class period or more. Your task is knowing how much preparation is needed and providing means for the students to acquire it regardless of the time it takes. The interest and competence of the students are guidelines to keep in mind in determining when enough preparation has been made.

During the **II.   Reading the material silently** step of the lesson procedure, you have the opportunity to extend individual assistance to any student who has a question or who has difficulty in reading the selection. Many secondary teachers claim that they do not have opportunities to give attention to individual students because of the large number of students they meet in class each day. However, when the student reads silently in your class, you can extend individual help when he needs it and the material demands it. Assistance can be extended to note the author's organization of information, to note structure words, to clarify the meanings of words, and word structure. At this time you can help specific needs which you may have noted from previous class work. Often, silent reading is assigned for outside of class and this is also proper procedure. In such cases the student has to be independent in reading—a skill he must acquire. But, of course, there can be no individual help given when the assignment is read outside of class. Perhaps a balance needs to be struck here with some assignments read, or at least started, in class and others read outside.

In the **III.   Developing comprehension** step of the lesson, the following are accomplished:

1. Purposes are clarified.
2. New vocabulary terms are discussed, especially those which the student has failed to master independently and which the teacher considers important to the understanding of the material.
3. Important understandings are developed.
4. The basic structure of the information is noted—the interrelationships of main ideas to details, cause and effect relationships, author's purpose and so on.
5. Pertinent reading skills are developed and apparent needs of the class and of individuals are noted.

In the traditional lesson of times past this step corresponded to the recitation, in which the teacher both tested informally and clarified the understandings that were intended. This step still has in it the ingredients of a recitation. However, there is an added dimension—through discussion the students are guided to apply pertinent skills. For example, paragraph analysis may be used with paragraphs and sentences, from which the pupil must be able to obtain accurate meaning. For each lesson the teacher will delineate behavioral objectives based on specific tasks to be accomplished by the students.

Step **IV.**   **Rereading** is done for clarification. When rereading is needed, new and specific purposes are set. The rereading may be of the entire selection or of parts. It may be a written assignment for which the rereading must be done or it may be done during a class discussion where some specific point is to be clarified. It may be silent or oral. The students can use information gained thus far to extend their understandings through specific details, relationships, conclusions, nuances, and so on. If there is a specific skill need the rereading may pinpoint the application of the skill in obtaining the required information. The skill is taught during the step in developing comprehension. Now the students apply the instruction with further evaluation resulting from the ensuing discussion and written assignment. This step may be thought of as the "clincher." The student applies under direction both his knowledge and skill. Groundwork may also be laid for extended reading and research.

The **V.**   **Follow-up** step is designed to increase the student's knowledge and to give him the opportunity to apply his basic knowledge to related problems. In the follow-up the following can be accomplished:

1.   Develop and extend interests, attitudes, and appreciations.
2.   Develop further the ability to evaluate data in terms of point of view expressed, emotive language, use of facts or opinions, author's qualifications, and the students' own views and prejudices.
3.   Conduct research on a problem related to the content.

In this step, various projects related to the problem may be engaged in that might involve creative writing (plays, essays, an original plan, etc.) and various art activities (murals, models, pictures, etc.). A basic aim of the followup is the student's application of the skills and information he has been taught. It is also another prime opportunity for you to extend individual assistance.

Review of this procedure brings up certain considerations for the teacher. (1) The purpose of the five-step procedure is to guide the student in his ability to think. It attempts to provide the student with both the information and the skill he needs for thinking. (2) Teachers often become concerned with time. This procedure may seem endless, especially in light of a year's crowded curriculum. No specific time limit can be placed on the directed lesson procedure. As we have noted, the time spent on a specific selection is dependent upon the student's background, the length and difficulty of the selection, and the importance of it to the total curriculum. A lesson may take only a class period or it may take more than a week. In cases of material which is not of essential importance and is not fundamental to the understanding of the subject, and thereby used only to give the students supplementary and enriched data, steps four and five may be deleted. It is not always necessary to reread or to follow up with various activities. Rereading at times may be incorporated into step three—developing comprehension. (3) The class procedure is teacher-directed. You are in command to guide, instruct, and develop the student's ability to think about the material. The procedure is similar to the SQ3R study formula which the student uses on his own when he is studying an assignment. Since there is this similarity, the student should be alerted to the basic steps of the lesson procedure as well as the variations upon it which you employ. In this way he will begin to realize the fundamental steps of study procedure.

The SQ3R and the directed lesson have a similarity shown in the diagram comparing them step by step.

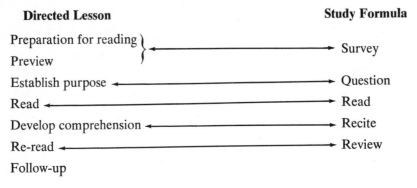

Directed Lesson		Study Formula
Preparation for reading	⟶	Survey
Preview		
Establish purpose	⟵	Question
Read	⟵	Read
Develop comprehension	⟵	Recite
Re-read	⟵	Review
Follow-up		

The efficiency of the study formula as well as of the directed lesson is readily apparent. A minimum of three readings of the material is accomplished, each for a different purpose. The first reading is the preview or the survey which gives an overview of the information covered, notes the author's organization and study helps included, and alerts to new and specific vocabulary. Necessary background is established for effective comprehension. The second reading is the silent reading to get the essential important understandings. The third reading is the rereading or review to clarify details and to note the interrelationships of the factual data which the student is able to do because he can now draw upon the understandings from his previous readings. It is interesting to note that these three readings parallel the basic essential structure of a well-written essay or article: introduction (survey, preview), body (the silent detailed reading) and summary or conclusion (rereading or review to clinch the ideas).

Unit Procedure

The unit procedure, which usually encompasses a long period of time—two to six weeks—also follows the basic structure we have been describing. The procedure, demonstrated in Appendix II (page 303ff.), shows the similarity.

Introducing the unit	⟶	Preparation for reading
Developing the unit	⟶	Read
Pupil-teacher planning for research	⟷	Developing Comprehension
Conducting research	⟶	Re-reading
Culminating research	⟶	Follow-up

The introduction of the unit includes evolving the unit problem with the students, establishing the scope of the problem, surveying the areas to be included, and filling in needed background. Developing the unit is the investigation into the basic subject matter pertinent to the unit. It is similar to the student reading an individual assignment to gain basic information pertinent to his purposes for reading. Pupil-teacher planning for research results in research projects developing from the study of the basic subject matter. The subject information is studied and discussed leading toward the research problems. This is similar to developing comprehension of a separate selection. Then, conducting research includes much the same pattern as the re-reading which is done for separate purposes just as the research is done around a specific problem. Finally culminating the unit—the presentation of the research—can be equated with the follow-up step of a lesson procedure.

The unit procedure is a huge umbrella encompassing the entire scope of a specific problem or topic. The directed lesson and the individual study are small segments which fit under the umbrella of the unit study.

DEVELOPING INTERESTS

Effective classroom procedures have another dimension beside the important one of developing and guiding the student's ability to think while reading. Effective teaching can also increase students' interest in reading for both information and pleasure. This additional dimension sometimes seems elusive, particularly with the competition of other adolescent interests and other media which can provide the student with both. You know that interest does not develop just by telling the student to be interested. But, there are considerations for classroom procedure which tend to foster it.

Classroom Procedure to Develop Interests

1. *Material must be available.*   One of the obvious ways to develop interest in reading is to surround the students with books. Books related to the topic under study should be placed in various places around the classroom. They should be in effect, if not in actual fact, within arm's reach. Very few students can resist looking at interesting and related books when they are available. It is as important for classrooms at the high school level to have classroom libraries as it is for elementary classrooms.

The classroom library should number three to five books per student and they should be about various facets of the topic being studied as well as on different levels of difficulty. The books can be single or dual copies of reference material, textbooks other than the one(s) used for intensive study, and trade books. The collection would include both fiction and nonfiction. The cost of the classroom library can be kept to a minimum by using paperbacks, collections from both the school and public libraries for the period of time a topic is being studied, and by books some students may be able to bring in. The classroom library can and should grow over a period of years with new titles being added constantly.

The classroom library is of tremendous importance in developing both interest and skill in reading. Yet, I have observed classroom after classroom in the high school which are barren of any additional or supplementary material. Everything we are discussing in this volume requires an adequate supply of reading material. Reading cannot very well be taught without books!

2. *The teacher's enthusiasm is contagious.*   The teacher who likes to read usually does, and is predisposed to develop this interest among his students. Obviously, if books are available, increased use of them is sparked by incorporating their use in your procedure, talking about them, and giving time to the students to examine and read them. There must be involvement with the books.

3. *Give the students time to read.*   Though it may be maintained that a student will find time for his interest—and will find time to read if he wants to—many adolescents have daily schedules which preclude wide reading. We need only to reflect on the typical student's schedule—time in school, time for homework, an out-of-school job or responsibility, and interests in avocational and social activities —and it will soon become evident that many students do not have time "hanging on their hands." Therefore, some time should be set aside in class for the students to read. Get them started in reading material of interest to them, and many students will make time outside of class to continue it.

4. *Materials at different levels are essential.*   None of us voluntarily chooses material which is too difficult for us to read—certainly not for pleasure. Students may choose highly technical material voluntarily if it is about a strong interest and is pertinent to a student's problem which he is trying to solve. But the fact remains that the student must feel competent with the material if he is to read it voluntarily.

5. *The style of the material—how it is written—is equally important.* The level of the student's reading is a determinant of the style of writing he enjoys. Obviously, long and involved syntax, figurative language, and passages of description are not barriers to the competent reader, while the slow and reluctant reader is particularly susceptible to the style of the material. His skills of reading are usually woefully inadequate which may cause an unfavorable emotional association with reading. Reading for such a student is not an activity in which he can appear competent, even to himself. Therefore he reacts best to a natural style that is simple though not condescending. He understands more easily simple direct sentences and short paragraphs consisting largely of familiar words. He likes a fast-moving story with little description and mood setting. A story that pulls him along with much dialogue, a simple plot and familiar life situations appeals most. With nonfiction, the reluctant reader likes easy-to-comprehend material with many pictures and other graphic aids. The format of the book should be attractive and the book should not look too hard. Yet, the slow reader may be defensive about reading a book that looks like it is intended for the primary or elementary school level.

6. *The material must be pertinent to the reader.*   The reasons why a high school student reads differ little from the reasons why the population as a whole reads. They read for enjoyment and for information pertinent to their concerns. These concerns and problems center around their social relations with both sexes

and with vocational choices. They read in accordance with their special interests and their hobbies as well as stories and information pertinent to the current social and political issues of the day, especially those which affect them directly. The stories they read must be true to life. Essential to their voluntary choice is material which relates to their background of experiences and that which helps them to choose alternatives or to solve problems they face. Carlsen lists the types of stories enjoyed most by early, middle, and late adolescents:

Early Adolescence (Ages 11–14)
    Animal Stories
        Boys tend to prefer stories about animals in the wild
        Girls tend to prefer stories about animals dependent upon humans
    Adventure stories
        Preferred by boys
    Mystery stories
        Boys like the stories in wild and unusual spots
        Girls like the stories set in familiar locations
    Tales of the Supernatural
    Sport Stories
    Growing up around the world
        Girls are particularly interested in adolescent life in various countries
    Home and family-life stories
        Preferred by girls
    Broad bold slapstick
    Settings in the past
        Girls prefer stories—not historical fiction—which use the setting and life style of times past

Middle Adolescence (Ages 15–16)
    Non-fiction accounts of adventure
        Boys prefer first hand accounts
    War Stories
        Preferred by boys
    Historical novels
        Preferred by girls
    Mystical Romance
        Preferred by girls
    Stories of Adolescent life—contemporary stories of adolescents
        Both sexes like these

Late Adolescence (Ages 16–18)
    The search for personal value
    Books of social significance
    Strange and unusual human experience
    The transition into adult life[6]

---

[6] Robert G. Carlsen, *Books and the Teen-Age Reader* (New York: Bantam Books, 1967), pp. 25–30.

Specific Techniques for Developing Wide Reading

Specific techniques can be inserted into lesson procedures to accomplish a two-fold goal of increasing the student's interest and competence in reading while contributing to the purposes of the lesson. Techniques which are to increase interest should not be developed in isolation. They are best accomplished when they are natural parts of the lesson. Suggested techniques include:

1. Establish in each classroom a library corner for browsing. Books related to units being studied should be available.
2. Discuss books with students. Encourage student reactions (in which there is no correct or incorrect reaction) and the telling of related personal experiences.
3. Let students illustrate stories.
4. Let students write a dramatization of a story.
5. Use "story-teasers." Tell or read a story up to the climax and leave off at that point so that the students will not know what happens unless they read the story.
6. Provide for reasearch reading in which the students find additional information on a topic being studied by the class. Use the problem solving approach which would include basically:
   a. all of the locational skills—reference and library skills as well as parts of a book.
   b. adapting the manner of reading to the type of material and the purpose.
   c. skills needed for exact understanding—main idea, sequence, etc.
   d. interpretative skills—checking the validity of information, seeing relationships, etc.
   e. skills involving the relationship of the material to the topic being studied—drawing conclusions and making inferences.
   f. skills of organizing the information into a complete report—sequence, relevant vs. irrelevant, etc.
7. Have a group of students prepare an annotated bibliography of references for a topic to be studied in class.
8. Have committees of students prepare bulletin board displays of favorite books or stories. Bulletin board displays should not be allowed to grow stale, but should be changed often.
9. Have a sampling of books related to a unit of study displayed in the classroom—especially at the beginning of the unit. Talk about the books.
10. Set up a place map using either a map of the world, region, or country with a pin marking the place where a story takes place. Attach a ribbon to the pin leading to the side of the map with the story title labelled.
11. Take a sentence from a story and let the students develop their own story. Let them compare their story with the story from which the sentence was taken.
12. Let students compare points of view from stories. For example, one author may be laudatory of some person or animal and another may be deprecatory.

THE PLACE OF THE SCHOOL LIBRARY IN CLASSROOM PROCEDURE

The school library is central to all school reading programs. It is a valuable resource to both teachers and students. Incorporating the use of materials in the library into classroom procedure enables the teacher to enrich his course offering and to individualize his instruction. The student finds that he can locate information pointed to his needs and desires. Competence in library usage is a mark of independence.

Ellsworth and Wagener state that the library offers facilities for independent study and list the activities that students may engage in when using the library.

Find answers to specific questions that arise either from the teaching process or from ordinary curiosity.

Go alone or as a member of a committee sent to get information.

Carry out study hall assignments; that is, spend a specific amount of time studying in the library.

Find material for projects such as a written report, a book review, a debate brief, or a research paper.

Learn how to use the keys of a library—card catalogs, bibliographies, reference books, periodical indexes, etc.

Look at motion-picture films, filmstrips, or other audio-visual materials. Study with a teaching machine, listen to phonograph records or tapes, listen and record voice for language study.

Locate quotations, excerpts, or data for speeches or projects.

Read just for the fun of reading—one book or a hundred.

Browse through current magazines and newspapers or look at the new book shelf.

Talk with other students.[7]

The library is the school reservoir of reference materials which students can use in all of their content courses. Students need to have the opportunity to learn to use the reference materials. To require a student to do outside reference reading without instruction in the techniques of it is a "sink-or-swim" procedure. It is not conducive to success and satisfaction on the part of either the student or the teacher.

Perhaps the first prerequisite is that the teacher understand the nature and content of reference materials and their appropriate uses. He is the one best qualified to guide students in the use of the reference material most pertinent to his subject. Some reference materials such as the encyclopedia are pertinent to all areas, but such reference materials as the *U.S. News and World Report* are likely to be used mostly in the social studies class. Hence the social studies teacher would be the one to guide students in their use.

The use of reference materials must be deliberately taught. Again, you will need to plan specific behavioral objectives in the cognitive domain. Though many high school students will have some of the skills needed, the high school teacher

---

[7] Ralph E. Ellsworth and Hobart D. Wagener, *The School Library* (New York: Educational Facilities Laboratories, 1963), p. 25.

has to be ready to teach all or any of the skills in which the students need guidance. These skills include: locating information, alphabetizing, use of key and guide words, card catalogs, indexes and knowledge of the library shelving system. Other skills include those of skimming and the use of book aids such as the table of contents, headings and subheads, and structure of the material to be aware of in introductions and summaries. The various reading skills of comprehension used for notetaking and for organizing information into a report are essential. All of the skills should be taught as necessary whenever they are used in each content area.

That the student must have practice in the use of reference materials is a third consideration. Pupils become competent in the use of reference materials by using them constantly with the necessary direction and instruction from you.

A fourth consideration is that the materials be readily available. Ideally, the library is available to the students whenever reference materials need to be used. If, because of the total school population, the library is not always available to all students, then you should arrange to have the reference materials brought to the classroom.

Some specific types of assignments requiring the use of reference materials are:

1. Use open-ended questions which require numerous references. For instance, instead of a topic assignment such as the gold rush of 1849, ask a question such as "What was the effect of the gold rush of 1849 upon the westward expansion of the United States?" Use the problem solving approach.
2. Organize groups and committees of students to work together in developing a report.
3. Use the reference material to develop background for a topic under study in class.
4. Encourage the students to organize panels, demonstrations, debates, as a means of presenting their topic.
5. Use reference material as sources of background information for field trips, for current events.

The librarian is a valuable resource for you. Whenever time allows, librarians do instruct students in reference reading techniques, especially the locational skills needed for the effective use of the library. However, you cannot rely completely upon the librarian because of the size of the typical school; time is simply not available. Librarians can aid teachers in the following ways:

1. By preparing bibliographies to help in research and reference projects.
2. By providing books and materials to aid professional study and improve in-service training programs.
3. By assembling material which would help improve instructional methods.
4. By participating in curriculum committee work and assisting in the development of new courses of study and units of work.
5. By helping teachers interpret test data and gain an understanding of the reading difficulties of the students.
6. By discovering the reading interests of pupils by means of reading records.

7.   By assisting counselors in observing students with a view toward noting personality traits—day-dreaming, dawdling, worrying, and reading difficulties—and leading the boy or girl to selection of books and materials that will help the problem.

The major goals of bringing the library into classroom procedure are to develop the competence that leads to independence in study as well as to develop within the student the orientation and habit of using the library both for research into information and as a means of providing pleasure.

A teacher's procedures in the classroom must hold the development of the student's ability to think as the primary objective. The acquisition of information and understandings is for this purpose. The growth in mastery of the use of reading-study skills that enable the student to be independent in gaining, judging, and applying information is for the purpose of increasing his ability to think. Such is consonant with the broad aims of education—to have students become effective and constructive members of society at all levels.

SUGGESTED QUESTIONS AND PROBLEMS TO BE CONSIDERED IN REFERENCE TO YOUR OWN CLASSROOM

List A (For readers who are training to be teachers.)

1.   Prepare cognitive and affective objectives for a specific lesson. Translate these into student purposes.
2.   Select a topic and note the necessary background the students must have in order to understand the factual data.
3.   Select a topic and note the concepts the student must acquire. Determine your role as the teacher in helping the student.
4.   Determine the amount and type of practice necessary to indicate competence after instruction in a skill.
5.   List ways you might help a student to achieve success in your classroom.
6.   Plan a complete lesson using as your guide the five basic steps of the reading-thinking plan. Show how you would implement the fusion of instruction in both skill and content.
7.   Compile a listing of materials in your subject to include in your classroom library.

List B (For readers who are teaching.)

1.   Plan for the incorporation of the services and facilities of the school library into your classroom procedures. Then, consult with the librarian to determine how the plan can be implemented.
2.   Review your subject syllabus and your basic classroom procedures and determine ways to have the students become actively involved in their learning.

3. Plan lesson procedures in which you determine the amount and nature of background information your students will need. Determine when and how you will present this information to them.

4. Go through the reading assignment for your students and note (1) the concepts they should know and are needed for comprehension and (2) the new concepts.

5. For each unit of study, compile a listing of supplementary reading.

6. Plan lesson procedure to show how and when you would give instruction and then practice in a reading skill. Fuse the instruction in subject data and skill.

CHAPTER SEVEN

Individualizing
Instruction

Every high school teacher faces a range of capabilities and levels of competence in each of his classes. If the class is composed of a heterogeneous group the range may encompass a span of eight or more years in reading level. If it is scheduled as a homogeneous class, the span of reading levels presented may be reduced by two or three years, but a range of several years is not uncommon. To add to the teacher's dilemma, his effectiveness in meeting the needs and level of each student increases the span. The highly competent student, who may be able to read material considered to be difficult for his enrolled grade, will develop his skill to even higher levels under effective teaching. The incompetent student who is unable to read the material required by his enrolled grade will, if he has limited capacity, fall further and further behind because of his inability to achieve one year's progress in one year. Thereby the range in student competence grows if the pace of instruction is adjusted to each student. It is only as the teacher adjusts his teaching to the average group of the class that the range may appear to narrow. It is only as the individual levels of competence are not dealt with in class that these levels seem to remain static or to converge.

Education under a democracy calls for the education of all students, for each will become an adult citizen who is expected to contribute to the implementation of governmental activities. Education for all students implies mass education—that all students master the same level and body of content. However, another tenet of the democratic process is that each individual is unique in each aspect of his being within the continuum of commonality regarded as the average or the norm. In other words, students as a group have similarities, yet as individuals they are different.

Very few teachers would deny the uniqueness of each of their students. Very few would maintain that mass teaching is appropriate. And yet, many teachers

147

would attest to the fact that they do not individualize as much as they would like. A number of reasons may be given. One is the large number of students they meet each day in their classes (around 150 individuals). Another reason is the demands of a full and growing curriculum. Faced with these two conditions the teacher sometimes takes the position that students should be competent in the skills of reading and study when they come to high school, thereby enabling the curriculum to be fully implemented.

Teachers, then, find themselves on the horns of a dilemma: the ideal of individualized teaching on the one hand and the realistic day-to-day experience of teaching on the other. Indeed, many teachers know that, in addition to knowledge of content, their ability to "reach" each child is a measure of professional competence.

What does this mean to the teacher who has in each class a group of adolescents who exhibit characteristics in common but who are at the same time unique individuals? How does this situation direct his implementation of class procedures? The answers to these questions compel the teacher to review his role in education and his basic understanding of his students. He knows that society expects him to impart a specific body of information and to develop within his students a specific level of skill competence. He knows also that as a group adolescents have certain interests, problems, and reactions. Yet within each class there are as many individuals as there are students enrolled. There are varying amounts of information known by the individuals because of differing prior experiences and capacities. There are different levels of competence in the skills of reading, writing, and study. Likewise within a group there are variations of interests, aptitudes and reactions. There are, as in the whole of society, different personalities. Therefore, though there may be a common body of subject matter, it has to be fitted to the characteristics of each student. But how is this done? There are no foolproof prescribed methods. However, specific guidelines and suggestions can be useful when you adapt them to each class.

CONSIDERATIONS FOR IMPLEMENTING INDIVIDUAL PRACTICES

The methods you choose for individualizing instruction are determined by your expertise in implementation, by the goals and demands of the curriculum, and by the needs of the students. They vary from total class instruction to complete individualization on a one-to-one basis. Whatever method or combination of methods you use, the implementation must be in accordance with the following considerations for effective learning.

1. The form of individualization in the classroom is determined by the goals to be accomplished. Whatever the type of classroom organization you employ, it should be chosen because it will enable you to accomplish specific goals with the students. For example, if you see that a small group of several students are having difficulty in mastering the basic vocabulary of the subject, these students may be organized into a temporary group for additional helpful instruction in learning the vocabulary.

2. You need to know your students—their strengths as well as their weaknesses, their best modality of learning, their interests, and specific pertinent information about them. You cannot very well differentiate or individualize blindly. There must be continuing and varied means of diagnosis.

3. Diagnostic teaching enables you to individualize as you note specific needs of individual students. Indeed, it may be assumed that the degree to which you individualize is determined by the extent of daily diagnosis as the student's performance is noted in each class. Individualization cannot be accomplished without it.

4. No one method of individualization is adequate. Ideally you use various methods to accomplish the purposes of instruction in accordance with the needs of the student. For example, some students may be able to embark on individual study while another group may need intensive work in a specific skill of reading. Or, one student may respond well to programmed materials while another does best through the use of tapes and films.

5. You must be flexible in your use of instructional methods. Student needs, as they develop, change. Your purposes may change in the course of a year's instruction. The classroom procedure therefore does not become fixed, but changes as the conditions require. Consequently, there will be times when you are with the total class and times when you are with specific groups or individuals.

6. Individualization requires the student to have capacity for self-direction and independence, since the teacher cannot be with all groups and individuals at the same time. Still, some teachers hesitate to allow students to exercise self-direction for fear of losing discipline and direction of the class. Student self-direction and independence is not always easy to achieve, especially if the students have not had the opportunity to exercise it. It can, however, be developed. First, you must believe that self-direction is a valid goal of education. Second, you must have high expectations for the students' ability to mature into self-directing individuals. Third, you must look upon your students as co-partners in the learning process. This means that the students should know their strengths and weaknesses in the reading skills, should know enough about the reading process to realize their degree of competence, should understand the relationship of the reading skills to the content, and should understand the goals, purposes and relevance of what they are studying. Then the student and the teacher can plan together for mutual effectiveness.

7. Individualization requires planning. You must plan how you will proceed prior to classroom implementation. When you plan with the students, you still must know what needs to be done so that as you flexibly incorporate student suggestions you are able to hold to your purpose. Cooperative planning fosters student self-direction and independence of study.

FORMS OF INDIVIDUALIZATION

Individualization can take many forms in a classroom. The combination of methods you choose will be determined in part by the realities of the external conditions of instruction such as materials available, furniture arrangement and class size. Another factor is your philosophy and the purposes you have in mind. Uppermost are the needs and characteristics of the students and the mode of instruction that will be best for them. Also, your preference and feeling of security with both the procedure and the class may be factors in determining the type of individualization used.

It may seem desirable for you to use a combination of forms incorporating flexibility in moving from one to the other. Russell states:

> Some research studies, particularly in the field of reading, indicate that the teacher may be teaching and pupils may be learning most effectively if some activities are individual, some undertaken in small groups, and some shared by whole classes or even larger groups.[1]

Blackledge then goes on to say,

> The best teaching, therefore, will make use of a wide variety of procedures and materials in an attempt to suit the task to the characteristics, needs, and interests of the individual children. This kind of teaching will take into consideration the basic concepts and understandings in the subject matter areas and will utilize the content found in these areas to help the children develop basic skills and abilities, social skills, and a method of working.[2]

Consequently you may become involved with techniques of differentiating assignments and of directing various types of groups. Materials organized to help the student become self-directing and self-helping may consist of printed learning programs as well as instructional media such as TV, audio tapes, films, teaching machines, and learning laboratories. Further, two or more teachers may incorporate more individualization into their procedures by engaging in a team approach. The truly skillful teacher obviously does not rely on just one of these various ways to individualize, but uses whichever form seems appropriate to the purposes of the instruction and the characteristics and needs of the students.

Forms of grouping

No grouping of students should take place unless you see that such a form of classroom organization is most conducive of the desired objectives. However, once you decide to use grouping as a means of individualization, different purposes will designate different types of grouping. For example, if you wish to use materials on different levels of difficulty the grouping will be set up on the basis of reading competence; each group will read from material commensurate to the reading level of

---

[1] David H. Russell, "Finding Out More from Research Sources," *Learning and the Teacher* (Washington, D.C.), Association for Supervision and Curriculum Development Yearbook (1959), p. 178.

[2] Helen V. Blackledge, "Reading Procedures and Materials for Content Areas in Grades Four Through Six," in *Reading Instruction in Various Patterns of Grouping,* ed. Helen M. Robinson, Supplementary Educational Monograph No. 89 (Chicago: University of Chicago Press, 1959), p. 75.

the students in it. Or, if you note specific needs of pupils either by observation in class or by more formal diagnosis, groups may be organized to give students help and practice in specific skills. If you desire to have the pupils work together on research problems, the group will have as its purpose the investigation of the problem, probably with a culminating report. You may assign topics or allow students to choose the research group. Interest groups might be organized for research. For instance, in a unit on ecology a group of several students may wish to investigate the ecology of the sea. This would be a grouping around an interest as well as a grouping for the purposes of research. Sometimes you may designate certain students to work together for the purpose of having their respective traits and abilities supplement each other. Guidance grouping takes place when you have a withdrawn student or an isolate in the class work with a student or students who are not withdrawn and who might be the popular leaders. Another type of grouping would occur in the situations sometimes called paired grouping, duos, or trios in which one student helps another in mastering a specific skill. The goal of such a grouping is for the helpers to benefit as well, for explaining a skill or process to another student helps him to achieve complete mastery or to get experience in extending himself to less able students. Finally, grouping can become completely individual such as in independent study. Obviously, various self-helping materials, tapes, and programmed materials enable you to encourage complete individualization as the student develops at his own pace. At times, the class may require no intra-class groupings. The whole class can be treated as a unit in such activities as hearing and reading a literary selection, the viewing of a film, the presentation of a basic concept, and the discussion of information.

In summary, the various forms of grouping may range from the total class as a unit to individual assignment. Within this continuum groups for the purposes of appropriate level, need, research, interest, social, and specific pairing of students would be employed. Obviously, there are pros and cons to each type of grouping which become more pronounced if only one type of grouping is used. Grouping and regrouping students continually for many different purposes blunts any possible stigma which a student may attach to a specific grouping—particularly the grouping set up on the basis of competence level.

Forms of Grouping

Group	Purpose	Advantages	Disadvantages
Reading Level	Study of content in books of differing levels, so that each student can succeed.	Materials suited to students' instructional level. Students can acquire skills at level of competence.	Students may feel stigmatized if in low group.
Need	Follow-up to give specific instruction for an observed skill deficiency.	Adds to pertinence of instruction to fit student needs.	

Group	Purpose	Advantages	Disadvantages
Research	Investigation into aspects of subject to supplement basic textbook materials.	Gives practice and application in reading-study skills. Leads to independence of study.	
Interest	Expand student interest through opportunity to investigate additional information.	Gives practice and application in skills. Motivates by giving opportunity to develop own interest.	If used at all times may impede balanced acquaintance with a subject.
Social	Allow students to work on specific topics with peers of their choice.	Motivates the students.	May not give students opportunity to work with wide number of their peers.
Guidance	Allow disparate students to work together in order to foster greater social development and tolerance.	Brings about opportunity for experience in working with students of dissimilar interests, ability, and competence.	Depending upon student understanding such grouping may prove to be negative in results.
Duo or Triplet	Two or three students work on a problem to the mutual advantage of each.	Gives special help to student.	Student can be exploited if he is expected to "sub" for the teacher.
Tutorial	Student who needs intensive help because of lack of competence or has a special skill need.	Gives intensive help to student.	Tremendously time consuming if used constantly, as often the need requires.

Planning for Groups with the Students

The success of grouping with a class depends in large measure on the planning you do with the students. The planning has two aspects. One is your own plan gauged to the purposes you have developed from what you wish to teach and from the needs of the students, individually and collectively, within the class. The other is the planning you do with the students so that they will understand why the procedure is chosen and how it must be implemented. The fundamental characteristic of any grouping requires students to work constructively while not under your direct supervision. For this to occur, the students must be apprized of the objectives to be accomplished and the way they are to be implemented. Many a well-planned group has failed to operate as desired because the students did not know what to expect and many times were suspicious of the effect of the procedure upon them. When students are set into groups without adequate discussion of the purposes and techniques of operation, a chaotic situation in the classroom can result. Some teachers do not group for this reason—they fear losing control. One teacher announced in the teacher's room before school, "I decided on the way to school today to group my class." After the period, she came out of her room and said, with an exasperated sigh, "Well that's that! It was a madhouse. I know now that grouping doesn't work. It's just another one of those 'new' ideas in education!" What this teacher had failed to do was to plan adequately so that she would have a clear idea of what she was about to do and then to discuss and plan further with the students so that they would know what was to be accomplished. Planning with the students is necessary to get them to work *with* you rather than merely *for* you. Though it is more difficult to get the students to work with you, the results are far more satisfying in increased motivation and self-reliance.

There is no reason why you should not take the time to let the students understand the reasons for methods of classroom procedure. You do not abdicate authority by so doing. Rather, it is a means of you and the students working together. Whatever form of grouping you plan to use, the students should be told about it, help to plan for its implementation, and realize the goals to be achieved. Specifically, you need to plan with the students the following:

1. the goals of the class—understandings and skill needs as shown by informal diagnostic measures.
2. the ways the goals can be accomplished—types of groups, materials available.
3. the responsibilities of everyone involved, evolved from the students themselves, for the successful implementation of the procedures, and
4. evaluation of the procedure to note improvements for the further implementation of the procedure.

As noted in the chapter on diagnosis, the students can plan with the teacher with maturity if they know their specific strengths and weaknesses. When students are informed about the procedures to be employed they will usually show maturity in assisting the implementation. For example, one seventh grade teacher spent the first two weeks at the beginning of the school year diagnosing levels and skill needs of her students in English. Each day she would have a reading selection, or some vocabulary or English syntax exercise. She would tell the students the approximate level of the material. One day she had material at the sixth grade level, another day a selection on the eighth grade level and so on. She would identify the skill she was diagnosing such as main idea, organization, connotative use of words and so on. The teacher and the students kept a record for the two weeks of the students' competence at each level and with each skill. Finally she announced what had become an obvious fact to all the students: some were stronger than others in certain skills and some could read more difficult materials with success than others. She said she wished to place them in groups at specific levels so that she could fit the classroom instruction more pertinently to each of them. She asked them to group themselves in the appropriate level within the framework she outlined. It was indeed interesting to note that in a class of thirty-five students all except two placed themselves exactly where she would have grouped them. The two who did not, placed themselves higher. After two days one requested another more appropriate placement, and the other was able by intensive voluntary effort to remain in the group he had chosen. Though this was a reading level grouping, the teacher did not feel that the students were defensive about any stigma attached to the group they were in. They had chosen the group themselves through informal but objective means.

Another teacher of English in the eleventh grade decided to try three reading levels in her class. She planned meticulously but did not inform the students except to say one day, "Class, we have three literature anthologies, each at a different level. Therefore I am going to place you in groups." At this point, one young lady in the class stood up and said, "Just why are you doing this? Do you think some of us are dumber than the others?" The teacher wisely saw her neglect in bringing the students along with her in her thinking. She cancelled her plan for the day immediately and for the next three days explained her planning to them and also conducted informal objective class tests of skill and reading competence. Reading and skill levels were noted as well as expectations of the eleventh grade. The students became aware objectively of their reading status. When the teacher went back to her plan of grouping by reading levels, the class worked with her. They understood what was being done and why.

In both of these illustrations the often maligned reading level grouping was successful with little or no feeling of stigma by those students who were in the lower groups. Neither their peers nor their teacher held them in low esteem. True, they would have preferred to be in the group commensurate with their grade; but they also saw, in both instances, the wisdom of the grouping plan. In both cases, the teacher had a tremendous sensitivity to the feelings of the students and also, by her action, complimented the students' maturity to accept irrefutable facts when they were realistically and objectively given and when the attitude of both their peers and their teacher was not demeaning.

The necessity of student understanding of grouping applies to all types of groups if the procedures are to accomplish desired purposes. In all content areas, reading level groups can be organized. Appropriate materials are a requirement for this type of grouping. But, in the absence of multilevel material, some degree of this type of grouping can be accomplished by the method of using the text. Though not ideal, the readers who find the textbook too hard can be helped by reading and discussing small sections of material at one time, making full use of the graphic aids, by establishing thoroughly the important vocabulary and by additional supplementary materials such as models, records, tapes, films, pictures. More adequate readers can be assigned larger assignments with more attention given to the subtleties of the language used. With groups of need, the students (even though they are in reading level groups) can be grouped again to bring together those students who need specific help in a skill such as seeing the author's organization. Or, if they are doing research, all those who are having difficulty taking notes could be given instruction in this while the other students continue with their research. Research, interest, social and guidance groups can all be used as desired when students work on research projects. In such groups, level of competence is not a criterion. The poorest and the best reader may be in the same group, while in reading from their textbook(s) they may be in reading level groups. Individual tutorial assistance or the pairing of students can be accomplished by the teacher as the other students are working. In the pairing of students, the teaching student should realize he is getting specific help while the other students are being given help. He needs to see that explaining the skill or information to his peers will help him in his mastery. (The teaching student is the one who understands but who has not mastered the information or skill.) All of these types of groups can be incorporated into a typical unit of study.

Throughout the grouping procedures, three basic considerations of an interpersonal nature stand out. One, you must accept each student and have a sensitivity to each student's feelings and desires. Second, you must be objective and realistic and thereby be truthful but helpful about each student's reading needs. Third, you should expect student maturity to accept and then attack a problem.

Flexibility, diagnosis, preplanning, objectivity are all key concepts to effective grouping. One final requirement is to have the student apply instruction immediately—instruct and then do. Such a plan shows the student the pertinence and immediacy of his learning.

Differentiated Assignments

Differentiating assignments is a means of fitting each assignment to the capabilities and reading levels of the students in the class. As Karlin has pointed out, ". . . all students in the group might read the same selection but would not be expected to attain the same levels of understanding from it."[3] Another form is to assign differing amounts of material to read. In some instances the teacher designates who among the class is to work at a specific level. Direct assignment to the students can create problems since the poorer readers are singled out and sometimes the better readers question why they are given more work. Open objective atmosphere in the classroom may ease the situation, but the better procedure is to allow the individual students to choose which level of assignment they wish to do. Some teachers handle differentiation by having a basic and minimum assignment with various possibilities of extension and enrichment. For example, in such a situation, the assignment sheet given to the student may have activities, problems, and questions under such headings as "Required Study" and "Additional Optional Study" or "Basic Requirements" and "Suggested Extensions." Since the teacher should know the goals of each of his students, he can suggest assignment possibilities to the student.

One basis for differentiating assignments as well as for grouping can be the informal reading inventory. When used for diagnostic teaching, as it should be, the teacher obtains information about student competence in the reading skills required and thereby has one basis for diffentiation and for grouping. In a typical graph of the results of an informal reading inventory (p. 156), the following information is apparent for classroom implementation.

---

[3] Robert Karlin, "Methods of Differentiating Instruction in the Senior High School," in *Developing High School Reading Programs,* ed. Mildred A. Dawson (Newark, Delaware: International Reading Association, 1967), p. 73.

SOCIAL STUDIES READING INVENTORY
CLASS & INDIVIDUAL PROFILE

(Checks denote weaknesses)

	Parts of Books	Library Skills	Graphic Aids	Vocabulary	Main Ideas	Details	Dr. Concl.	Organization
Cynthia		✓		✓			✓	
Bill	✓	✓	✓	✓	✓	✓	✓	✓
Gloria					✓	✓	✓	
Steve		✓		✓			✓	
Stephanie							✓	
William	✓	✓		✓				✓
Lauren			✓	✓	✓	✓	✓	✓
Jessica				✓			✓	
Bruce	✓	✓	✓	✓	✓	✓	✓	✓
Julia							✓	
Jeff				✓			✓	
Mary	✓	✓		✓	✓	✓	✓	✓
Dan					✓	✓	✓	✓
Isabel				✓			✓	
Ginny	✓	✓					✓	
Gayle							✓	
Mary Ann				✓	✓		✓	✓
Wendy				✓	✓			
Gavin		✓		✓			✓	
Douglas	✓	✓		✓	✓		✓	✓
Thomas								
Frank			✓	✓	✓		✓	✓
Stevie	✓	✓		✓			✓	
Gloria				✓			✓	
Ann		✓						

Read horizontally to note individual student weaknesses.

These students need simpler supplementary material

These students are able to use more difficult material and to acquire more depth of understanding

Read vertically to note class pattern

1. The skills in which nearly the entire class needs instruction—vocabulary and drawing conclusions.

2. A basis for assignment of materials for differentiation of assignments—those students who need simpler supplementary material, those who can master the basic textbook with normal classroom guidance and explanation, and those who are able to read more difficult supplementary material and acquire more depth of understanding.

3. A basis for grouping in accordance with skill need—all students who need specific instruction in using library skills, or noting main ideas, or organization, and so on.

4. Further differentiation may be implemented by letting Thomas, Stephanie, Julia, and Ann undertake independent study.

5. Complete individualization or a small group of two (Frank and Bill) in the skill of using graphic aids.

6. Research and/or interest groups may be comprised of students having different skill needs. For instance, Dan, who is weak in noting main ideas, could be in the same group as Stephanie or Tom, who are not weak in noting main ideas. In the process of coordinating their research into a group report, Dan would receive peer instruction in a natural setting thereby getting practice in his skill weakness.

Various forms of grouping bring about differentiation since each group works on its assignment. Even in such groups as those doing research where the constellation of students may comprise various reading levels, differentiation occurs. As the students meet in their committees and plan their work, each student works in accordance with his level and strengths. For instance, the student(s) with the greater competence may do much of the organizing and synthesizing of information into a report while those with less competence may be charged to research specific parts of the topics, contribute illustrative materials and participate in skit or roleplaying the committee may decide to do. In the participation within the committee the less competent student is able to work with his peers and learn from the committee discussion.

Individualization

Complete individualization can be accomplished only as you know the strengths and weaknesses of each student. The concept of each student reading a book of his own choice and appropriate to his needs and characteristics fits in logically among the various classroom procedures as the students read library materials for recreation and enrichment, or when one works on an individually assigned topic. Individual study can contribute strongly to the student's interest and initiative. On the other hand, if the teacher is not readily available, the student may bog down in the reading. He must have material to read in which he can achieve the feeling of success. He needs material in which the vocabulary and skills of comprehension do not present insurmountable difficulties for him.

Niles and Early describe a means of individualization through the use of job sheets. Their description notes the need for diagnosis so that the job sheets can be appropriately assigned to each student.

Job sheets are particularly useful in developing the more mechanical skills, such as word analysis techniques, finding main ideas, and following the author's sequence. They are not so effective with higher reading skills, such as distinguishing between fact and opinion, where group discussion is essential to growth in skill.

The preparatory steps (in preparing job sheets) are as follows:

—Collect or construct exercises in the various skills. The series of exercises for each skill should represent varying degrees of difficulty.

—Paste copies of the exercises on sheets of oak tag of uniform size. It is best to have two or three copies of each, so that more than one pupil may work on the same exercise at the same time.

—Label each sheet as to type of exercise.

—Number the sheets within each type in order of difficulty.

—Provide answer keys on the back of each oak tag sheet.

—Study each pupil's diagnostic test record.

—List by name and number the exercises which each pupil is to do.

—Give each pupil his own personal list.

—Instruct the pupils in the filing system so that they can find the appropriate sheet.

—Prepare a series of mastery tests which the student may take after he has done a given series of exercises.[4]

MATERIALS THAT HELP YOU TO INDIVIDUALIZE

The versatile teacher uses materials of many different levels and types for greater effectiveness of grouping and individualization. Two prerequisites to the use of varied materials are (1) the availability of them in the classroom and (2) your knowledge about them.

Books

Books and printed matter are the traditional school materials. They can be easily applied to individualization. Each student can use them for his particular interests and they can be read in different ways in accordance with the reader's desire to obtain an overview or to study and reflect in depth. In comparison with many of the newer automated materials, they are still the cheapest form of instructional material. Oddly, there are still classrooms where books are not in an adequate supply. Not only should there be textbooks on different levels of difficulty, but also each classroom needs a collection of supplementary materials. Many types of grouping depend upon an adequate supply of printed materials. For example, groups designed to help the student at his level of competence and for research and interest projects depend upon the adequacy of books in the school and classroom.

---

[4] Olive S. Niles and Margaret J. Early, "Adjusting to Individual Differences in English," in *Teaching Reading in High School: Selected Articles,* ed. Robert Karlin (New York: The Bobbs-Merrill Company, Inc., 1969), p. 374.

Self-help Materials

Numerous reading textbooks have specific directions to explain procedures and skills especially for the students' understanding. Other materials are packaged in such a manner that the reader is given instructions in how to attack a reading assignment with comprehension checks and answers provided.

Self-help materials include both printed materials and automated materials. These materials, aimed at helping the student to note and chart his individual progress, are based upon sound educational principles. First, the student can progress at his own rate through the material. Second, the design of the material is such that the student usually can see his errors as he proceeds. Third, the student is informed of the nature of the skill being taught as well as the subject matter covered, thereby providing him with the knowledge he needs in assessing his strengths and weaknesses. And, fourth, the student is put in charge of his own progress. It compels active participation more directly than is often accomplished through teacher-directed assignments from printed materials.

But, there are cautions that all teachers need to observe. The student often needs guidance when he meets an obstacle. He may not know why he is making an error. Or he may need more intensive instruction in a skill before he can apply it— even through the self-help material. Further, he may need more background for understanding than is provided. Obviously, the teacher cannot assume a *laissez-faire* approach thinking that the self-help material is self-teaching. The thorough teacher correctly uses such material to provide for a high degree of individualization but *will keep informed of his students' progress with self-help material, and provide additional instruction when necessary.*

Programmed Materials and Teaching Machines

Programmed materials, based upon specific behavioral objectives in which the subject is presented to the student in minute self-learning steps, is a type of self-help and self-teaching material. One of its greatest values lies in the degree of individualization which can be accomplished with it. Komoski and Sohn state an unproven hypothesis derived, they believe, from indications thus far:

> The nature of programming is such that when a teacher programmer programs his subject, he also teaches the reading of it. Because he does test his programs on students selected from the audience at which he aims his teaching, and because he analyzes his feedback from his audience, revising until he does his best teaching, while he teaches his subject, he also teaches the reading of it. If he is a chemistry teacher, he teaches his students to think as chemists think and to read chemistry. If he does not do this, his program will not teach well. Therefore, our hypothesis is that by *working through a good program, a student improves his reading ability.*[5]

---

[5] Kenneth P. Komoski and David A. Sohn, "Programmed Instruction in the Field of Reading," in *Teaching Reading in High School: Selected Articles,* ed. Robert Karlin (New York: The Bobbs-Merrill Company, Inc., 1969), p. 391.

In programming, a subject is analyzed into its component strands which are arranged in proper sequence and divided into the smallest possible bits of instruction. A student's understanding is tested at each step to minimize error and to reinforce correct responses. The advantages are many: (1) the techniques of a master teacher are used, (2) the classroom teacher is released from drill work and free to work individually with each student, (3) each student progresses at his own pace, (4) reinforcement (correction or reward) is given at each step of learning, (5) automatic teachers are inhumanly patient, (6) the student's errors are recorded and show where he is having trouble, and (7) programs show records of progress. On the other hand, you should also be aware of disadvantages. (1) Mature reading skills are complex and learning situations can be diverse for which there are not, as yet, adequate programs. (2) Much more is needed to include the entire repertoire of reading behavior such as telling stories, experiencing and accomplishing research, or group discussions of ideas. (3) The sequence of child development and readiness to learn do not relate to programmed instruction—the program is individual in that the student progresses at his own pace, but it is not geared to the peculiar individual needs of the student. (4) Programmed instruction cannot answer a spontaneous question. (5) There is still the inability to program long reading selections. (6) The skills of creative reading based upon the open-ended question cannot be programmed. Still, programmed instruction, under teacher guidance, is one means of individualizing instruction.

Tapes

Tapes and cassettes are especially useful to the teacher who needs to provide instruction for the reluctant or disabled reader. Tapes can be used individually or in group situations. They can build the student's background of information, establish concepts and vocabulary. They can enrich and supplement printed material. You will find that blank tapes and cassettes offer the opportunity to tape specific instructions to be given to a student or a group for an assignment while you are engaged with other students in the classroom. Cassettes, by being easy to use, are particularly effective for smooth classroom conduct.

GENERAL CRITERIA FOR THE USE OF AUTOMATIC MATERIALS

Whatever the type of material used, the use made of it in the classroom determines its effectiveness. Therefore specific criteria must always be kept in mind.

1. The automated devices are valuable adjuncts to instruction. They are aids for you and you must not abdicate your position in favor of them.
2. The automated devices should be designed and used to foster the findings of research in how students learn.
    a. Is the process of self-development fostered so that students can draw their own inferences and become thinking persons who have learned how to learn?
    b. Are the students able to proceed at their own rate?

    c. Are there opportunities for self-instruction, self-correction, and self-evaluation?

    d. Is the material meaningful and pertinent to the learner?

    e. Is there adequate reinforcement?

    f. Is the love of reading fostered?

    g. Is emphasis placed upon reading comprehension?

The basic purpose of the automated devices is to provide you with a more complete battery of instructional materials with which to accomplish the ends of education. The value of the materials rests with your use of them.

CLASSROOM ACTIVITIES FOR SPECIFIC TYPES OF STUDENTS

The Superior Reader

The superior reader is usually a superior student who is reading above his enrolled grade level. He is usually an avid reader and one who seems to learn rapidly and easily. He is the reader of whom you may think as needing no further help in the skills and techniques of reading and study. Yet, I have observed superior groups who show the need to (1) develop more effective techniques of study, (2) develop the comprehension skills of interpretative and critical reading, (3) refine the precision and depth of their vocabulary, and (4) increase their general speed of reading. The Bulletin for the National Association of Secondary School Principals points out many needs of the superior student among which are:

> They need help in becoming well-qualified academically, for this acts as prime mover for further effort in learning.
> They need the informal techniques of instruction in which group planning, group execution, and group evaluation are continuous.
> They need and demand overviews of subject matter where the pursuit of knowledge starts with the whole, progresses to the parts, and then terminates as a whole.
> They need individualization of instruction in order to broaden those interests they already hold and to open new fields of endeavor and new interests.
> They demand opportunities for being creative and critical in the realms of expression, of opinion, and of behavior.
> They want opportunities to draw generalizations and to apply them in concrete situations.[6]

Specific classroom activities might include:

1. Dramatizing stories

    a. Doing some of the things that the characters did to show insight into the mood and personality of each character.

    b. Rewriting the story as a play.

---

[6] Bulletin of the National Association of Secondary School Principals, "Reading for the Gifted in the Secondary School," in *Reading in the Secondary Schools*, ed. M. Jerry Weiss (New York: The Odyssey Press, Inc., 1961), p. 93.

2. Making graphic representations of a story
   a. Showing a story in serial form; writing or telling what is happening in each scene.
   b. Making a picture to illustrate an event or a description from the story.
3. Oral and written presentations of stories
   a. Telling a story up to the point of climax.
   b. Rewriting an ending to a story.
   c. Writing about a story or book and showing why it was enjoyed or not liked.
4. Planning with the teacher for help in diagnosing the student's own abilities in reading and in working out a plan for the development of those abilities.
5. Doing self-motivated independent research around an area of interest for practice in use of reference materials and library reference guides and finding information independently.
6. Working alone or with others in writing original stories and essays, analyzing authors' patterns of thought and organization, and determining new application of principles and of actual data.
7. Practice in the scientific method—the problem solving approach
   a. Discovering and clearly stating problems.
   b. Planning and executing ways of determining what is true.
   c. Checking with reliable sources and determining what is true.
   d. Making applications of what is learned to the environment.
   e. Making use of simple records.
8. Extensive reading of library materials for information, enjoyment, and enrichment.
   a. Reading a wide variety of books.
   b. Scanning and classifying reading materials for the school library.
   c. Setting up displays of books to supplement and enrich classroom work.
9. Engaging in vocabulary study.
   a. Noting special words pertinent to each content field.
   b. Determining general words with specialized meanings.
   c. Analyzing an author's connotative use of words.
   d. Becoming aware of an author's use of sensory words.
   e. Noting and defining figures of speech.
10. Classroom discussion. Superior students learn from each other by increasing their own depth and scope of knowledge and by sharpening their vocabulary in the communicative process which is basic to discussion.

The Slow-learning Student

The slow-learning students, sometimes called the academically untalented, are generally viewed by teachers as those who are below the average in achievement. They become known through their inability to master basic content. Less than average mental capacity separates the slow learner from the disabled student who is capable but not fulfilling his potential. In heterogeneous groups the slow learners comprise the few at the low side of the normal curve of ability within the population. In homogeneous grouping whole classes may be comprised of those students who are unable to achieve to normal expectations and who, at the same time, achieve better than those who are scheduled for classes for the mentally disabled. They are not the students who are intellectually stimulating to teach. They are the students who require intensive teaching with much practice and practical application. Vick suggests:

> to teach the severely retarded reader in the classroom, try a new approach. Get really acquainted with each pupil so that you can know his potential and his needs. Recognize the voids in his educational background and plan for the reteaching of these skills or concepts.
>
> Plan a variety of ways to teach any single item . . . This method is necessary for many reasons. These pupils have an extremely short span of attention; therefore, several approaches must be available to provide an adequate amount of drill. Also, different pupils learn in different ways.[7]

The same suggestions can be effectively applied to the slow-learning student.

Slow-learning students do not differ markedly from other students in most characteristics. As a group they may show a slight inferiority in physique and health. Mostly the inferiority shows up in academic matters—they do not learn as rapidly as other students, and reading is often a laborious task for them. They may show a marked lack of interest in reading due to the difficulty they have with it; in fact, they may avoid it whenever possible. As a result of their lack of success in reading and academic achievement they often show the characteristic of a negative self-concept which in itself can be defeating to their progress. For many, school means reading; they are faced with it each day. Each day they are reminded of their deficient ability. We can understand why they may manifest attitudes expressed as, "I can't learn, I'm stupid, school has nothing for me." Also, we can understand why many will seek to avoid an unpleasant situation in which they feel they cannot compete by dropping out of school. In situations where instruction is not geared to capabilities, the negative self-concept is almost certain to develop.

Procedures for teaching the slow learner are not markedly different from procedures used with any group. They must be geared to the level of the student. The major differences are the need for intensive practice, and the need for concreteness.

1. Instruct the slow learner with material he is capable of reading successfully.
2. Give systematic instruction in tools of study and in the development of concepts. They are less able than average students in the ability to learn incidentally or to draw conclusions voluntarily.
3. Show how the tools of learning and the information in various content subjects have a practical application. The more direct the application is

---

[7] Nancy O'Neill Vick, "High School Reading for the Severely Retarded Reader," in *Vistas in Reading,* ed. J. Allen Figurel. Vol. II, Part I, Proceedings of the Eleventh Annual Convention (Newark, Delaware: International Reading Association, 1967), p. 229.

to the content, the more motivated the slow learner will be. The practical application should encompass the basic goals of the students.

4. Go as slowly as necessary. The educational goal should not be curriculum coverage but successful learning by the student.

5. Try to understand the slow learner by noting how he feels about himself. Diagnose to find his strengths and weaknesses. Be objective and truthful with him about his level of competence; however, suggest ways he can work successfully.

6. Use suitable procedures which provide for building background and pre-reading activities to help him meet success.

7. Show him specifically how to read and study in each content area. Give instruction in pertinent skills as necessary. For example, show him how to break words into syllables, how to get the meaning of a word from the context when the need for such skills is apparent. This must be done for all basic skills.

8. Urge the slow learners to communicate with each other. Let them talk. They need to become increasingly fluent with words. Meanings can be sharpened and new words introduced in discussion sessions.

9. Use newspapers, magazines, commercial brochures and other current printed matter as sources of reading material. Use the materials of daily life (i.e., driver manuals, job directions, business forms, and directions).

10. Use a wide variety of audio-visual aids to widen the students' background and provide alternative modes of learning which may be more appropriate for the slow learner.

11. Differentiate assignments in the class in any of the various ways described on pages 155–158.

The Disabled Reader

The disabled reader is the student who, as far as can be ascertained, is able to do the usual level of work for his grade but because of disability in reading competence is unable to achieve adequately. Many schools have remedial classes for these students, especially if they are two or more years retarded in their reading level. These students need the extra help of the remedial classes, but they also need all the help they can get from the content teachers in how to read material in each discipline. They need the coordinated attack from both the remedial and the content area teachers for several reasons. First, the results of improvement from the remedial classes are usually gradual and therefore do not enable the student to effect improvement in his content reading immediately. Second, the remedial teacher usually does not give specific practice in each of the content fields, but rather attacks the reading skills from a variety of materials without a direct consistent application to a content area. Third, the disabled remedial reader is enrolled in content classes concomitantly with the remedial reading class, and needs direction and help in content reading even while he improves his skill in the remedial class. Fourth, you cannot assume that the student will automatically transfer learning from one class to another. Disabled readers are often not aware that reading skills need to be applied to each content area. Their full attention is merely on content. Also, they often fail to note how a transfer can be made with material which is different from the type they have worked with in the reading class. Fifth, a skill should be applied immediately where it is needed for the best results. For example, the intensive reading needed for mathematics problems is best practiced and applied in the mathematics class as a result of the instruction given by the mathematics teacher. Sixth, the ideal program for the disabled reader coordinates the efforts and procedures of all teachers in order to provide the comprehensive help that is needed.

Activities in the classroom may include:

1. Developing the knowledge of writing patterns in each of the content fields as a means of helping the student to see how authors in each field tend to structure their information.
2. Establishing adequate readiness for reading material in each content class. Investigate and expand the student's background for the topic, preview the material with him, clarify the basic conceptual terms, and help him see specific purposes for reading.
3. Giving specific instruction in study techniques when they are needed. Give instruction in a study technique, then have students apply it immediately.
4. Providing multilevel materials so that materials are available for each student which he is competent to read.
5. Differentiating assignments to take into account levels of competence and skill needs of the students. Also use differing modes of classroom organization to meet specific needs.
6. Evaluating the student's level of work with him to enlist his thinking and cooperation in attacking his deficiency in reading.
7. Using audio-visual materials to help the student increase the depth and scope of his background of information.
8. Using different applications of the skills to increase reading competence, particularly the application of writing. Have students apply, for instance, their knowledge of paragraph patterns by writing their own paragraphs.
9. Alerting students to the use of structure words (see pages 92–93).
10. Giving consistent help in developing word meanings, in classifying information, in precision of thought.
11. Using well planned and structured classroom procedures that employ simple and clear-cut directions, well-thought-out questions that will foster logical thinking and concentration.

The Reluctant Reader

The reluctant reader may be either a disabled reader who has weaknesses in reading skills, or an adequate reader who does not read voluntarily. Obviously the student who does not read with ease and fluency will turn to a more satisfying means of using his time for recreation. Individuals have different preferences and with some, reading may not be one of them. They may like to be involved with more active projects. However, you should attempt to foster wide reading as a means of pleasure as well as for extending background of experience. The goal should not be to develop all students into avid readers, but to be sure that they do have the skill they need to read for pleasure.

When you find the reluctance to read, interest may be fostered by finding out what the student's interests are and then by providing related books suitable to his reading level. And though the teacher may note a wide range of skill needs, the goal of developing student interest in reading must be kept in sight. Share and discuss the information in books. Enjoy an author's use of language. Analyze the author's line of reasoning. In short, discuss and evaluate the ideas of the author. You will find it propitious to read to your students occasionally and to provide time in class for them to read. And, of course, your enthusiasm as well as an adequate supply of books are essential ingredients.

The Culturally Different Student

The culturally different student is often puzzling to the teacher. Within a composite group, composed of individuals with different interests, desires, strengths, and weaknesses, you find this student with a different language style and different sets of values. The language of the culturally different student is different from the standard English which you speak, and which is used in most textbooks. Viewed from the position of school academic requirements, the student has many weaknesses and is in need of intensive remedial instruction.

Coupled with the language difference can be the problem of attitude. The culturally different student reflects the teachings and experiences of his home and school environment just as any student does. Depending upon the attitudes in the student's home and the experiences he has had in his years in school, the student's attitude toward learning and even toward society may range anywhere from complete negativism to full acceptance of his situation expressed by striving to achieve. A culturally different student who has failed each year in school, who has perhaps been humiliated by either overt or subtle discrimination, may well look upon school as a highly distasteful place for him to be.

Life style and language usage are intricately interwoven. An individual's life style and style of communication are in large measure intrinsic parts of his personality and of his attitudes toward life and society. The student may see no point in changing and may even resist change from the life style and language which serves him in his home environment. The very act of trying to change the culturally different child says to him that he is not adequate. All individuals tend to react negatively to such attempts. In fact, change in language pattern is *not* the chief aim. Rather, the culturally different student needs to be taught the generally-accepted language patterns of standard English so that he is able to communicate in that pattern when he needs to.

The basic principles of remedial teaching are of extreme importance when working with culturally different students: the need for immediate success, direct practical application of the learning, objectivity with the individual, acceptance and genuine concern for the student and his language, and goals and strategies planned with him—all must be aspects of any classroom technique or procedure.

Suggested activities for this student are

1. Organize class sessions in the psychological study of language. Determine with the students the functions of language and how people use it and are used by it. For example, investigate and discuss the connotative use of words. Have the students suggest expressions they use for emotional impact. The objective discussion of language will be less of a threat to the individual than a direct attack upon his level of usage.

2. Discuss the goals of the students with them. Map out strategies for accomplishing their constructive goals.

3. Provide wide opportunities for students to hear and use language. Emphasize all aspects of the language arts.

4. Enable the student to see immediate application of what he is being taught. In the planning with him on how to accomplish his goals, help him to see where in the overall strategy the specific learning occurs.

5. Spend much time and emphasis on concept development with the attendant vocabulary. Use audio-visual and actual experiences to build background.

6. Surround the students with books of their interests and levels of competence. Help them to become familiar with the library. Create a reading atmosphere. However, also use other modalities for learning which will be more appropriate to them to supplement the reading.

7. Some specific activities:

   a. Arrange a bulletin board using attractive book jackets and captions which excite interest. Have the books under the display.

   b. Have a class discussion to identify favorite books, authors, book characters as well as favorite TV programs and comic strips.

   c. Utilize hobby interests to create reading needs.

   d. Use word games, listening centers, experience charts, crossword puzzles.

   e. Read to the class selections of high interest.

   f. Make a card file of magazine pictures that students can relate to. Have the student write a paragraph about the picture to show narration and/or description as a means of communicating with language.

   g. Have the students write instructions for: (again practice in language communication)

      1. changing a tire
      2. preparing breakfast
      3. making a bed
      4. preparing for work in the morning
      5. tying a shoe

   h. Give the students a hypothetical $100.00 and a mail order catalog. Help them with a budget for their Christmas shopping. Instruction would give them the opportunity to fill out an order blank, figure sales tax, postage fee, and so on.

    i.   Give each student a telephone directory. Explain the yellow classified pages and formulate questions to require their finding specific information.

Effective instruction is pertinent to the individual student. Though the subject content of the class may remain essentially the same for different classes, each group of students exhibits different learning needs and different learning strengths. The perceptive teacher notes these and incorporates them into his planning. He diagnoses daily. He uses many different types of classroom organization, selecting the one which best suits the purposes of his teaching and the needs of the learner. Even at the secondary level the student must be taught rather than the subject.

SUGGESTED QUESTIONS AND PROBLEMS TO BE CONSIDERED IN REFERENCE TO YOUR OWN CLASSROOM

List A (For readers who are training to be teachers)
1. In your subject, plan how you could incorporate the various forms of grouping. On what bases would you organize them? How would you have more than one form operating with the same class?
2. Develop a differentiated assignment job sheet for your class.
3. Compile a file of reading skill activities pertinent to your subject which can be used individually and with groups of students.
4. Compile a bibliography and listing of books, self-help materials, programmed materials, tapes, film strips, films, and recordings pertinent to your subject.
5. Prepare an interest inventory as a means of determining the interests of your students.

List B (For readers who are teaching)
1. Determine the goals of instruction for your class with a specific unit of study. Plan the forms of individualization you can employ to contribute to the accomplishment of your goals.
2. Poll your students concerning their thoughts about the goals of the class, how the goals can be accomplished, their responsibilities and what they think your responsibilities are. Discuss your findings with them with the view in mind that mutual strategies will be evolved.
3. For your class develop specific activities for your superior readers, your reluctant readers, your slow learners, your disabled readers, and your culturally different students.
4. Evolve with your class the duties of a group leader, of the recorder, of the process observer.
5. If there is a negative attitude toward reading in your class, plan through discussion and diagnosis to find the cause of it and how you can counter it.

CHAPTER EIGHT

Applying Reading Skills to the English Class

Lefevre states that "ideally, the English teacher would embody the attainments of a Renaissance man." He is responsible, according to Lefevre, for organizing and directing developmental learning experiences in language, literature, and rhetoric. He is also concerned with and must develop within his students the arts and skills of communication. These include the aspects of the language arts of reading, writing, speaking, and listening, and also appreciation, creativity, criticism, and performance as they are applied to them.[1] In essence, the English teacher, as he teaches students to think and to communicate their thoughts, is primarily concerned with the formulation and expression of ideas.

GOALS OF THE LANGUAGE ARTS

The goals of the language arts are basically the same as those of education in general, since language and communication are intrinsic to all curricula. Therefore, the goals may generally be listed as (1) cultivating within the student the qualities needed for a satisfying life, (2) developing social sensitivity and effective participation in the activities of society, (3) helping the student toward a vocational competence. To attain these goals the student must learn to use language as an effective instrument of thought and communication, to gain insights from literature about the world of people, and to develop curiosity and the capacity for critical thinking.

---

[1] Carl A. Lefevre, *Linguistics, English and the Language Arts* (Boston: Allyn & Bacon, Inc., 1970), pp. 18–19.

Lefevre sums up by saying that "language and language learning are the most important of all learnings—to the individual, to his speech community, to the larger society, and to the world."[2]

THE INTERRELATIONSHIPS OF THE LANGUAGE ARTS

The language arts curriculum consists of many parts linked in an interrelationship based upon the nucleic core of language itself. Early points out that studies have shown improvement in reading, for instance, as a side effect of instruction in spelling, since practice in phonetic and structural analysis and the use of the dictionary improve both reading and spelling.[3] The study of written language patterns as implemented through composition instruction and practice seems to improve the students' ability to comprehend the written language.

It seems, however, that many students do not see the interrelationships of the language arts, or to make the transfer from one to the other. One reason for this may be the compartmentalization of the language arts curriculum. In many schools the language arts curriculum is broken into time segments of two weeks to two months in which composition, literature, and grammar are taught as separate entities. Even these major divisions are often broken into tight compartments. For example, literature may be broken into distinct units of the novel, drama, essay, short story, and poetry. Grammar, instead of being related to composition, is often a dreary practice of examples governed by rules. Choice of words or style in literature is not related to composition. Composition is not related to reading comprehension. Organization of ideas in speaking is not related to effective composition. The same use of structure words is not pointed out in each of the four aspects of the language arts.

Early indicates further that students must be guided in making the transfer from one aspect of the language arts to another.

> The imperfect relationships among language skills warn teachers to pay sufficient attention to each. As reading skills improve, for example, listening skills often deteriorate. Good readers may be relatively poor speakers and writers. Without conscious attention to each of the four major language skills, students may not make useful transfers from one to the others. The cluster of skills sometimes labeled "organizational" provides a vehicle for emphasizing transfer. Thus, we teach students to perceive patterns of organization in reading and show them how to use these patterns in their own writing. Studying main ideas in paragraphs is an excellent basis for teaching the topic sentence, or controlling idea, as a tool for composition. Outlining another's ideas demonstrates the usefulness of planning before writing.[4]

---

2 Lefevre, p. xvi.

3 Margaret J. Early, "The Interrelatedness of Language Skills," in *Developing High School Reading Programs,* compiled by Mildred H. Dawson (Newark, Delaware: International Reading Association, 1967), pp. 106–108.

4 *Ibid.,* p. 107.

The following chart shows the major interrelationships. The conclusion which can be drawn from the chart is that each of the language arts skills has an application in each of the four branches of the language arts.

Integration of the Language Arts Skills

Listening-Reading Skills	*Speaking-Writing Skills*
Getting the main idea	Finding the topic sentence Paragraphing Note-taking
Reading for details	Outlining Giving directions Organizing ideas in sequence Summarizing
Determining author's meaning of a word	Vocabulary development Use of dictionary Dramatic interpretation
Using context skills	Understanding sentence structure and paragraphing
Word analysis skills	Spelling
Oral reading	Pronunciation Enunciation Dramatic interpretation
Interpreting poetry	Choral reading Creative writing
Visualization	Descriptions
Understanding modifiers and referents	Use of pronouns, adverbs, adjectives, clauses, and phrases
Drawing conclusions	Logical organization of material
Social sensitivity to ideas presented	Expressing emotional feelings[5]

The English curriculum has a content of its own which includes utilitarian as well as literary uses of language. Strang lists those reading skills applicable to all parts of the curriculum which should be taught in English classes.[6] Vocabulary building is aimed toward more effective oral and written communication as well as listening and reading comprehension. The aim is to increase the student's effectiveness of communication and precision of thought. Understanding sentence and para-

---

[5] Paul S. Anderson, *Language Skills in Elementary Education* (New York: The Macmillan Company, 1964), p. 271.

[6] Ruth Strang, "Teaching Reading, An Essential Part of Teaching English," in *Reading in the Secondary Schools,* ed. M. Jerry Weiss (New York: The Odyssey Press, Inc., 1961), pp. 351–357.

graph structure is essential if the student is to be able to perceive the author's structure as he reads and to create his own language structures when writing. Locating information is an important research skill which should be taught generally in English class and then applied to other subjects by the teachers of the other disciplines. Likewise the reading-study process (SQ3R) can be taught in English class and then applied to each discipline. Interpretation and appreciation skills are fostered through the study of literature. Critical reading, especially of current selections, is important. The students should be directed to find out to whom, by whom, when, where, and why specific ideas have been stated. The communication skills involving the use (especially oral) of language, are pertinent parts of the English curriculum. Denotative and connotative meanings of words and the structure of thoughts are investigated to show their effect upon the clarity and impact of the communication. Finally, voluntary reading is fostered so that it becomes a rewarding and enjoyable activity.

The goal of language arts teaching is the student's development of the capacity for independent learning, and his development of the ability to use language effectively. Though this is an evolving process throughout the school years, each year the goal is for the student to become independent of the teacher at that specific stage of development. Obviously, the skills of the reading-study process must become known by the student to the extent that he uses the process as he reads and studies on his own. Lesson procedures should encourage and expect the student's use of the process as he studies, with you serving as a guide and monitor. Further, the student should learn the attitude that he can use what he has learned. Relevance of the skills must be apparent. This means, of course, that the student must be aware of what the reading skills are. He should be able to identify them, know how to apply them, and when to use specific skills.

Early has listed a series of questions which each teacher may use as a basis for analyzing his own procedures.

Do [you] frequently develop concepts and introduce vocabulary *before* students read an assignment?

Do [you] help students to identify the reading tasks required by a particular assignment?

Do [you] then demonstrate how to apply the necessary skills?

Is attention paid not only to what a textbook says but to how it is said, that is, to the author's choice of words, his sentence structure, and his organization of ideas?

Is the author's purpose examined?

Are comparisons made among treatments of the same subject?

Are students not only encouraged to make judgments but shown how?

Are [you] aware of the different kinds of reading abilities students possess?

Do [you] help them to make the best use of their various abilities by providing books and other reading materials on varying levels of difficulty?[7]

---

[7] Margaret J. Early, "Reading: In and Out of the English Curriculum" in *Teaching Reading Skills in Secondary Schools: Readings,* ed. Arthur V. Olson and Wilbur S. Ames (Scranton, Pa.: International Textbook Company, 1970), p. 249.

LITERATURE AND THE READING SKILLS

Reading instruction and the study of literature are two very different processes. Reading instruction emphasizes specific skills of word recognition, word meaning, levels of comprehension, and is a means to an end. Skill instruction is usually best accomplished with nonliterary selections that can be analyzed to give specific guidance in the skills, which can then be practiced by application to literary selections.

Literature is usually considered to be the body of writing belonging to a people which includes their legends, myths, experiences, beliefs, values, and aspirations—expressed by an expert implementation of language. Dwight Burton has pointed out that there are four major relationships that permeate literature. The subject deals with man and deity, man and other men, man and the natural world, and man and himself.[8]

Literary writing is discursive and imaginative and tends to be descriptive and narrative. Usually, factual data is not listed or explained as in the writing of science and mathematics. In literature, vocabulary usage is the precise and appropriate use of general words. There is little technical vocabulary as is found in factual subjects except as the craft of literary writing is investigated. Further, the use of diagrams, maps, charts, and tables is not generally found in literary writing.

The basic comprehension skills, as pertinent to literature as they are to all prose writing, are the abilities to:

1. read sentences of all types.
2. develop scope and depth of vocabulary.
3. note the main idea.
4. be aware of sequence.
5. read to note and recall details and see their relation to the main idea.
6. see the author's organization—recognize the plot structure.
7. summarize the main points.

Specific activities which apply directly to literature are:

1. Develop word meanings by:
   a. investigating interesting word origins.
   b. noting words with multiple meanings.
   c. examining word structure—prefixes, suffixes, roots, inflectional endings.
   d. noting shifts in the meanings of words.
   e. being aware of subject matter words.
   f. noting words from other languages.
   g. investigating idioms.
   h. noting onomatopoeic words.
   i. determining the differences in meaning between denotation and connotation.

---

[8] Dwight L. Burton, "Literature in No-Man's Land: Some Suggestions for the Middle School," in *English for Junior High Years*, ed. Stephen Dunning (Champaign, Ill.: National Council of Teachers of English, 1969), p. 134.

    j. becoming aware of words of classification.
    k. noting abstract and concrete words.
    l. thinking of antonyms, synonyms, homonyms.
    m. investigating words not common in speech but used in writing.
    n. recognizing slang.
    o. noting strange words an author uses over and over.
2. Note main ideas and summarize by:
    a. giving in a sentence the events of a given scene or situation, the character or nature of the situation, the personality or general appearance of a character.
    b. selecting a revealing name for a character.
    c. choosing an alternative title.
3. Show sequence by:
    a. charting the main events or happenings, or story structure.
    b. using outlines or marginal type explanations.
    c. listing the events in order.
4. Note details by:
    a. selecting a character which the reader likes or dislikes and noting the details which substantiate the feeling.
    b. listing the details in the description of the setting or mood; noticing the things that give the description a mood of gloom, gaiety, impending doom, mystery.

The implementation of the skills through classroom procedure require specific considerations. Mersand has listed them as misconceptions which must be cleared up before a positive program can be established.[9]

1. *All students entering the secondary schools do not have the ability to read on their assigned grade level.* Therefore, to expect all students in a grade, or even all students in a class to be able to read a single literary selection with understanding, enjoyment and appreciation is unrealistic. There must be differentiation, individualization, and flexibility in approach as well as in the selections. For example, students may be assigned by groups to literary selections of differing levels of difficulty. In one instance a teacher had her class divided into two groups, each reading a different story. The stories were related in that they were both about lions. Though the stories were on different levels of difficulty, both were interesting to the students. One portrayed the lion in a very positive manner and the other portrayed him negatively. After discussing the two stories individually with the two groups, the teacher brought them together so that they could share with each other. Different impressions of the lion were noted. The natural development of the ensuing discussion centered upon the respective authors' points of view, and each author's use of language and incident to present his point of view. Finally, open-ended questions were asked in which the students searched their own previous knowledge about lions to support one or the other viewpoint, or both.

---

[9] Joseph Mersand, "How Can We Help Students Enjoy Literature?" in *Reading in the Secondary Schools,* ed. M. Jerry Weiss (New York: The Odyssey Press, Inc., 1961), pp. 357–377.

If for some reason the class as a whole is expected to read the same selection, then you can vary the procedure by (1) providing background and relevance, (2) having the students read only certain sections, (3) reading some sections to the students, (4) using films and recordings, and (5) using open-ended questions to stimulate the students to think about their reactions to the language, the characters, incidents, and the general mood.

2. *Secondary school teachers must cease to castigate the lower grades for a lack of student competence.* Mersand goes on to say that teachers have the responsibility to maintain those skills acquired in the earlier grades, provide remediation and correction where necessary and guide the student toward the acquisition and refinement of new skills. You will know what is to be accomplished with each selection. For example, if the students are to note the author's use of the setting to establish the mood of the story, then practice exercises should be discussed prior to and different from the story, which would give the students some insights and competence in this skill.

3. *Flexibility of literary selections is required.* To have the entire class read and analyze to a minute degree one literary selection is not consistent with our knowledge of individual interests and abilities. In one instance a teacher had her students select their own novel to read. She established only a specific general theme. Prior to the students' reading she presented to them in diagrammatic form the academic development of a plot. The overall assignment was to compare their novel with the standard plot presentation and development. After the students had completed their reading, class discussions were conducted in which each student told the class about his novel and how it compared to the standard plot. In the process, the students learned not only how a novel can be developed, but also many of the variations. They discovered possible reasons for the variations such as the flashback technique, and noted the pertinence of the technique to the author's purpose, thus recognizing the reasons for some aspects of style.

4. *We cannot assume that growth will come automatically by exposure to literature.* Too many of our secondary school students do not return to the literature they were exposed to. In my mind is the picture of a young college student on an airplane reading a stack of comic books. He admitted he was an American Literature major in college. "But," he said, "one doesn't read that stuff for pleasure." How literature had been presented to this young man is not known. One can only surmise. One point we must keep in mind—the students must become involved with the story. They must be guided to relate some aspect of it to their own life experiences and style.

5. *We should not bewail the onslaughts of the mass media.* It is true that TV cuts into time that might be used for reading. Yet, we know that such media can also build background and interest in reading for further information and enjoyment. It is a medium of learning as well as a means of communication. Through the movies and plays presented on television, we have one graphic means of presenting selections of literature.

6. *We stimulate enjoyment of literature best by our own enthusiasm for it.* Your own background in literature and true enjoyment of it will do more than anything to stimulate the students' desire to read and enjoy it. If you like to read, and

share at times casually some of the material you are reading your enthusiasm will prove contagious. If you say sometimes, "I read the most interesting story last night. It was about _____," or "I did not like the author's point of view, but he presented his points so well. Listen _____," the students will learn from you to enjoy reading and might even wish to share in class some of their outstanding reading. If, on the other hand, you teach literature merely because the curriculum requires it or "it's good for the students," then the program is doomed to failure.

7.   *Growth in literature as in anything else comes over a period of time.* It does not come in one class period or even in one year alone. It comes as a result of a school-wide approach to literature through all the years of school.

Student involvement (in the story, the action of one or more characters, or the author's handling of the story) seems to be one of the secrets of developing in students an interest in and liking for literature. Questions centered around student experience and reaction such as the following may help to involve the student:

What would you have done if _____?

What would your reaction to such a character be? Why did he do what he did? Explain what you would have done. Discuss the characterization and motivations of the character.

What would you have expected from such a description? How important is the description and setting?

How would you have solved the problem? What is the crisis of the story? How is it resolved? What is your evaluation of the resolution?

Why do you think the author wrote the selection? What is his theme? What is his approach to the subject? What reaction does he want from his readers?

What techniques does the author use to foster his theme? For a specific reader-reaction?

Lois Claus has pointed out that students learn to conform to what the teacher expects. She would ask such questions as, "Explain the importance of the setting; Discuss the characterization and motivation of _____; Tell the crisis and the resolution of the story; Give examples of symbolism," in order to have the students discover as they read and thereby stimulate their thought. She goes on to say that the starting premise is that we must direct students to what to look for in their reading. Then, she says,

> To appreciate fully a short story, for instance, they need to be aware of structure, particularly setting, plot, crisis, climax, and resolution, and such subtle literary techniques as symbolism, irony, and metaphors. Students should be able to distinguish between theme and moral, between summary and characterization.[10]

Students can see the universality of a subject, especially when the subject is related to their own experiences. Selections chosen for high school students should be within the reach of their level of maturity and experience. Even then, the teacher

---

[10] Lois M. Claus, "The Role of Discovery in Teaching Literature," *The English Journal* 53, No. 9 (Dec. 1964): 687–688.

sometimes needs to bridge the gap for them between their experience and that in the story.

The student's depth of appreciation is not likely to be the same as yours. As he develops toward maturity and as he has continuous positive contact with literature through his school years, his depth of perception and appreciation of literature will grow. Knowledge about literature increases appreciation, and this is a gradual development. Awareness of the universal themes of literature and their relevance to his own life experience, knowledge of an author's purpose and techniques, and the ways language can be used to express ideas contribute to increasing depth of appreciation.

You must adapt your instruction to the student you have in class. For some, a cursory reading of the story may be all that is required, while other students may begin to interpret and evaluate characters, uses of language, setting, and so on. Ideally, the teacher will gently lead the student from where he is to deeper and deeper levels of appreciation, giving him only as much challenge as he is able to meet at any one time.

Skills and Student Involvement

For an understanding of literature, which is a prerequisite to appreciation, the student must understand the author's use of language. He must be able to identify and give meaning to the words. He must see their relationship to each other in the sentence. The basic comprehension skills must be applied. Then he has the data to interpret, to enjoy the nuances and to apply to his own life style.

The essence of literature for the student reader is his interpretation of it and how he is able to relate it to his own experiences and thoughts. It is the insights he gets from it about his own life and life situations that are important and interesting to him. Interpretation involves both skills and attitudes; the student's application of his reading skills is affected by the conditioning he has received, and by his own self-concepts and wishes. His life style in large measure determines how he suspends judgment, whether or not he weighs evidence objectively, and the degree to which he can fuse intellectual and emotional reactions.

Those skills in which attitudes are most involved may be listed as:

1. recognizing the emotional reactions and motives of story characters
2. making inferences
3. forming and reacting to sensory images
4. anticipating outcomes
5. making judgments and drawing conclusions
6. perceiving relationships such as cause and effect, sequence, time, and place
7. interpreting figurative, idiomatic, or picturesque language
8. identifying and evaluating character traits
9. comparing and contrasting
10. identifying and reacting to mood or tone
11. identifying the author's purpose or viewpoint
12. evaluating and reacting to ideas in light of the author's purpose

13. asking questions of critical evaluation
14. identifying techniques of propagandists
15. relating literature to personal experiences
16. contrasting form and style through the type of language used, repetition and rhythm, and person (first or third)
17. understanding the use of signs and symbols
18. sharing reactions to selections.

General Guidelines for the Lesson

General classroom procedure can be varied depending upon your preference, the selection used and perhaps most important, the needs of the students in the class. When teaching a selection of literature one to several days may be required to complete all of the procedural steps. In teaching a novel or play, the time span may be even longer and consist of a number of individual lessons as each new section is read.

The teacher will need to ascertain first the objectives to be accomplished. Many literature textbooks have a teacher's manual or guide book which can give help toward this end. The effective teacher will also adapt the content to his class. As he learns the capabilities of the students—their strengths and weaknesses shown by the diagnostic inventory—other objectives such as developing a greater vocabulary, practice in noting sequence or cause and effect may become lesson goals.

Adequate preparation should be provided for the students to aid their understanding and appreciation of the selection. The teacher would do any or all of the following items as needed, taking as much time as is required.

1. Provide background information pertinent to the time, setting, and nature of the selection.
2. Probe and expand student experiences relevant to the selection—help them begin to relate known experiences.
3. Introduce selected vocabulary and language usages of the author that are needed for a basic understanding and appreciation of the selection.
4. Provide information about the author which would add to the understanding and appreciation.
5. Set up purposes for reading the selection.

These five aspects of reading preparation may be accomplished in numerous ways. Discussion, reports, recordings, films, pictures, models—all can be used as needed, as available, and as appropriate.

The students will read silently all or parts of the selection. The amount of reading assigned is largely determined by the student capabilities and interest as well as by the length and nature of the selection.

Comprehension of the story follows with a discussion of the purpose questions. From these the teacher may pose questions to help the students gain adequate comprehension and greater insight. The key questions should be identified as to type, i.e., do they require the ability to get the main idea, sequence, factual information, use of specific words, inference, conclusion? Open-ended questions will compel the student to think about his own views and feelings.

Rereading may or may not be required. If it is, new purposes for reading are also required. At this stage new vocabulary may be investigated, or students may be asked to find evidence of various techniques employed by the author, such as use of exaggeration, flashback, sensory imagery, suspense, dialogue, word choice, and so on. (The textbook and the teacher can suggest many other literary techniques.) The author's attitude may be noted as well as the characteristics of a literary genre.

Follow-up activities, if the teacher wishes to go further, may include creative assignments in which the students attempt to emulate the technique(s) portrayed by the author, or further reading and/or research pertinent to the author, time, setting, or subject of the selection. When such assignments are contemplated, instruction in the skills required must be given. For example, if the students are to emulate an author's technique, samples of it should be reveiwed and an analysis of the technique made. Class practice through discussion may be necessary before the individual student works independently. If the student is to do supplementary reading and/or research, the sources and skills of research need to be reviewed and taught as necessary.

Another type of followup is an extension of skill development into practice material other than the selection. This is done as student weakness is discerned in the reading of the assigned selection, and as the teacher has knowledge of specific student needs through diagnosis.

A Good Unit in English

A unit approach is often suggested which allows for the development and application of the major skills. The organization of the unit can be thematic or it can be centered around a literary genre or a single classic.

An effective unit of study in English will encompass all of the aspects of the language arts and emphasize their interrelationships. Alm has listed the criteria for a good unit in English.[11]

1. It must deal with an idea, a problem, or a theme.
2. It must have a sense of direction observable to both the teacher and the students. Students must know why they are studying the material in the unit.
3. It reflects the interrelationships of the language arts.
4. The teacher focuses upon the learning activities necessary to accomplish the objectives of the unit.
5. The students must be involved in the learning commensurate to their level of development and ability. (This involves means of individualization and grouping.)
6. There is self-discipline needed by the student to learn and to practice those skills needed for the successful execution of the unit.
7. It will give the learner increased and fresh perspectives about himself in relationship to the unit theme.

Suggested Steps of an English Unit

(The numbers to the left of each step indicate which of the above criteria are being implemented.)

---

[11] Richard S. Alm, "What Is a Good Unit in English?" in *Reading in the Secondary Schools,* ed. M. Jerry Weiss (New York: The Odyssey Press, Inc., 1961), pp. 377–83.

(1)   1. Select a universal theme for the unit. Many literature textbooks are organized around themes with stories, poetry, and essays selected to contribute to the student's understanding and appreciation of the theme.

(2)   2. Note the skills which would be required and emphasized by the selections. If there is a teacher's handbook accompanying the text, such a catalog of skills may be compiled either in it or in the teacher's edition of the textbook itself.

(2)   3. Give an informal reading inventory, if not already administered, to determine the students' strengths and weaknesses in reading skills. (It usually is not necessary to give an inventory with each unit.) Discuss the strengths and weaknesses of the students with them.

(2)   4. From the requirements of the theme and the skill needs of the students evolve the behavioral objectives for the unit.

(3–6) 5. Provide instruction and practice in the deficiencies. This teaching can be accomplished with the entire class if the need is apparent, or with temporary groups organized around specific needs.

(5–7) 6. Begin teaching the literature selections of the unit using the various methods of grouping and individualization as may seem appropriate. Use flexible classroom organization. If different textbooks are in use, there will be grouping based on level. There can also be grouping based on need as different students may be required to work on applying specific skills. Also, groups of two and three students can work together in applying the skills so that their mutual discussion is a learning situation for both.

(3)   7. Provide opportunities for wide reading around the theme. Most textbooks suggest supplementary readings. Use this list and others to extend the opportunities of reading. The librarian may be of assistance here in preparing bibliographies or in obtaining the related books. A classroom library of related materials can be set up.

(3)   8. Provide opportunities for the students to report on their reading.

(3–7) 9. Other follow-up activities may be implemented. The students may conduct research reading on a theme. In this instance, the teacher will need to insure student competence in research skills by teaching and then reinforcing them through student implementation. Also written compositions may be assigned to foster student involvement through relating his own experiences and feelings to those in the selections. Or the compositions may be designed to have the student practice a specific writing technique or word usage.

Free Reading

One goal of literature is to develop and foster the student's desire to read widely as a means of enjoyment. Enjoyment of literature and the wide reading of it work in conjunction. Usually, the more a student reads, the more he enjoys it. You may wish to consider the following stimuli to wide reading:

1.   Use pop-rock lyrics to introduce students to poetry. These investigate many of the themes concerning young people in today's world. Nancy Larrick writes of this approach:

> That's a very different approach to reading from the traditional one. It's a very different kind of reading material, too. But the pop/rock syndrome is tremendously significant in understanding our children and guiding them to pleasure from print. Here is the one great factor in our culture which is youth-centered. It screams out the importance of sound over sight, and it shows us that listening is the road to reading. It illustrates the power of first-person commentary in a rhythmical, conversational style. It exacts an emotional commitment that young people long for. It puts feeling above meaning and invites each listener to sing from his own senses.
>
> Pop/rock culture is not what many of us grew up with, and most of us still feel strange about a development which our children take for granted. But we can't turn back the wheels of time and make now into then. We can't re-cycle the children to fit the old patterns, although some adults are making that foolish effort.
>
> Our only choice—and it is actually an opportunity—is to become so immersed in the sounds of our children's language and in the sense of their feelings that we can sing and listen with them.[12]

2.   Provide time in the school day for recreational reading for students and teachers alike. Richard M. Petre in describing a total school-wide involvement states that this approach basically depends upon four steps:

> Administration and faculty should schedule a daily thirty-five minute reading break for the total school.
>
> Students should select their own material to read during the reading break.
>
> Administrators and teachers must read during the break.
>
> A faculty-student reading committee should be appointed to select a variety of paperbacks to be placed throughout the school, conduct a monthly promotional idea, and evaluate the ongoing progress of the reading environment.[13]

Mr. Petre noted also that students requested two things: more time for reading and an opportunity to discuss books with others who had read them.

3.   Use paperbacks which are less expensive than hardback books and are often more manageable and less formidable in size and appearance. Most publishing houses publish paperbacks both as single titles and as collections around specific themes.

4.   Let students read what they wish to read, what they think will be meaningful to them, what appeals to their interests.

---

[12] Nancy Larrick, "Pop/Rock Lyrics, Poetry and Reading," *Journal of Reading* 15, No. 3 (December, 1971): 189–190.

[13] Richard M. Petre, "Reading Breaks Make It in Maryland," *Journal of Reading* 15, No. 3 (December, 1971): 191–194.

5.   Provide the students with opportunities to share the books they read, such as the following book-reporting activities.

   A.   About a week before the book report is due, present a list of thought questions for class discussion. Each student then chooses two or three questions relevant to his particular book and uses them as the basis of a written report. Examples:

> What hardships or difficulties did the main character overcome?
> How does the setting affect the action?
> What part does coincidence play in the plot?
> Show how one character influences another.
> Show how responsibility changes a character.
> How is the main character typical of a boy (or girl) of his age?
> How is he different from the boys (or girls) you know?

   B.   Pupils can pretend that the book is to be filmed and:
   —select the cast for the leading roles, justifying their choices
   —decide on possible locations for the shooting of various scenes
   —decide which scenes would be suitable (or not) for inclusion in a movie and explain why
   —explain how they would change the ending to make it appropriate for a movie

   C.   The class makes a project of compiling a useful outside reading book file. Cards list author, title, type of book, specific opinions and reasons for reading. The file is made available to the class for consultation. Cards may be distributed from time to time for discussion.

   D.   Students discuss how the author feels toward various characters.

   E.   Students write an imaginary conversation between two characters.

   F.   Students write a book review consisting of author and title, type of book, setting, identification of chief characters with one detail about each, a brief summary of two important incidents, and a few reasons for recommending (or not) the book. The class may be prepared for this activity by analysis of reviews in the daily or Sunday newspapers.

   G.   Students report on ideas gained through their reading.

   H.   Pupils choose a point of view for their reports from a series of suggested topic sentences: i.e., *This book made me see—wish—realize—decide—wonder—believe.*

   I.   Pupils compare their own neighborhoods or communities with localities described in the book.

   J.   Students describe their own reactions to various characters.

   K.   Students make oral reports to committees, whose members take notes.

   L.   Pupils report through art work projects:
   stage to illustrate a scene, with paper dolls for characters;
   illustrated booklets of clues for a mystery novel;
   literary maps for historical or regional books indicating locations of scenes, birthplaces of characters, places connected with author's life, etc.;

illustrated bookmarks or booksellers' posters with brief book reviews
lettered or pasted on the back;

vertical lettering of title,—thus:

L
O
V
E   Pupils write a brief phrase applicable to the book for each letter
in the title.
S   If the title is brief, pupils may write phrases starting with the
T   letters of the author's name in the same way.
O
R
Y

READING AND LANGUAGE STRUCTURE

Part of the English teacher's task is to teach English grammar and syntax. The
goal is to help the student attain mastery over his language as he uses it. It would
seem that knowledge of English structure would aid the student's ability to comprehend in his reading. O'Donnell, however, points out that there is no statistical
evidence to conclusively prove that the mastery of grammar guarantees success in
reading. He does say, though, that

> The reader whose native language is English may not be able to intelligently
> discuss the syntax-structure of his language but it seems that he would have
> to have some awareness of the varying functions of different elements of a
> sentence if he is to accurately interpret what he reads.[14]

Perhaps there are two considerations which should be investigated. One, the
student must learn the structure of English so thoroughly that he does not have to
concentrate on it *per se as* he reads. Rather, his attention should be on the content
of the reading selection with an awareness and analysis of the structure operating
at a subsidiary level. Second, instruction in grammar should emphasize the thought
being expressed with the specific detailed mechanics and rules learned and applied
only as the thought is changed. Emphasis should be on the functions of grammar
in the thinking processes. This would mean that all of the various aspects of grammar would be approached from the point of view of the effect upon the thought.
The student should be guided to note the effects of punctuation on the thought expressed in the sentence. Sentence patterns should be approached as ways of expressing ideas. For instance, the thought element of the basic parts of a sentence,
the effect upon thought of a subordinate clause, or what structure words signal the
condition upon the main clause—these are the understandings we seek. Paragraph

---

[14] Roy O'Donnell, "Awareness of Grammatical Structure and Reading Comprehension,"
in *Improving Reading in Secondary Schools,* ed. Lawrence E. Hafner (New York: The Macmillan Company, 1967), p. 361.

patterns should be analyzed as schemes of thought organization. Any textbook on the language arts will list and discuss the many grammatical and syntactical rules and analyses. However, it would be interesting from the point of view of reading comprehension to note whether an effect would be generated if the thought emphasis were made and if students were guided to "play" with grammatical and syntactical forms in expressing ideas.

The English teacher is charged with developing student competence in language. In this capacity he must relate the four aspects of the language arts to the student's complete knowledge, use and appreciation of his native language. An understanding of the theory and structure of language is necessary. Further, an appreciation of masterful examples of written language is desired to serve as examples of the beauty of language as well as examples of effective communication. The skills of reading are one means of developing student language development and appreciation. A major concern of skill instruction is to enable the student to receive the author's communication as fully as possible. Competence in a skill as an entity unto itself has no value. The emphasis must be toward the greater goal of communication.

SUGGESTED QUESTIONS AND PROBLEMS TO BE CONSIDERED IN REFERENCE TO YOUR OWN CLASSROOM

List A (For readers who are training to be teachers)

1. Plan how you will provide for different reading levels and needs in your literature program.
2. Compile approaches that will foster student interest in literature.
3. Identify the reading skills you wish to apply to each selection of literature. Work these into your lesson procedure.
4. Plan a teaching unit in English and make provision for developing appreciations, teaching the pertinent language arts skills, and differentiating the study to the competence level of each student.
5. Set up a classroom library. Compile bibliographies of books related to each theme for your students to read.

List B (For readers who are teaching)

1. Review the goals of your language arts curriculum. Note the areas where both cognitive and affective objectives would be included.
2. Review the content of your language arts curriculum. Note where instruction in reading, writing, speaking, and listening would be included. Determine the skills you would wish to include in each area.

3. Review the literature selections you will be teaching and plan questions and activities to stimulate student involvement in relating them to their own life experiences.
4. Through the results of a diagnostic informal reading inventory and/or in conjunction with the guidance office, determine the reading levels of your students. Plan how you will provide for these levels in your literature program.
5. For each unit in your curriculum, compile a bibliography of the appropriate and available books in your school library.

CHAPTER NINE

Applying the Reading Skills
to the Social Studies

The social studies is an area of study which draws its information from the various disciplines of the social sciences. The disciplines usually comprising the social studies curricula are geography, history, economics, sociology, and civics. The content of these subjects describes the interactions of human beings in small and large groups throughout the world. The social studies direct the students' attention toward the record of mankind's activities as well as toward the study of his current structures of government. Government is a formalized system of regulating the interaction of people—ostensibly for the good of all. The main thrust of the social studies, therefore, is the chronicle and analysis of the interactions of people.

The objectives of the social studies relate to the desires of society—what it wishes the student to know, to achieve, and to become. They are pertinent to the time and to the mode of government and life-style promulgated by society. Whatever the specific objectives may be, the teacher has a three-fold responsibility: first, to impart a body of basic information which is considered to be important for the student to know; second, to help the student acquire specific skills which will foster his independence; and third, to inculcate specific attitudes deemed necessary for the constructive working of society.

In this chapter we will concern ourselves with the second objective: the acquisition of skills that will enable the student to use tools for acquiring information and understanding which he will need throughout his life as a functioning member of society. The emphasis will be on the skills of effective reading.

THE RELATIONSHIP OF READING AND THE SOCIAL STUDIES

Except in instances when a reader reads orally to others or when discussion of a topic results from information gained from reading, the reading act itself is a solitary activity. The social studies, on the other hand, centers upon the interrelationships of people. But we know that reading is one aspect of communication which affects the degree and the nature of the interaction among people. It would be obvious to point out that the level of communication, which affects the degree and the nature of the interaction, would be reduced to the level of the higher animals without our systems of language.

The student's understanding in the social studies depends upon his ability to use his language. There is a vital and direct relationship between the two. He must rely in large measure upon his ability to read in order to acquire understanding and concepts which are expressed in language. He must be able to discuss the information; he must be able to listen intelligently in class; and he must be able to express his thoughts in writing. Holmes and Finley concluded that acceleration and retardation among fifth grade boys were more closely related to linguistic abilities than to those of a quantitative nature such as knowledge of subject matter.[1] Without an effective skill in language usage the student will be unable to acquire understandings in the social studies. Reading is one of the major avenues of gaining information.

The social studies teacher realizes the vital, all-pervasive nature of language, but he most often sees his emphasis as one of content. The content comes first with the reading skills subordinate to the nature of the content. In practice that means that reading is taught if there is time. However, no such decision should have to be made. The teaching of content and the skills of reading are fused. Reading is the means, and the end is content acquisition and understanding resulting in the development of specific attitudes.

STUDENT DIFFICULTIES IN READING SOCIAL STUDIES MATERIALS

Social studies material is often difficult for the students to read with understanding. Much of the reason for this is the student's lack of background and actual experience with social studies information and concepts. This consideration alone suggests specific direction to the teacher for implementing classroom procedure which will provide the needed background.

Textbooks in the social studies provide a barrier to the student. Much of his reading instruction through the years has been based on readers, which are comprised of story-type reading material. With the social studies the student is faced with factual prose jammed with data. Marksheffel states:

> Most textbooks are excellent sources of information, facts, and ideas pertinent to learning in specific content areas. The material is usually of the highest

---

[1] Jack A. Holmes and Carmen J. Finley, "Relative Importance of Curriculum Areas for Grade Placement Deviations in Grade V," *California Journal of Educational Research,* VI (Nov., 1955): 213–18.

caliber because it is written by experts in the particular area of concentration. The fact that textbooks are written by experts is at once both a major weakness and a major strength. Specialists in subject matter are usually amateurs at writing. They understand so well the materials about which they write that they appear to forget that the sudent has but a meager knowledge of the vocabulary and concepts necessary for understanding.[2]

Other difficulties attributed to social studies materials are:

1. Contractions of subject matter in which many facts and ideas are condensed, thereby omitting much of the concrete factual and anecdotal material that would both make the subject more alive and provide the bases for the student to relate the ideas to his own background.
2. Difficult ideas which are largely removed from the experience of the students. This problem is often compounded with the condensation of the subject matter.
3. Sentence length adds to difficulty in that complex ideas often seem to compel complex sentences. Involved sentences add to the student's difficulty with the organization and treatment of ideas. Though many textbook authors have striven to simplify the language, complex writing still persists. For instance, a sentence taken at random from a paragraph of a senior high school American history textbook: "The Americans had none of the largest vessels afloat, ships of the line; but their frigates, the second largest type of ship, were bigger, faster, and carried more guns than their British counterparts."[3] To the competent reader who understands language structure and syntax such a sentence is not difficult. To the less competent reader, the sentence, with its subordinate clauses, series of adjectives and apposition, can be confusing.
4. Organization may elude the student in that he may find it difficult to note the sequential development of ideas, cause and effect relationships and relevant or irrelevant data.
5. Vocabulary is a basic difficulty. The words used are either general words used in a social studies context or technical words pertinent to the social studies. The student may know the meaning of the general words, but may not know the meaning applied to the social studies. There are many such words in the social studies: for instance, *storm, grant, revolution.* Then there are the specialized social studies terms such as *federalism, treaty,* and *capital,* abstract terms which represent whole concepts.
6. Teaching procedure is often a further cause of student difficulty with the social studies. Students may not see the relevance of the information they are reading. They may not see the connection between the social studies information and what is happening in the world today.
7. The student may lack the skills necessary for thinking about and using the ideas within the subject. Obviously these difficulties, experienced by many students, require direct assistance through instruction by the teacher. The

---

[2] Ned D. Marksheffel, *Better Reading in the Secondary School* (New York: The Ronald Press Co., 1966), p. 174.

[3] T. Harry Williams and Hazel C. Wolf, *Our American Nation* (Columbus, Ohio: Charles E. Merrill Publishing Company, 1966), p. 231.

teacher, with his richer background and broader base of experience, can help the students to see the relevance of the information, to delineate purpose, to work with ideas, and to acquire competence in the necessary study skills.

SOCIAL STUDIES VOCABULARY

Word–concept–understanding is basic to comprehension in the social studies. Only as the student understands the concept which is labeled by a word is he able to think about social studies ideas. A concept is a mental construct which the student develops, or rather evolves. It grows and is refined by experience and the acquisition of factual knowledge which bears upon the idea. Vocabulary in the social studies represents the concepts by labeling them.

The meanings a student develops for words can be on two levels. The first, the superficial level, which is hardly adequate, is a memorized meaning of words. Whether or not the student knows the idea the word represents is doubtful unless he has an experiential base and can make a concrete application of the term. Often vocabulary study is complicated by the high school student's glibness with language which enables him to use the correct words in the correct context because he has the experience and understanding to use word patterns correctly. But he may not be able to explain the ideas represented. In such a case, vocabulary development is reduced to jargon.

The second level of vocabulary development, and the desired one, is the student's understanding of the concept labeled by the word. It is at this level that he will be able to think creatively and critically with interpretation and precision. Teaching the language of social studies, then, must be involved with the development of concepts.

Many words in the social studies vocabulary are abstract. They represent ideas rather than objects which can be experienced through the senses. They can be made concrete only through situations where they would apply. For instance, the word *constitution* is concrete in that a written form of it can be seen. But, the idea of what it is and represents can only be understood as it is applied to a structure of government. The student can only realize the concept as he sees it in context with its function. Obviously, the student's background of information and understanding will determine the degree of meaning. In the case of *constitution,* the role of the Student Organization constitution of his school, of which most students would be aware, would help him to relate the word to his experiential background. If background and experiences are lacking, the teacher's role is to build them, as part of concept development.

Things to do in Developing Social Studies Vocabulary

1. Write new words on the blackboard during a discussion to focus the student's attention upon them. At the same time quickly review the syllabication of the word, its root, and various forms of it. If the word is *democracy,* note the two Greek roots and the meanings of each (demos—people; kratein—to rule) and the forms: *democratic, democrat, democratization,* etc.

2. Have students list and identify names, places, and events related to the word to add to the richness of its conceptual base.
3. Suggest that the students list the words peculiar to a period of history such as *whig, feudalism.*
4. Have the students evaluate the definition of some figure of speech, slogan, or expression. Note the significance and the impact. For instance: What did Thomas Paine mean in the statement, "These are the times that try men's souls?"
5. Use films, recordings, tapes, drawings, dramatizations, models, and exhibits to add to the conceptual background of the words.
6. Have the students note the emotional use of words. Suggest that the students use other less emotional words and notice the difference in the impact of a selection.

STUDY AND COMPREHENSION SKILLS PERTINENT TO THE SOCIAL STUDIES

The study skills are those which enable the student to attack a reading assignment in accordance with a stated purpose, to locate information, and to determine the structure of thought of the author. Obviously, the social studies teacher gives guidance and instruction when needed. The study skills common to all content subjects are listed in Chapter Five, pages 101–125, in which a general discussion of the hierarchy of many of the study skills is presented.

These specific principles of teaching will help the student become effective in use of the study skills:

1. Use material in the student's instructional materials (textbooks) when teaching the study skills. These skills are best developed as they apply to the instructional material in class. Direct application should be made to the specific paragraph, chapter, graph, picture, etc., which is needed for clearer understanding of the subject information.
2. Be cognizant of sequence in the study skills. If the students seem to have difficulty with getting the main idea of a paragraph in which it is only implied, you will probably need to return to a simpler structure such as determining the main idea of a paragraph in which it is stated. Then, through discussion of various clues develop the skill to the implied main idea paragraph.
3. Teach the skill when the need for it arises. This practice usually brings about the best results. Motivation is highest when the students see the direct application of their learning.
4. Fuse the teaching of the skills with the teaching of content. This principle is really an extension of the first. The essential point for you is that greater competence in the skill should bring about greater mastery of the content. The content is the body of information through which the skill is taught.

Specific Suggestions for Instruction in the Study Skills

A.   Developing purposes for reading
1.   Ask the students questions, or get them to formulate them, about the possible causes or results of a historical event.
2.   Help students to formulate questions of *why, what, where, when,* and *how* as guides in determining basic information.
3.   Have the students read the introduction to a chapter and note whether the author suggests questions to be answered.
4.   Show the students how to formulate questions from the topical headings.
5.   From the preview of a chapter or section, have the students speculate about the information or note what they do not know but would like to. Formulate questions accordingly.
6.   Have the students list the facts they already know about the subject under study; then have them formulate questions about information they would still need to know.
7.   Have the students evolve purposes and then find the paragraphs or sections in the textbook where they are answered. This can help the student see the significance of the paragraph. A reverse of this is to have the student read a selection and determine its main point or significance.
B.   Using parts of a textbook
1.   Getting information from a table of contents
     From the perusal of a table of contents, have the students answer the following questions:
     a.   How does the book seem to be organized?
     b.   What are the major topics?
     c.   Is the content organized by units or chapters? What is the significance of the organization when the chapters are grouped under unit topics?
     d.   What is the scope of the book?
2.   Using an index
     a.   How are the topics listed?
     b.   What is the difference between a table of contents and an index?
     c.   What is the purpose of the itemized sub-topics listed under a major topic?
     d.   Give the students topics to look for in the index. Ask how they can find a topic when they may have a question such as: "Why are the trade routes basically East-West in direction rather than North-South?" "What are the entry words to use to find pertinent page references?" (The key entry word is *trade* and the term is *trade routes.*)
3.   Using study aids in a textbook
     a.   What is the purpose of an introduction to a unit and a chapter? What does the introduction tell the reader?
          Have the students find the sentence which may best express what information is to be covered.
     b.   What is the purpose of a summary?

    c.   How can the vocabulary list at the end of a chapter or unit be of help to a reader?

    d.   What is the purpose of the questions following each chapter? (Determine the information the students are to acquire.)

    e.   How does the textbook facilitate the reader's problems in discerning the important ideas in review?

    f.   Have the students read the chapter headings, subheadings, and marginal headings, look at the pictures and other graphic aids, to get an overview of the material. Direct the students to express in a short paragraph the material to be covered.

  4. Noting the importance of the foreword or preface.

    a.   What is the author's purpose in writing a preface?

    b.   What reasons can we find that tell what the author hopes to accomplish with his books?

    c.   What point of view can we note?

    d.   How does the author think his book could be read and used?

C. Using graphic aids

  1. Whenever the students use a map have them note what the map shows, or what the author's purpose is, the type, date, and parts of the map.

  2. Have students use maps to determine trade routes, ocean currents, climatic zones, etc.

  3. Have students compare types of maps such as one showing population distribution and the climatic zones. Note relationships.

  4. Suggest that the students maintain a bulletin board map showing the places where current events of note are taking place. Have them attach a ribbon from the place on the map to the newspaper clipping describing the event.

  5. Help students interpret cartoons. Note the symbolism, the hyperbole. Deduce the main point or inference.

  6. Discuss the impact of cartoons upon the reader.

  7. Discuss pictures and determine what the purpose of each is. Note the significance to the topic under study.

  8. Guide the students in using any key, symbol or scale accompanying a graphic aid.

  9. Have the students read the caption for a chart or picture. How does the caption relate to the information given by the chart or picture? How does it relate to the reading of the material?

 10. Suggest that the students write a summary of a topic using only pictures, maps, graphs, and other graphic aids as their sources of information.

 11. Have the students make a chart showing the comparisons and/or contrasts between two countries, two types of governments, etc.

 12. Have the students draw a time line showing the evolution of a condition or the progression of a period in history.

D. Locating information—library sources

  1. As a class project develop a topic with the students to review the use of:

    a.   the library card file

    b.   the *Reader's Guide to Periodical Literature*

     c.   specific references such as encyclopedias, atlases, almanacs, biographical dictionaries and other available and needed references.

   2.   Have the students determine the particular values of types of source materials and the kinds of information found in each type.

E.   Finding the main idea

   1.   Have the students read the chapter headings and subheadings and determine the topic that is discussed under each heading. Have them express each topic in one sentence.

   2.   Ask the students to restate in their own words the author's statement of the main idea of each paragraph in a chapter or section of a chapter.

   3.   Have the students use the main ideas of the paragraphs in a chapter or chapter section to write a summary of the material.

   4.   Have the students read several paragraphs in their textbook and determine where the main-idea sentence is found in each paragraph. Have them note the function of the details included in each paragraph.

   5.   After the students have read a chapter in their textbook, have them think of a different but appropriate title for the material.

   6.   Select a series of paragraphs from the textbook and list four possible main ideas for each paragraph. Have the students choose the correct one. Discuss in class the reasons for the correct choices. This type of exercise can also be done with longer selections.

   7.   Collect a group of news articles and cut the headlines from them. See if the students can match the appropriate headline with the article. (This exercise increases in difficulty when all of the articles are about a single topic.)

   8.   Analyze paragraphs from the textbook to determine types. Have the students apply their knowledge of paragraph structure to determine the main idea and organization.

   9.   Determine the main ideas of several paragraphs. Draw a conclusion about the author's basic style of paragraph structure.

F.   Recognizing important details

   1.   Have the students find paragraphs in which the main idea is explained by details.

   2.   Have the students note ways in which the author may indicate the relative importance of facts. Look for:

     a.   more space to the discussion of one fact than to another;

     b.   the use of introductory remarks, such as "above all," "preeminent," "the chief factor," "probably the most crucial";

     c.   questions at the beginning of the chapter, or at its end, that indicate the most important facts;

     d.   the use of italics.

G.   Noting organization

   1.   Test the ability of the class to report an exciting event giving the main idea and the supporting details.

2. Have the students read about the organization of a type of government. Have them show how such a government would operate and how it would affect the lives of people under its jurisdiction.

3. Have the students use facts obtained from reading to list ways in which problems of the past have been solved or that problems of the present are being solved.

4. Have the students write a term paper or an essay, using an organization that will show a comparison of one or more facets of a country with another, such as comparison of the governmental structure of one country with that of another.

5. Suggest that a committee of students gather data on local history and local problems. Have the committee organize the data and present a report to the rest of the class.

6. Have the students list the chain of events leading up to a historical crisis or incident. Point out the words which suggest each step such as: *second, finally, in response to this,* etc.

7. Have the students trace the growth of a group of people or of a nation.

8. Have the students write a summary of the facts they have studied about some topic.

9. Suggest that some of the students describe a historical event in the style of writing used by newspapers of the time.

10. Have the students write a short biography of some historical figure.

11. Guide the students to prepare a forum, round-table discussion, or panel on some such topic as the causes of war or possible methods of preventing war.

12. Have the students classify topics under headings such as *causes* and *results.* Group historical figures in an event as they would be representative of specific countries or aspects of historical events; or in a discussion of the geography of a country make columns entitled: Climate, Topography, History, Industry, Customs, Agriculture, Trade. Comparisons can be made easily if such is done for several countries.

13. Give the students a partial outline with instructions for them to complete the sub-headings. Example:

    I. Issues Facing the Continental Convention
        A.
        B.
        C.

    Outlines of increasing complexity or steps can be gradated to develop competence.

14. Have the students include two or three related points into a single sentence as a means of developing competence in summarizing.

H. Newspaper Reading

Newspaper reading is an important source of information for the social studies student. Current information is not available from textbooks but from the materials such as newspapers which are published daily. Gaining information from newspapers requires its own application of skills, so the student will need instruction in the specific application. The following outline highlights the skills and techniques needed:

I.   Skills needed for newspaper reading
  A.   Skimming
    First paragraph of a news story contains an account of "who, what, when, where, why, how."
    News articles have the "lead" paragraph which is the summary and "the body" which is the story in detail.
  B.   Newspaper Make-up
    Use of the newspaper index
  C.   All of the basic skills:
    Previewing a reading selection
    Finding the main idea
    Reading for details
    Establishing purpose—change headlines into questions
    Noting key words and phrases
    Increasing vocabulary

II.   Planning for newspaper reading (budget time)
  Example:

Skimming	2 minutes
News	15
Financial pages	3
Sports	2
Drama, Music, Books	2
Radio, TV programs	1
Editorials	2
Columnists	1
Advertisements	1
Comics	1
Total time	30 minutes

III.   Plan of attack
  A.   Skim all headlines on the front page
  B.   Skim through entire paper. Make mental notes of what is to be read in more detail later.
  C.   Read the news stories on the front page. Sometimes the first one or two paragraphs of an article will suffice.
  D.   Read widely throughout the paper. Select the most informative, interesting articles.

READING SKILLS REQUIRED BY THE NATURE OF THE SOCIAL STUDIES

Social studies writing requires the application of specific skills if the reader is to comprehend and use the information. These skills involve the use of the common study skills and go beyond to higher levels of thinking. The student must become acquainted with the skills and how to use them. He must also have a background of experience and knowledge to serve as a base upon which he evaluates the new information. The student's competence in the skills and the language of the social studies increases as his background of knowledge increases. He becomes better acquainted with the patterns of writing used in the social studies. Smith discerned six patterns in social studies writing: picture and map; cause and effect; sequential events with dates; comparison; detailed statement-of-fact; and propaganda.[4] In addition, the social studies requires the student to discern fact from opinion as a means of arriving toward historical accuracy; and he needs to appreciate time, place, and space concepts.

The Picture and Map Pattern

In a well written social studies textbook the pictures and maps are included to supplement the information given to the printed material. As obvious as pictorial aids may be to a competent reader, the average student may get little from them. One student told his teacher, "I never look at the pictures and maps, but I like them in the book because the more pictures there are, the less reading." As the teacher discerned in this case, the student needed to realize that the pictures and maps could give much information, especially if the student knew how to use them and if he had a purpose (information to find) in looking at the pictorial aids. Teachers have found that students have not realized the relationship of the picture to its legend. With maps, the students may not understand types of projections, how to use the map key and scale, or know such basic map features as longitude and latitude. All students need to become adept in the use of pictorial aids. And, as many teachers have noted, a poor reader especially can get much information from such sources.

The Cause and Effect Pattern

This pattern is a common and predominant one in the social studies. The interaction of peoples is characterized in large measure by a chain of causes and effects—sometimes with effects being the causes of further effects through a continuous flow or movement of man's activities. An example of cause and effect within a single paragraph from a social studies text shows a cause with a number of effects.

Increased Production, More Jobs. By 1923 the American economy had weathered the postwar depression. The automobile industry had grown rapidly, spurring prosperity in iron, steel, glass, and rubber manufacturing. Its development created all kinds of new jobs in the oil industry; road construction, as well as that of office buildings and dwellings, boomed and so did the demand for workers. In addition, other industries soon copied Henry Ford's assembly-line production techniques and his installment-plan sales procedures. As

---

[4] Nila Banton Smith, "Patterns of Writing in Different Subject Areas, Part II," *Journal of Reading*, VIII (Nov., 1964): 97–102.

Americans purchased more goods, both necessities and luxuries, production increased and created new jobs and eventually still further demands for goods. Long before the political convention of 1924, general prosperity made the political outlook for the Republicans very good.[5]

_____Cause

_____Effect

Suggestions for classroom procedure:
1. Have the students list the factors that led up to a certain event.
2. After listing the factors that led up to an event, check each one to see how or if it may have been a cause leading up to the event.
3. Find similar situations in history. List the points that make them alike and those that make them different.
4. Suggest that pupils use facts as a basis for making predictions.

The Sequential Events with Dates Pattern

History evolves chronologically with the passing of time. One of the understandings students will need to acquire is the large movements of history and the overlap of historical movements. They must learn to appreciate the fluid nature of historical development and realize when they study a historical movement that it did not begin at a specified date or end with one. For instance, the study of the Westward Movement in the United States: the movement did not occur only around the Gold Rush Period of 1849 (a time when this movement is described in many textbooks), but started with the first settlers and, according to the current census reports, is still continuing.

Suggestions for classroom procedure:
1. Construct a time line showing the development of a historical period and to show the overlap with other periods.
2. Have the students note important dates relative to a period of history.
3. Make a chart of a historical period showing the chronology of events and persons involved. Use arrows to show interrelationships between persons, and between persons and dates.
4. On an outline map record the place, name of person(s), and date of historical events.
5. Direct the students to note the introduction of another step in a chain of events by such words as *then, finally, second, another, subsequently,* etc.

The Comparison Pattern

Students use this pattern when likenesses and differences are to be noted on such topics as countries, theories of government, policies of different political lead-

---

[5] Williams and Wolf, p. 664.

ers, and historical periods. Obviously, the student's purpose for reading should presuppose that he look for likenesses and differences as he reads.

Suggestions for classroom procedure:

1. Have the students compare and contrast the governmental structures of two or more countries.
2. Have the students compare the resources, economic conditions, and living standards of two or more countries.
3. Have the students compare two historical documents of different points of view or of different countries during the same period.
4. Have the students compare living conditions of the present with a time in the past.
5. Compare means of travel today with a period in the past.

An example of the comparison pattern is shown on pp. 202–203.

Detailed Statement-of-fact Pattern

This pattern of writing is designed to give information about some social studies phenomena for the purpose of building the student's background. The student uses this information on which to base, in large measure, his comparisons, interpretations, and conclusions.

Suggested classroom procedure:

The procedures of this pattern are similar to those for noting the main idea, the pertinent details, and in seeing the organization of information.

1. Have the student tabulate or chart the information as indicated in the following example:

	Facts about Hoover
As a mining engineer whose work had taken him all over the world and brought him a small fortune, and as an ①efficient wartime food administrator in Europe as well as in his own country. Hoover was accustomed to directing the work of the offices he held. As ②Secretary of Commerce he had been determined to ferret out every kind of opportunity for American business. ③He had kept close watch on other Cabinet departments, alert for activities which might be correlated with those of his own department to the advantage of business. He tried, Coolidge had complained, to be undersecretary to every other Cabinet member. As ④President, he expected to be equally active. He would make his own studies of current issues and suggest his own corrective legislation.	1. Wartime food administrator-directed work. 2. Secretary of Commerce—looking for business opportunities. 3. Kept close watch on other Cabinet departments—note opportunities to help business. 4. President—would suggest corrective legislation.

The Farm Problem

Since the farm problem seemed more pressing than any other, Hoover called a special session of Congress to consider it. When Congress assembled, he was ready with a program. Two months later, the lawmakers approved an①*Agricultural Marketing Act* based on his suggestions. Farmers were urged to join voluntarily in marketing cooperatives which would be aided by the federal government. Supporters of the measure believed it would enable farmers to control production and distribution in much the same way that many manufacturers did. To aid the effort, the act created an eight-member Federal Farm Board with a half-billion dollar revolving fund for loans to cooperatives or to organizations which the board might set up to purchase, store, and market possible surpluses.

Farmers responded at once.②During its first year of operation the board loaned over 165 million dollars.③The advice it gave on limiting the production of crops already in oversupply, however, was to some extent canceled out by Agriculture Department and agricultural school advice on how to increase production.④But cooperative marketing did not curtail the rapid decline of wheat and cotton prices.⑤The board then exercised the second power which Congress had given it and established a Grain Stabilization Corporation and a Cotton Stabilization Corporation. In an effort to raise prices, each corporation purchased and stored the surplus of its particular commodity.⑥By mid-1931, the Grain Corporation, with 257 million bushels of stored wheat (but no buyers), suspended purchases.⑦Wheat dropped to 57 cents a bushel. ⑧The following year the Cotton Corporation also stopped its purchases, and cotton fell to 5 cents a pound. Within another year the Farm Board, having spent 184 million dollars, gave up the stabilization program, and the farm problem remained unsolved.[6]

The Farm Problem

1. Agricultural Marketing Act. (description of function)
2. Farmers responded.
3. Advice on how to increase production cancelled out limiting production by acreage.
4. Prices continued to decline.
5. Establishment of Grain and Cotton Stabilization Corporations (description of function)
6. Government grain surplus with no buyers —purchases suspended.
7. Wheat prices dropped.
8. Cotton purchases stopped. Prices declined.
9. Stabilization given up, farm problem unsolved.

The Propaganda Pattern

Propaganda has been in use by people throughout the history of man. The interaction of people involves points of view and the various techniques of per-

---

[6] Williams and Wolf, pp. 680–681.

suasion. This pattern calls for the skills of critical reading. Students will find this pattern in newspapers and in written materials by authors who wish to convince readers of a point of view. Generally speaking, most school textbooks are bland in regard to a specific point of view.

Suggested classroom procedures:

1. Have the students decide what great power (or powers) control(s) the various strategic spots on the earth. What techniques of control are used?
2. Have the students evaluate the information used by the author to prove an important point. Direct them to note the words he uses to see what emotional impact or impression they convey.
3. Have the students evaluate a historical figure of speech, showing its origin, application, and emotional appeal.
4. Suggest that students draw cartoons illustrating the effect of some historical event.
5. Have the students show how some country takes advantages of its geographical position.
6. Have the students describe the methods of leadership used by various historical leaders. Analyze the techniques of their leadership.
7. Have the students prove or disprove a statement with concrete factual information.
8. Have the students decide what the author's purpose is in writing propaganda and note his use of words to foster his purpose.
9. If an author presents two sides to a problem and draws a conclusion, have the students note the author's treatment of the facts for each side and have them determine the author's preference—if there is one—and the validity of his preference.

Noting Fact from Opinion

This is also a part of critical reading. The student will need to note the author's use of words which indicate his conclusion. The information needs to be evaluated to determine if it is founded in statements of fact, or statements of conjecture. Then, a finer distinction is often required in which the student must judge conclusions based on fact, or statements presented as fact but based on accumulated circumstantial evidence. Such statements are often generally accepted ideas which are based upon common empirical knowledge about human activity throughout the ages and which are generally accepted as true.

Suggested procedures:

1. Have the students note statements in their textbooks which are based on fact and are therefore logical conclusions. Note the difference between these and statements of opinion which may not have factual support. For example: *The Continental Congress completed the Constitution in 1787 and voted to submit for ratification.* (fact) *All of the leaders in the congress were enthusiastic about the new constitution.* (opinion, not based on fact) *Many of the leaders of the Congress had reservations about the new Constitution but submitted it for ratification since it represented the best*

Comparison of Plymouth

Difficulties of the First Years

Their choice of site was ill-advised, for they built James-town in a low, marshy, malarial spot without an adequate supply of drinking water. Then, because the promoters were demanding an immediate return on their investment, the Virginians feverishly searched for gold and prepared stocks of New World products such as lumber, pitch, tar, and iron ore to ship to England.

> Site, location
> Site, drinking water

The first settlers worked so diligently to accumulate money-making goods that they neglected to grow food to enable them to survive. The stores they had brought with them and the food they did grow were kept in a common storehouse and given out as needed. This system permitted "gentlemen" who labored only a little to draw the same rations as those men who worked hard. A great deal of resentment resulted, and dissension developed among the men. Not until Captain John Smith, a professional soldier employed by the company, silenced the wrangling by laying down some stiff rules did the colony begin to get on its feet.

> Food supply

In 1609 Smith had to return to England for treatment of a severe powder burn. During his absence about 440 of the 500 settlers died for lack of food. Those who survived this "starving time" decided to return to England in the spring of 1610. They turned back when ships arrived with supplies and new settlers.

> Survival

with Jamestown

Setting up the Colony

Colonial Hardships. At Plymouth the Pilgrims had
chosen a site with a supply of good drinking water, near hills
of good timber and tracts of cleared land. In the bitter December cold, the whole group lived on the crowded Mayflower while the men built homes and a storehouse. When
the meager supply of food brought from England ran out,
obtaining more became a major problem. The sea could yield
fish, but the colonists had no boats or fishing equipment. The
woods were full of game, but the newcomers were not yet
skillful hunters.

Site, drinking water
Site, location

Food supply

The most heartbreaking experience of the winter was the
epidemic that the colonists called the "general sickness." Its
victims suffered from pneumonia as well as from scurvy
brought on by a diet without fresh fruits and vegetables.
Half the Mayflower passengers died during that first winter.
Among the dead was the colony's first governor, John Carver.
William Bradford succeeded to the office.[7]

Survival

---

[7] Williams and Wolf, pp. 45–46, 49–50.

solution to government they could devise. (factual conclusion based on arguments during the writing of the Constitution)

2.   Have the students be aware of the use of such words as *think, perhaps, in my opinion, maybe,* etc., which may indicate statements of opinion.

Time, Place, and Space Concepts

An awareness of time and its passage; of places and their characteristics of climate, topography, importance, etc.; and of space involving an appreciation of distance is essential to the understanding and appreciation of human history and activity. The chronology and sequence of history and, to some extent, cause and effect relate to an understanding of time. Providing information about places and comparing them with the students' own environment aids understanding. Distance can be determined by map study and an understanding of map scales. An important concept involving distance is the interpretation of past events in history which must be made with the consideration of the time taken to traverse distances— particularly as compared to today's rapid means of transportation. Students are intrigued by the effect of the time-distance ratio in historical events. An understanding of time which includes a "feeling for it" as it were, helps a student to see the fluid and continuous roll of human history. The time line is a means to help students achieve this feeling of history. One technique which intrigues students is to note on a time line the space equivalent to their own life span to date. The contrast of the small segment on the time line of their life span to the whole of human history helps them to realize the long period back into time that human history has evolved. An understanding of the time, place, and space concepts is needed for an adequate comprehension and interpretation of social studies information.

PLANNING A SOCIAL STUDIES UNIT

The unit is like an umbrella which embraces many individual lessons. In it all forms of classroom organization are employed, all types of material used and instruction is given in all of the appropriate reading skills. The unit outline may extend over whatever time span is needed for an adequate study and investigation of the information. The basic structures of the unit plan parallel the structure of a standard lesson procedure:

UNIT PLAN	DIRECT READING ACTIVITY
1. Introducing the Unit Investigate and expand student's background Survey—preview the materials Clarify basic vocabulary Evolve unit purposes	1. Preparation for reading Evolve lesson purposes
2. Developing the unit Read the material	2. Silent reading

3. Establish basic background Student-teacher planning for research	3. Developing the comprehension
4. Conducting research	4. Re-reading
5. Culminating the unit	5. Follow-up

The unit procedure is basically a DRA pattern. Furthermore, within the unit many lessons on specific aspects of the unit will be conducted. The basic steps of a lesson procedure are also followed whenever a portion of the information within a total unit is read.

Sample Highlights of a Social Studies Unit

(The entire unit is not developed. Only types of suggested questions, activities, and procedures are given.)

The unit is entitled "How the Seeds of Revolution Were Planted and Bore Fruit." It consists of three chapters: "Mercantilism and Conflict," "A Clash of Interests," and "The War for American Independence." The unit has a three paragraph introduction before the first chapter. Each chapter has a short introduction before the beginning section. As expected, there are topical headings. Each chapter has a review section consisting of vocabulary reviewing, main ideas, and activities to extend knowledge and for using judgement. At the end of the unit are activities incorporating knowledge of the entire unit, and a list of books of interest. Numerous maps, pictures, and documents supplement the information in each chapter.

I. Introducing the unit

    A. Explore the student's background. Ask questions during the preview of the material. A sample of such questions:

        Against whom were the colonists fighting in the American Revolution?

        Why did the colonies want their independence?

        What kind of taxes did England levy on the colonies?

        What other countries owned parts of the North American continent during this period?

        When was the Declaration of Independence declared? When was independence secured?

        Who was Benedict Arnold? Why did he become a traitor?

    B. Develop basic concepts of the unit as a preparation for reading. In this unit the basic concepts are:

        revolution
        independence
        conflict
        mercantilism

The students will probably be able to give definitions of all except *mercantilism*. This word may become a purpose for reading in the lesson which will direct the students to read for specific information.

C. Preview the unit. Call attention to the introduction, graphic aids, study helps at the end of each chapter. For instance, have the pupils read the unit introduction:

The American Revolution is an exciting episode for a student of any age to study. <u>One reason</u> why it is exciting is that historians are not in complete agreement as to what caused it. Some of them think that the Revolution was primarily an economic protest—that the Americans rebelled because they thought that the English government had placed unfair restrictions on colonial economic development. Some believe that the Revolution was a movement for democratic reform—that the Americans wanted to break away so that they could institute a democratic society without British interference. Still others argue that the Revolution was an uprising for "home rule"—that the Americans desired merely to keep certain rights that they had always had and considered basic. Thus any study of the Revolution has to begin with an intriguing challenge: What was it all about?

Two reasons why The Revolution is an exciting episode

The Revolution is exciting for <u>another reason.</u> It is the story of how a people won their independence in a war against a nation of superior numbers and resources. In that war the Americans received important aid from some European nations, especially France, but essentially they achieved victory by their own efforts. It is a story of determination and valor and sacrifice, along with some less desirable qualities, and Americans have always taken pride in it. It is a story that features a cast of strong and interesting men, headed by the first national hero, George Washington. It is finally, the story of the birth of a new nation, the American nation.

Perhaps if there had not been a Revolution the American people would have separated from the mother country in another way at a later time. This is an "if" of history. But the Revolution happened and the American nation was born and the history of the future took a dramatic new turn.[8]

Discuss what the "dramatic new turn" means.

1. Discuss the introduction with the students:
   - What three possible reasons are given for the American Revolution? Which do you think is the basic reason?
   - Why do we take pride in the events of the Revolution?
   - What was the result? What is your view about the possibility of the United States becoming an independent country if the Revolution had not occurred? How is your view linked to your view of the causes of the Revolution?

[8] Williams and Wolf, p. 94.

2. Direct the students' attention to such graphic aids as the pictures showing trade routes, the territories owned by various powers of Europe, and military campaigns.

3. Help students to relate the information to their background of experience. Use such ideas as:
   - Discuss the concept of trade. What do the students require when they trade something? What conditions, if any, do they apply?
   - Relate, in a broad sense, the concept of war to disagreements between individuals and between groups. Discuss ways disagreements can be solved. Have the students think of their actions when they have been in disagreement.

D. Establish Unit purposes. Evolve some from the students if possible.
   - What were the different points of view between England and America in regard to the place of the colonies in the British Empire?
   - How did England become the major political power in North America?

II. Diagnosis of student proficiency in the skills (See pages 24–26.)

III. Developing the unit

A. Research problems
   Develop research topics:
   In addition to topics which you and the students may suggest, the questions in the textbook under the heading, "Extending Your Knowledge" can be used. (Most textbooks have such a listing at the end of each chapter.) A sample follows. "Give the arguments for and against *mercantilism* as a sound economic policy for a nation."[9]

B. Reading skills
   Emphasize instruction in the reading skills in which the students seem to be deficient. For instance if organization of the subject matter seems to be a problem for the students the teacher may evolve an outline of the material with them. Such an outline may be taken directly from the sectional and topical headings in the textbook thereby helping the students to see the structure of information as presented in the textbook. An original outline could be evolved in the attempt to have the students think about the topic and determine what should be included. Such an outline about mercantilism may be something like:
   Mercantilism
   A. Definition
   B. Relationship of colonies to mother country
      Colonial products
      Mother country products
      Mercantile relationship

---

[9] Williams and Wolf, p. 113.

    C.   Parliament's attempts to foster mercantilism
          Navigation Acts
          Royal controls
    D.   Advantages
          Colonies
          Mother country
    E.   Disadvantages
          Colonies
          Mother country
    F.   Historical efforts of mother country to control trade
    G.   Colonial reaction to strict enforcement

Teach vocabulary and use of graphic aids as needed to enable the students to acquire and understand the information.

IV.   Student-Teacher Planning for Research

    A.   Organize committees.

    Evolve the topics and have the students elect or assign them to investigate a topic, thereby setting up the committees. Then—*Give Instructions* in how the committees will function.

    B.   Discuss and review resource material.

    You should give guidance to the students by using a problem and developing it as a class exercise throughout the time the students will be doing research. This extends the instruction with the immediate follow-up of application. The teacher may evolve the illustrative topic in the following steps:

    1.   Topic: "Compare the English trade policies in effect after 1763 with the present trade policies in effect among members of the British Commonwealth."[10]

        a.   Delineate the topic by determining the key words (entry words) to use in finding information. In this case such words are *trade policies* of England in 1763 and today.

        b.   Discuss and give instruction in the use of possible sources of information.

        c.   Give guidance in library aids: the card file, the periodical index, *The Reader's Guide to Periodical Literature,* guide words, cross references, the library shelving system and even alphabetizing is necessary (the librarian may assist in this instruction).

        d.   Teach techniques of skimming—use of key words, topographical heads, etc.

        e.   Give instruction in reading for the information: main ideas and related detail, organization (and in this instance, comparison).

---

[10] Ibid.

f. Teach the students how to take notes from a reference. When using reference books, which will be read by the student only once, the following ideas and practices should be made clear to them:

- The length and detail of the notes depend upon the amount of reading material and what the problem requires; the purpose; and what limitations have been set up by the assignment.
- In order to organize and to reorganize the notes, the student will probably find notes recorded on cards most convenient since these can be shuffled into the required sequence.
- Each card should carry the complete bibliography of the reference and list the ideas relevant to the purpose of the assignment.
- All notes should be brief and stated in the student's own words unless a quotation is to be used.
- The student may copy word for word important definitions, formulas, tables, etc.
- The student will use various hints to structure in both his own note taking and his reading, such as *"first, finally, remember, most important, the essential feature is_____."*
- The student may wish to invent his own code of note taking.

g. Instruct the students in the techniques of compiling and organizing the notes from many references into a unified report. This step leads into the writing skills needed for the report. In using more than one source the student will need to be particularly cognizant of:

- Recording the bibliography and page references of each book.
- Writing brief summaries on cards of the most important ideas and information pertinent to his purpose which can be shuffled later into the proper order for the report.
- Organizing and using the outline for the report as the basis for its structure.
- Writing skills of paragraph construction, unity, sequence, and relevance of ideas will need to be used. The student will now use structure and transitional words to point up his emphases and organization.

h. Apply the information gathered to the problem.

V. Conducting Research

The teacher will give individual and group guidance as necessary when the students are conducting research following the steps as listed above for the illustrative topic.

VI.   Culminating the Report
The teacher will help the pupils to:
   Set standards for giving reports so that students can take notes.
   The structure of the report must enable the students to take notes from it
   in outline form as it is given.

   A.   Give the report so that the students in the class can take notes in out-
        line form.
        1.   Give introduction defining the scope and emphasis of the report.
        2.   Give each main point in sequence using such structure words as *the
             first, finally, next, the main differences,* etc.
        3.   Present a summary which reiterates the scope of the main ideas.

   B.   Be cognizant of the importance of speaking clearly and correctly.

   C.   Use pictorial aids as necessary to clarify or make more concrete essen-
        tial ideas.
The teacher will assist pupils in listening to take notes. In listening to the re-
port the students will use essentially the same skills as are needed in reading,
writing, and speaking. The skills are used from another vantage point.
Standards may be evolved with the class which would include:
   A.   Listening for the purpose and scope of the report.
   B.   Listening for the main ideas and essential information.
   C.   Discriminating between what is important and what is not.
   D.   Being courteous to the speaker. Asking for clarification if necessary when
        the report is completed. Not interrupting unless the speaker asks if there
        are questions.

See Appendix II, beginning on p. 303, for a complete sample unit.

   Two basic premises in teaching reading in the social studies class are: (1) the
social studies teacher is a teacher of the language used in the social studies, and (2)
the skills of language usage are taught at the same time that content is studied, resulting in a fusion of skill instruction and content teaching. The suggestions and
techniques presented in this chapter derive from these two premises.

SUGGESTED QUESTIONS AND PROBLEMS TO BE CONSIDERED
IN REFERENCE TO YOUR OWN CLASSROOM

List A (For readers who are training to be teachers)

   1.   Analyze the material of a social studies textbook to determine the dif-
        ficulties you think students might have in reading it. Then, plan how you
        may help the students with the difficulties.
   2.   Analyze material in a social studies textbook and note the various patterns
        of paragraphs.

3. Compile a bibliography of materials for each unit topic.
4. Identify the reading skills you consider pertinent to the social studies. Use a selection and compose two questions requiring the use of each skill.

List B (For readers who are teaching)

1. Discuss with your students the difficulties they experience in reading social studies materials. Evolve with them some corrective procedures.
2. In each reading assignment, note the various patterns of information as a means of planning the emphasis of the subsequent lesson.
3. By coordinating the requirements of the subject and the skill and informational needs of the students, plan a unit of study.
4. Identify the understandings which you wish the students to obtain in accordance with the skill(s) they must be able to use. Identify the discussion questions for developing the understanding with the reading skill needed.

CHAPTER TEN

Applying the Reading Skills to Science

The word *science,* which derives from the Latin verb *scire* (to know), means knowledge. The various branches of science—botany, zoology, biology, physics, chemistry, etc.—are systematized bodies of knowledge. These bodies of knowledge are not based upon supposition or point of view, but upon observable and provable factual data. Though hypotheses in science may be suppositions, their viability is dependent upon specific evidence which then may become accepted generalization or fact.

The scientist uses all of his senses to gather evidence. He observes, feels, smells, listens, and tastes as appropriate. He also uses language, to evolve the problem and hypothesis, to think about the findings produced by his evidence, and to conclude the significance of the findings. He uses language to communicate his discoveries to other scientists and to become aware of their discoveries.

THE RELATION OF READING TO SCIENCE

The science teacher helps students to gain scientific facts through the purposeful use of their senses, with the help of such means as observation, films, experiments, field trips, models, pictures, and reading materials. The facts are not very important, however, as isolated bits of information. The significance of the facts is deduced, and generalizations are formed which incorporate scientific understandings. Of course, students cannot concretely become aware of *all* scientific fact— there is neither the time nor need to rediscover all the scientific facts noted throughout man's history. In fact, the student may only illustrate a principle, not prove it.

He seldom hypothesizes new understandings, or proves new knowledge. Most scientific knowledge is made known to him by reading. Therefore, language and reading are vital tools for the discovery of scientific data, the interpretation of factual data, and the formation of generalizations.

The science teacher can be guided by three interwoven and sequential goals. The first is to endeavor to have the students obtain facts. Factual data is available through many sources including written materials. Therefore, this basic goal requires student competence in the skills of gaining information from the printed page. The second goal is for students to acquire understanding of the data. This involves their understanding of functional concepts, principles and the procedure of the scientific method, and requires many reading skills. These include generally the skills of vocabulary, interpretation, and evaluative reading. The final goal is that the student acquire scientific attitudes, appreciations, and interests. These goals are not too different from the desired goals of the reading process—to develop mature, effective, and interested readers who are able to read with judgment and perception.

STUDENT DIFFICULTIES WITH SCIENCE

The nature of scientific writing presents obstacles to many students. The intensity with which the information is written and the interrelationships of the concepts presented often put before the student a situation that is new to him. If his reading instruction has been largely from descriptive and narrative materials, he may be overwhelmed by the myriad of details and facts and their interrelationships. Carter maintains that not all students can be expected to read effectively and well materials of a scientific nature.[1] This will certainly be true if instruction in reading science material is not given in the science classroom.

Bamman lists difficulties encountered by students in reading science and mathematics:

1. Students have been accustomed to reading materials of narration, not the terse language of scientific writing.

2. There is little control over the number of concepts introduced on a page or within a chapter which require intensive and slow reading by the student who must not only understand the concepts but see the interrelationships among them. The number of concepts introduced in a specified space affects the readability of the material. And though the science teacher and author may be mainly concerned with the teaching of science, the reading-study skills required for learning the science are not abilities which the student has by instinct.

3. Concepts are developed on an ascending scale of difficulty in which the reader is required to use his background of previous knowledge. Indeed,

---

[1] Homer L. J. Carter, "Helping Students to Read Scientific Material," in *Reading in the Secondary School*, ed. M. Jerry Weiss (New York: The Odyssey Press, Inc., 1961), p. 341.

Carter maintains lack of background and mental content, the maturity and ability of the student to use his background, are chief obstacles to the student. Background and mental content, he says, are built up by reading and experience. Mental content determines the kinds and degrees of meaning and it develops from experience, and from mental and emotional maturity.

4. Science requires sensing relationships and thinking critically about what is already known and what is currently being read.
5. Critical reading is required as the student must often judge the relevance, authenticity and value of the data he reads.
6. A mastery of study skills is needed. Not only are techniques of using textbooks and reference materials required, but in science the ability to interpret charts, tables, graphs, and formulas is also necessary.
7. The vocabulary of science can be a formidable problem for the student. The problem of explosive growth in various fields of science adds to the sophistication of the materials with new and often complex vocabulary.
8. Materials used for wide reading are sometimes insufficient in quantity and highly varied in difficulty.[2]

Though these several difficulties may seem insurmountable, they are not. There are procedures which can be employed to help the student learn and achieve the objectives of the science course. But student success in science requires effort by both the teacher and the student. Whatever the thrust of the science teaching—whether to teach the processes of how to obtain information from printed material in science or to teach some factual background—student competence with the language of science is required. Science teaching must be a balance between process and factual content, for the two are interwoven and support each other. Therefore, there are skills of reading scientific language which the student must master in order to develop competence in science.

READING SKILLS REQUIRED BY SCIENCE

Generally there are three types of reading done by science students. One is the intensive study of textbooks and laboratory manuals. The writing in these sources tends to be technical and require a careful, slow and analytical reading. Another type is the assigned collateral reading in scientific journals, popular science magazines, and books on scientific research. Books containing scientific research and material in many scientific journals is intensive and packed with many small but important interrelated details. Analytical reading is required for these also. Finally the student reads material of a non-technical scientific nature which is found in biographies of great scientists and newspaper and popular magazines reporting

---

[2] Henry A. Bamman, "Reading in Science and Mathematics," in *Reading Instruction in Secondary School: Perspectives in Reading #2* (Newark, Delaware: International Reading Association, 1964), pp. 60–61.

current happenings in the field. This is the easiest material to read and to understand. In organization and intensity it is most like literary and social studies materials.

The skills needed for the reading of science are essentially the same as those needed in the other disciplines, but adapted by the reader to the nature of scientific writing. The science reading skills are:

1.   Skill in varying the rate of reading according to the purpose for the reading and the nature of the material.
2.   Skill in using parts of a book.
3.   Skill in locating and using sources of information.
4.   Skill in using the vocabulary of science which includes technical and nontechnical words and symbols.
5.   Skill in understanding and using formulas.
6.   Skill in gaining accurate information from graphic aids such as charts, diagrams, and graphs.
7.   Skill in reading for exact meaning—noting main ideas and supporting details, and seeing organization.
8.   Skill in reading directions accurately.
9.   Skill in evaluating science materials, in drawing conclusions, making judgments, and discerning evidence.
10.   Skill in applying data from reading to practical problems.

SUGGESTED ACTIVITIES AND TECHNIQUES TO FOSTER THE SKILLS

1. Varying the Rate of Reading

In that the science student may read different types of material within a science discipline he needs guidance in how to attack each type. His rate of reading is dependent in science, as in other disciplines, upon two considerations. One is his purposes. The complexity of his purposes will determine speed and concentration. For instance, if he is reading to find merely one isolated bit of detailed information, he may skim until the information is located by looking for the key or most essential word or number and then reading slowly to be sure of his information. On the other hand, if he is reading to see how an experiment is to be conducted or to understand the interrelationship of the factors concerning some scientific phenomenon or truth he will need to read intensively and slowly. This is similar to following directions and the student will need to be alert also to such structure words as noted on pp. 92–93. The other consideration is the nature of the material itself. Material of a technical nature that includes specific numbers and formulas requires slow intensive reading. Material which describes and explains the application of a scientific phenomenon or truth, or which introduces a topic, usually requires the interrelationship of major ideas with specific details. This reading will be faster and less intensive. Biographical material may be read as one reads a story—for enjoyment and for general information, but usually without the careful discernment and classification of detail. Background of information also contributes in determining the individual's rate in any subject.

Pages 218–221 show samples of different kinds of writing from a physical science text and a chemistry text. Also shown are guide questions for reading with comments about the intensity of reading required by the student.

2. Using Parts of the Book

Most science textbooks are designed to assist the student in the study of the information contained therein. Questions to guide reading, explanatory diagrams and pictures, review questions, word lists, and the outlined organization of the information as indicated by the headings in boldface print are aids for the student. Yet, surveys made of many students reveal that they make little or no use of these aids. They are usually skipped over. One of your responsibilities is to direct your students in the use of the aids until they get to the point where they see the purpose of them, and will use them independently.

Sample pages from a physical science text and a chemistry text, with the various study aids labeled, can be found on pp. 222–229.

3. Locating and Using Sources of Information

These are library research skills in which the student must be competent as he searches for additional information on a topic of interest. It is likely that the student will know general library skills from his use of them in other classes. However, the science teacher will need to check the student's competence and be prepared to fill in any gaps that may be apparent. Librarians will give valuable assistance in the library. Your particular responsibility is to alert the students to specific science resource materials. These would include specific books about scientific topics—trade books, textbooks, and specific references—magazines and journals such as *Scientific American,* U.S. Government publications, and bulletins published by various scientific organizations and foundations.

4. Using Correctly the Vocabulary of Science

Scope, depth and precision are essential in the mastery of vocabulary. In science the student may be faced with three types of words which present difficulty. One is the technical word peculiar to the subject. Another is the general word used in a scientific context. And the third is the difficult general word with multiple meanings. Those who teach science readily assume the responsibility for the technical words and the general words used in a scientific context. However, teachers must be alert to the difficult general words as well. For instance, in a single chapter on energy one might teach technical terms—*kinetic energy, heat of fusion;* general words used in a technical manner—*work, power,* and *heat;* and general terms—*substance, standard,* and *expands.*

Deficiency in scientific vocabulary can be due to the lack of knowledge that words can have multiple meanings. Students may not realize that the precise meaning of a word depends entirely on how it is used in a sentence or expression, or the

[text continues on p. 230]

Introduction to help students think about the topic

*Introduce Chapter 1 by having students read the intro-
ductory paragraph. Have them make a list of objects in
motion and at rest. Examples of objects in motion:
earth, second hand in a watch, beating heart, digestive
tract, blood in arteries, moon. Let students speculate
on answers to the last question which is answered in
detail in the sections that follow.*

Forces Part of preview (overview)

*Review briefly the major concepts in MAIN IDEAS at end
of each chapter prior to intensive study of each chapter.*

Questions to stimulate
interest and thought

Is the second hand of a clock at rest or in motion? Look at
this page. Is it at rest or in motion? On a separate sheet of
paper, list five objects which are in motion and five objects
which are at rest. <u>Why are some objects in motion and other
objects at rest?</u>

Purpose question for chapter

Reading-
study
Technique—
purpose
questions

*Call attention to
questions in the
margins and explain
to students how
these questions may
be used as an aid
in reading and study.*

1:1 *Force and Resistance*

An object at rest can be put into motion only by a force. A
force is a push or a pull. For example, a boy can pull a wagon
or he can push it. In either case, he exerts a force to move the
wagon. Many forces are at work in the universe. A force pushes
against a passenger in a moving automobile. The force of gravity attracts the automobile to the earth's surface. The force produced in the engine of the automobile causes the car to move.

Specific
Topical
purpose
question

→ What is a force?

*See introduction to
Teacher's Guide at
front of book.*

List three examples of forces.

*All sports involve
forces and motion.
Relate these prin-
ciples to baseball,
basketball, foot-
ball, hockey, and
other sports. Have
students name the
forces they experi-
ence in their home
or school.*

Examples to help
students relate
information to
background of
experience

Figure 1-1. The force needed to start the wagon moving is larger than
the force required to keep it in motion. A larger force is required at the
start to overcome the wagon's inertia.

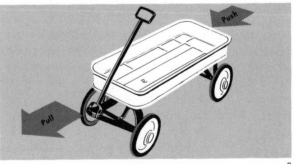

3

quadrivalence of carbon and the
linkage of carbon atoms
formulae

1. Ethyl chloride
2. Ethyl alcohol
3. acetic acid
4. acetamide
5. methyl formate
6. methyl cyanide

Friedrich August Kekulé
(1829-1896)

General
background
information—
biographical
writing

German chemist Friedrich Kekulé was considered by many the most brilliant of his day for his ideas on the linking of atoms. He was the first to speculate on the existence of bonds between atoms and he drew structural diagrams similar to those we use now. These ideas he developed while trying to elucidate the structure of carbon compounds. At this time he proposed that carbon was tetravalent. Kekulé explained that in substances containing several carbon atoms, it must be assumed that some of the bonds of each carbon atom are bonded to the atoms of other elements contained in the substance—and some are bonded to the other carbon atoms.

This concept led Kekulé to propose a ring structure as the logical arrangement for the atoms composing benzene. At this time, many felt that this was the "most brilliant piece of prediction in all of organic chemistry."

Many of our present theories on the structures of compounds were formulated by Kekulé. His teaching career was centered in Heidelberg, Ghent, and Bonn where personally trained investigators followed through with his theories after his death.

General purpose for the reading of this section might be: For what is Kekule noted? (Answer underlined above).

189

9 THE CHEMICAL BOND

Have you ever seen a lake on a windy day and heard the regular (periodic) splashing of the waves on the shore? Many things we see or experience in everyday living exhibit wave or periodic characteristics. We become so accustomed to them that we no longer notice or wonder why they occur. The strings of a piano produce a pleasant sound when you touch the keys. If you look at the piano string when it is producing sound, you will see that it is vibrating. Vibrations and waves are closely related.

Fill a glass with water and tap the edge of the glass. Do you see waves on the surface of the water? We are surrounded by waves of sound in the air and in the solids and liquids we see and touch.

Scientists were aware of waves and periodic vibrations long before Bohr, Planck, Schrödinger, and others explained atomic structure in terms of wave theory. These more recent scientists assumed that the minute particles of matter called atoms and the even smaller particles of which atoms are composed also exhibit wave or periodic characteristics.

From your study of the periodic table, you know that the elements can be arranged in regular periods and groups—they exhibit periodic properties. This periodicity results from the regular changes which occur in their atomic structure. In this chapter, as you study bonding, try to find as many periodic or regularly repeating characteristics as you can.

190

Purpose for reading
(Students may be
   directed to make
   a list of the
   characteristics as
   they read).

Use topical heading to determine purpose questions:

What determines the shape of molecules?

THE SHAPE OF ATOMS AND MOLECULES

9:1 The Shape of Molecules

When two or more atoms form a molecule, we say that the atoms are bonded together. The line joining the nuclei of two bonded atoms in a molecule is called the *bond axis.* Ordinarily, the orbitals formed by the bonding electrons are symmetrical about the bond axis. If one atom is bonded to each of two other atoms, the angle between the two bond axes is called the *bond angle.* The distance between nuclei along the bond axis is called the *bond length.* This length is not really fixed, because the bond acts much as if it were a stiff spring and the atoms vibrate as though the bond were alternately stretching and shrinking. Bonds also undergo a bending vibration which causes the bond angle to constantly change. However, the amplitudes of these vibrations are not large; and the bond lengths and bond angles which we measure are accurate, though average, values. We may think of them as the values for a molecule completely at rest. However, molecular vibration does not entirely cease, even at absolute zero.

Use italicized terms as sources for purpose questions; i.e., What is the bond axis? What is the bond angle? What is the van der Waals radius?

When two atoms approach, they cannot come closer than a certain minimum distance. Electrons of one atom repel the electrons of other atoms and, therefore, two atoms or molecules can never occupy the same space at the same time. In effect, colliding free atoms and molecules act as if they had a rigid outer shell which limits the closeness with which they may approach other atoms or molecules. Since the molecular bond consists of shared electrons, bonded atoms come closer together than atoms which are not

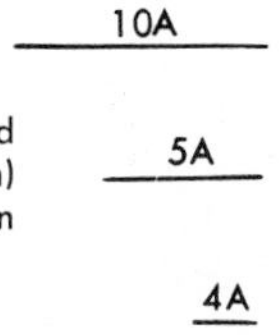

10A

5A

4A

FIGURE 9-1. Balanced repulsive (electron-electron and nucleus-nucleus) forces and attractive (nucleus-electron) forces determine the van der Waals forces and the van der Waals radius (point of closest approach).

Further purpose: What is the effect of the bond angle, the bond axis and the van der Waals radius upon molecule shape?

bonded. The radius of the imaginary rigid shell of an atom is called the *van der Waals radius.* (See Figure 9-1.) Figure 9-2 shows the relationship between the various dimensions which are needed to describe a water molecule. If we know these dimensions we can construct a physical model which represents a molecule to scale. The heavy circles represent the covalent radii of the oxygen and hydrogen atoms in the water molecule. The outer dashed line represents the approximate closest approach of the other non-[4]

---

[4] Robert C. Smoot, Jack Price, and Richard L. Barrett, *Chemistry, A Modern Course: Teacher's Annotated Edition and Solutions Manual* (Columbus, Ohio: Charles E. Merrill Publishing Company, 1971), pp. 189–191.

Book aids to study:

1. Word recognition

velocity (ve lahs′ et ee)

2. Study questions— purpose

How is velocity different from speed?

Why may the ground velocity of an airplane be different from its air velocity?

Figure 1-17. Velocity of airplanes is often expressed in knots. Plotting a course must include an allowance for wind speed and direction.

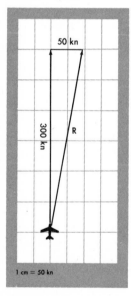

3. Diagram illustrating concept

In physical science, speed refers to how fast a body is moving. **Velocity** refers to both how fast a body is moving and the direction in which it is moving.

If the airplane in Figure 1–17 were blown toward the east by a 50-knot wind, what would be its true velocity? To solve this problem, draw a vector which is one centimeter long (equal to 50 knots) from the point of the first vector to the east at a right angle. Then connect the tip of this vector with the far end of the first vector. The line you draw to close the triangle represents the true velocity of the airplane relative to the ground over which it flies. In what approximate direction does the airplane travel? What is the speed of the airplane?

PROBLEM   4. Practical problems of application

1. A motorboat moves south across a river at 20 kn. The river current moves west at 5 kn. Use vectors to find the velocity of the motorboat.

MAIN IDEAS

5. Summary—students
advised to read before studying the chapter

1. Motion starts and stops through the action of forces.
2. Speed is the distance covered per unit time. Velocity is speed in a given direction.
3. Bodies in motion usually vary in speed or velocity; they are accelerating or decelerating.
4. Acceleration and deceleration result from the action of forces.
5. The size of a force may be measured in pounds, dynes, and newtons.
6. A vector is a ray representing both magnitude or amount and direction.
7. Force vectors are used to find the resultant of two forces acting together.
8. Velocity vectors are used to find the resultant or true velocity of a body in motion.

STUDY QUESTIONS

6. Sample test-like
questions to help the students check their
understanding.

A.   Matching

Match the following words and terms that are most closely related. (Do not write in this book.)

1. acceleration   **a.** unit of speed
2. deceleration   **b.** single force caused by two or more forces

3. dyne   c. unit of force
4. velocity   d. decrease in speed
5. resultant   e. speed and direction
                           f. distance/time
                           g. increase in speed

B. Multiple Choice

Choose the word or phrase which completes correctly each of the following sentences. (Do not write in this book.)

1. The (pound, inch, meter, liter) is a unit of force.
2. A car traveling 60 mi in 2 hr has an average speed of (30 mi/2 hr, 30 mi/hr, 30 mi/min, 30 mi/sec).
3. The formula for speed is $(v = \dfrac{d}{t}, v = \dfrac{t}{d}, v = \dfrac{s}{d}, s = \dfrac{t}{d})$.
4. Resistance (speeds up, opposes, has no effect on, starts) a movement.
5. When an automobile driver steps on the brake pedal, the automobile (accelerates, decelerates, gains velocity, changes direction).
6. An example of acceleration is (15 mi/hr, 15/min, 15 mi/min/sec, —15 mi/min/sec).
7. The opposite of deceleration is (acceleration, speed, velocity, force).
8. A dyne is the amount of force required to accelerate 1 g of mass (1 cm/sec, 1 cm/sec/sec, 1 m/sec/sec, 1 m/sec).
9. One newton equals (100; 1,000; 10,000; 100,000) dynes.
10. To find the resultant of two forces acting in the same direction, (add, subtract, multiply, draw a parallelogram).

C. Completion

Complete each of the following sentences with a word or phrase which will make the sentence correct. (Do not write in this book.)

1. ___?___ is a vector quantity.
2. Velocity has both speed and ___?___.
3. The resultant of three forces (30 lb, 50 lb, 100 lb) all acting in the same direction is ___?___ lb.
4. To find the resultant for two forces acting at a right angle to each other, draw a ___?___.
5. A vector shows both the amount and ___?___ of a force.

6. When a drag racer leaves the starting line and increases his speed, he must ___?___ his car.

7. ___?___ of an airplane is produced by the lowering of the airplane's flaps.

8. One ___?___ is the force required to accelerate 1 kg of mass 1 m/sec/sec.

9. Acceleration is produced by a ___?___.

10. The brakes of a bicycle cause it to stop by supplying the necessary ___?___.

D. How and Why

1. A boy rides a bicycle as fast as he can from his home to a store 1 mi away. On the way he goes over a hill. Look at Figure 1–18 and find:
   a. the rider's greatest velocity
   b. the rider's least velocity
   c. the time at which the rider is accelerating
   d. the time at which the rider is decelerating

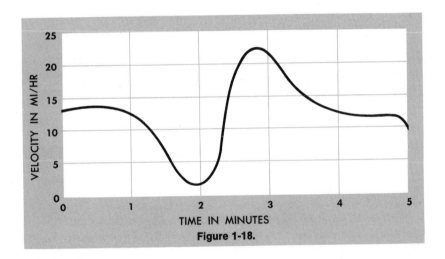

Figure 1-18.

2. A car travels 80 mi in 2 hr. What is its average speed in mi/min?

3. A car going 10 mi/hr accelerates to 50 mi/hr in 6 sec. Find the average acceleration.

4. A bobsled has an average acceleration of 1 m/sec/sec, starting from rest. How fast is it going after 6 sec?

5. What is the average speed of the bobsled in Question 4?

6. How much distance is covered in 6 sec by the bobsled in Question 4?

7. A car traveling at a speed of 80 ft/sec is stopped with a deceleration of 20 ft/sec/sec. How far does the car go before stopping? How long does it take to stop the car?

8. What acceleration will a force of 100 newtons give a 10-kg mass?

9. A sailor attaches a large fan to the stern of his sailboat. The fan is powered with a gasoline engine so that it will blast air against the sail. Will the fan move the boat? Explain your answer.

10. Why can a hammer exert a force many times its own weight?

7. Enrichment reading

INTERESTING READING

Burlingame, Roger, *Machines That Built America*. New York, New American Library, Inc., 1955.

Gamow, George, *Gravity*. Garden City, New York; Doubleday & Company, Inc., 1962. [5]

[5] Heimler and Price, pp. 16–19.

Book aids to study:

SUMMARY   1. Main ideas

1. The bond axis is the line joining the nuclei of two bonded atoms. The length of the bond axis is called the bond length. The angle between two bond axes is called the bond angle.

2. Electron clouds act as hard spheres when two non-bonded atoms approach each other. The radius of this imaginary sphere is called the van der Waals radius of the atom.

3. The shape of molecules can be approximated by assuming the mutual repulsion of electron pairs. This repulsion results because all electrons have the same electrostatic charge and are unable to occupy one orbital. Electron pairs spread as far apart as possible.

4. The shape of a molecule containing three or more atoms is determined by the number of bonding and non-bonding pairs. If the central atom has two bonding pairs and no non-bonding pairs, the molecule is linear. If there are three bonding pairs and no non-bonding pairs, the molecule is pyramidal. If there are four bonding and no non-bonding pairs the molecule is tetrahedral.

5. The actual bond angles vary from predicted angles, because a bonding electron pair does not repel another bonding pair as strongly as it repels an unshared electron pair. The repulsion between two unshared electron pairs is greatest; the repulsion between an unshared pair and a bonding pair is intermediate; and the repulsion between two bonding pairs is least.

6. Two atoms sometimes share more than one pair of electrons and this possibility must be considered when discussing molecular geometry.

7. All bonds are due to proton-electron attraction, and all bonds may be classified as principally one of the following: covalent, ionic, or metallic.

8. Ionization energy is the energy necessary to remove an electron from an atom, leaving a positive ion.

9. Ionization energy is determined by: (1) the size of the nuclear charge, (2) the shielding effect of inner-level electrons, (3) the distance between the nucleus and the valence electrons of an atom, and (4) the sublevel of the electrons.

10. Electron affinity is the attraction of an atom for electrons.

11. The relative tendency of an atom to attract electrons to itself in a bond with another atom is called its electronegativity.

12. The greater the difference in electronegativity between two atoms, the stronger the bond between them.

13. A polar bond is one in which a shared pair of electrons is attracted more strongly to one of the atoms, causing one end of the bond to be positively charged and the other end to be negatively charged. Unsymmetrical polar bonds in a molecule cause the molecule to be polar. Such a molecule is called a dipole.

14. Ionic bonds are bonds formed between atoms with a great difference in electronegativity and involve a transfer of electrons.

15. Polyatomic ions possess an overall charge just as other ions but they are composed of groups of atoms bonded together by covalent bonds.

16. Polyatomic ions form ionic bonds just as other ions do.

17. A metallic bond is a bond between atoms with few electrons in the outer level or levels. These bonds result in the circulation of free electrons and allow metals to carry an electric current. They arise because the difference between the energy levels in outer levels of metals is small, and the electrons are free to occupy almost all the space between the metallic atoms.

18. The relatively high number of free electrons of such metals as iron, chromium, and nickel makes these metals very hard and strong. In general, the transition elements are the hardest and strongest elements.

PROBLEMS   2. Applications of principles and information.

10. Try to predict the bond angles indicated in the following compounds:

a. HTeH in H_2Te
b. HPH in PH_3
c. CPC in $P(CH_3)_3$

d. ClAsCl in $AsCl_3$
e. FCF in $CClF_3$

11. Try to predict the bond lengths indicated in the following substances:

a. Cl—Cl in Cl_2
b. N—H in NH_3
c. C—N in $(CH_3)_3N$

d. H—Br in HBr
e. C—C in CH_3CH_3

12. By the use of appropriate reference materials, make a list of five stable polyatomic ions other than those listed in Table 4-2 and Appendix C.

13. Construct a graph of free electrons versus atomic number for the elements of $Z = 21$ through $Z = 30$.

14. Make a list of ten elements exhibiting more than two possible oxidation numbers.

15. Construct a table contrasting typical metallic properties with the corresponding properties of nonmetals.

16. Convert 384 mg to grams.

17. Convert 46.0 oz to kilograms.

18. What is the density of lithium if 476 g occupy 893 cm³?

19. How many significant digits are in each of the following:
   a. 74.8 meters   **c.** 0.0040 liters   **e.** 1.0 tons
   b. 800.9 g   **d.** 5.970 moles

20. Compute: $(1.12 \times 10)(4.62 \times 10)/(8.89 \times 10^7)$

21. Compute the molecular weight of the following:
   a. Cs_2S_3 **c.** Cu_2SO_3 **e.** $Mg_3(AsO_3)_2$
   b. $HgCl_2$ **d.** InTe

22. Convert 233 g of CaO_2 to moles.

23. Convert 6.21 moles of $Pb(C_8H_{15}O_2)_2$ to grams.

24. Find the percentage composition of $NH_4C_6H_4N_3O_5$.

25. Find the empirical formula of a substance with composition 81.7% Be and 18.3% H.

26. How many grams of HNO_3 are required to dissolve 43.1 g of Cu according to the reaction:

$$8HNO_3(aq) + 3Cu(s) \rightarrow 3Cu(NO_3)_2(aq) + 2NO(g) + 4H_2O(l) \ ?$$

27. How many calories are required to heat 148 g of water 32C°? How many kilocalories?

28. How many kilocalories are required to heat 789 lb of water 28F°?

ONE MORE STEP

1. Predict the ionization potentials for elements with atomic numbers of 31 through 38.

2. Using library resources, find the following bond angles:
   a. $C-C=C$ in CH_3CHCH_2 **b.** ONO in NO_3^-

3. Find a description and make a model of the following molecules:

    a. PCl_5 **b.** IF_7 **c.** Nb_2Cl_{10}

4. Investigate the methods used by chemists for determining bond lengths.

5. Make a graph of the electron affinities of the first 36 elements and interpret the shape of the graph.

6. Find an equation used to calculate electronegativities and try it on several elements.

3. For further understanding and enrichment.

SUGGESTED READINGS

Benson, Sidney W., "Bond Energies." *Journal of Chemical Education*, Vol. 42, No. 9 (September, 1965), pp. 502–518.

Bent, Henry A., "Isoelectronic Systems." *Journal of Chemical Education*, Vol. 43, No. 4 (April, 1966), pp. 170–186.

Brown, John F. Jr., "Inclusion Compounds." *Scientific American*, Vol. 207, No. 1 (July, 1962), pp. 82–92.

Companion, Audrey L., *Chemical Bonding*. New York, McGraw-Hill Book Co., 1964, Chapters 4 and 5.

Gillespie, R. J., "The Valence-Shell Electron-Pair Repulsion (VSEPR) Theory of Directed Valency." *Journal of Chemical Education*, Vol. 40, No. 6 (June, 1963), pp. 295–301.

Guggenheim, E. A., "Odd Molecules." *Journal of Chemical Education*, Vol. 43, No. 9 (September, 1966), pp. 474–476.

Gurnee, Edward F., "Fundamental Principles of Semiconductors." *Journal of Chemical Education*, Vol. 46, No. 2 (February, 1969), pp. 80–85.

King, L. Carroll, "Molecular Architecture." *The Science Teacher*, Vol. 33, No. 6 (September, 1966), pp. 27–34.

Luder, W. F., "The Electron Repulsion Theory of the Chemical Bond." *Journal of Chemical Education*, Vol. 44, No. 4 (April, 1967), pp. 206–212, and Vol. 44, No. 5 (May, 1967), pp. 269–273.

Ryschkewitsch, George E., *Chemical Bonding and the Geometry of Molecules*. New York, Reinhold Publishing Corporation, 1963, Chapters 3 and 4.

Sisler, Harry H., *Electronic Structure, Properties, and the Periodic Law*. New York, Reinhold Publishing Corporation, 1963, Chapters 2–4.

Snyder, Milton K., *Chemistry: Structure and Reactions*. New York, Holt, Rinehart and Winston, Inc., 1966, Chapters 5 and 6.

Verhoek, Frank H., "What is a Metal?" *Chemistry*, Vol. 37, No. 11 (November, 1964), pp. 6–11.[6]

---

[6] Smoot, et al., pp. 207–210.

concepts represented by the words may not be understood. Many high school students read in a superficial manner—they can recognize and call more words than they understand.

The teacher can enlarge the student's vocabulary in many ways by conscious and systematic concern.

a. Be a pace setter and show enthusiasm for the correct use of words. Develop a large vocabulary and use it in the classroom.

b. Search for ways to minimize differences between specialized words and those in everyday speech. When appropriate, a common term may be used as a translation or substitution for the technical term. The main thing is to help the student learn the specialized term by relating it to his experiential background.

For instance, the meaning of *density* in physical science is the mass per unit volume. In lay terms the words *body* and *thickness* may be used to give clues to the term. In another instance, for the term *equilibrium* which in one meaning is a condition in which two equal and opposing forces are operating in the same system, you can use *balance*. Fascinating vocabulary lessons can be taught quite spontaneously by comparing the looseness of the everyday terms with the precise scientific meanings. And such a device may well relate the scientific term to the student.

c. The complete understanding of a concept or phenomenon should be taught before citing the word that labels it. Isaac Asimov's *Words of Science*[7] does an excellent job of discussing the concept of each word presented.

d. Students should be guided to use the new words consistently in class discussion and in their writing.

e. Analyze the words with the students. Note acronyms (such as *laser*—light amplification by stimulated emission of radiation). Help the students to understand how many scientific words are directly related to roots—that a long word usually consists of strung-together word parts, each of which has a meaning, and that the putting together of the parts usually gives the meaning of the complete word. For example, the word *isotherm* consists of the prefix *iso,* meaning equal, and the root *therm,* meaning heat; *cycloid* consists of the root *cycl,* meaning circle, and the suffix *oid,* meaning that which resembles; *chlorophyll* consists of the root *chloro,* meaning green, and the root *phyll,* meaning leaf.

f. Strive for precision by encouraging students to say exactly what they mean. For example, would they be able to distinguish the meanings among the words *spherical, globular, round?*

g. Alert students to structure words which indicate the relationship between facts and ideas. Such structure words may indicate time order (*after, before, while, during*), cause and effect (*since, because, for, for this reason, therefore*), likenesses and differences (*unlike, different, same,* and comparative and superlative forms), and order of importance (*least, most, essential*).

---

[7] (Boston: Houghton Mifflin Company, 1959.)

h.   Alert the students to multiple meanings; for instance, *cell* as used in biology and in electricity.

i.   Classify words listed at the end of a chapter or unit in accordance with the interrelationships of the concepts they represent. For instance in a chapter of a science text entitled "The Atmosphere," the vocabulary listing at the end is presented alphabetically:

atmosphere	hydrosphere	stratosphere
barometer	ionosphere	temperate zones
climate	marine climate	transpiration
conduction	mesosphere	tropics
convection	nitrogen	troposphere

These words can be rearranged in an outline of the chapter done by topical headings. In this way students can see the total picture of their placement in the body of information. Not all of the possible new terms are included in the textbook listing; those in italics were the ones listed.

The Atmosphere
>   The atmosphere of the earth
>>   lithosphere
>>   *atmosphere*
>>   *hydrosphere*
>   Air Pressure
>>   *barometer*
>>>   aneroid
>>>   mercury
>   Composition of the atmosphere
>>   *nitrogen*
>>   oxygen
>>   argon
>>   carbon dioxide
>>>   evaporation
>>>   *transpiration*
>   Structure of the atmosphere
>>   *troposphere*
>>   *stratosphere*
>>>   *mesosphere*
>>>   ultra violet rays
>>>   ozone
>>>   meteoroids
>>>   meteorites
>>   *ionosphere*
>>   exosphere
>   Heat
>>   radiation
>>   *conduction*
>>   *convection*

Seasons
  tropics
  temperate zones
  frigid zones
Climate
  weather
  polar climates
  temperate climates
  tropical climates
  continental climates
  marine climates
  mountain climates
  desert climates

j. Other specific suggestions for students are:
  1. Note whether the new meaning is suggested by the content of the sentence or its appearance.
  2. Note whether there are any pictures, diagrams, charts, which may illustrate the meaning.
  3. Note italicized words or words in boldface print (usually new technical words) and determine the meaning as given in the textbook.
  4. Keep a list of new words in a notebook, each with its definition.

5. Understanding and Using Formulas

Formulas and the symbols used in them may be considered an extension of vocabulary, as they represent ideas by a symbolic code which can also be labeled by words. Often, the words are learned first. We may say that if words are abstractions of concepts, then formulas and specific symbols pertinent to a field are abstractions of abstractions. A specific symbol may be represented by a word alone. However, the formula is a type of shorthand that represents a thought. In language, the sentence carries the thought. Formulas are types of sentences. If the student understands the thought and the concepts contributing to it, the only additional skill needed is translation. Perhaps the formula can be presented as a type of language with its own vocabulary. For example, the formula for computing the size of a centripetal force is

$$F = \frac{MV^2}{R}$$

(Vocabulary)

F = force measured in newtons, dynes, pounds
M = mass measured in kilograms
V = velocity measured in minutes per second or feet per second
R = radius of the curve measured in milligrams
Expressed as a sentence the formula reads: "Centripetal force is equal to the mass times the velocity squared divided by the radius of the circle."

6. Gaining Accurate Information from Graphic Aids

Most science textbooks are amply filled with pertinent graphic aids which supplement many of the ideas presented. They are of value to all students, but particularly to the student who has difficulty in reading and understanding the words. The student may not give any attention to the graphic aids unless their importance is shown and unless he can understand them. In short, the student may not realize the interrelationship between the graphic aids and the language of the text—how they supplement each other. For example, figures 4–10 and 4–11[8] show the relation of time, distance and speed to each other. The figures summarize three paragraphs of printed text, and show succinctly the basic understandings. To fully grasp the information presented, the student may find that the arithmetical computation of the numbers given in the figures will help.

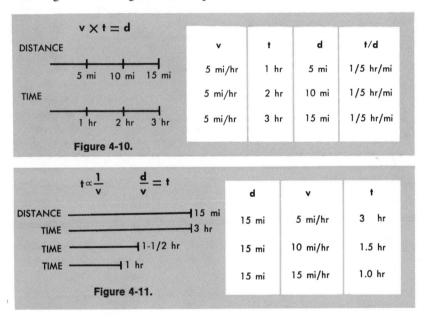

Figure 1–5[9] with the accompanying text (p. 234) shows pictorially the relationship of time, velocity and distance. Thereby the student is assisted in understanding the relationships in the formula.

In figure 4–12[10] (p. 235) no computation is necessary. The student merely notes from the numbers given the relationship between water depth and water pressure.

Figure 9–9[11] (p. 235) shows simply and pictorially an interrelationship of plants and animals.

---

[8] Heimler and Price, p. 70.

[9] *Ibid.,* pp. 6–7.

[10] *Ibid.,* p. 71.

[11] Margaret S. Bishop, Phyllis G. Lewis, and Richmond L. Bronaugh (Consultant), *Focus on Earth Science: Teachers Edition* (Columbus, Ohio: Charles E. Merrill Publishing Company, 1969), p. 164.

1:2   *Speed*

Objects in motion move a certain distance in a certain unit of time, such as a second, a minute, or an hour. Speed is the name given to this relationship between distance and time. The **speed** of an object is the distance traveled per unit of time, speed = distance/time. For example, an automobile speedometer indicates speed in miles per hour (mi/hr).*

Automobiles on a highway may move at a constant speed. *Constant speed* means that the same distance is traveled during each unit of time. For example, a car traveling at a constant

---

* See Appendix A, p. 460.

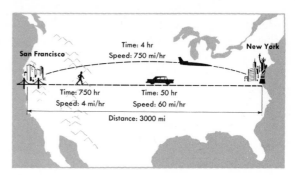

Figure 1-5. To find the average speed between San Francisco and New York, divide the distance (3000 mi) by total hours of time.

speed of 30 mi/hr will cover 30 miles in the first hour, 30 miles in the second hour, and 30 miles every hour that it maintains this constant speed.

Speed, distance, and time may be related in the equation:

$$v = \frac{d}{t}$$

In this equation, v represents speed, d represents distance, and t represents time. Here are two ways in which you can apply this equation to an actual situation.

What equation is used to calculate speed?

EXAMPLE 1

What is the speed of a truck which travels 5 mi in 10 min at constant speed?

Solution: a. Write the equation: $v = \frac{d}{t}$

b. Substitute 5 mi for d and 10 min for t:

$$v = \frac{5 \text{ mi}}{10 \text{ min}}$$

c. Divide to find the answer: $v = 0.5$ mi/min

EXAMPLE 2

What distance is covered by a police car that travels at a constant speed of 1.5 mi/min for 5 min?

Solution: a. Write the equation: $v = \frac{d}{t}$

b. Substitute 1.5 mi/min for v and 5 min for t:

$$\frac{1.5 \text{ mi}}{\text{min}} = \frac{d}{5 \text{ min}}$$

c. Multiply each number by 5 min:

$$\frac{1.5 \text{ mi}}{\text{min}} \left| \frac{5 \text{ min}}{} \right. = \frac{d}{5 \text{ min}} \left| \frac{5 \text{ min}}{} \right.$$

d. Simplify: $7.5 \text{ mi} = d$

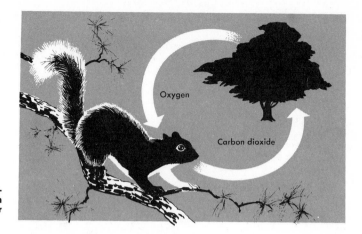

Figure 9-9. Plants and animals supply each other with substances necessary for their life processes.

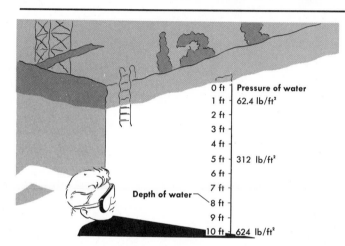

Figure 4-12. Pressure exerted by a liquid depends upon its depth and density. Pressure at any given point in a liquid is the same in all directions.

Pictured concept:
  Water pressure
  increases as
  water depth increases

Figure 4–13[12] shows another concept pictorially.

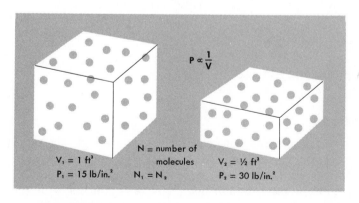

Pictured concept: Gas under pressure-number of molecules remain the same, volume decreased when under pressure.

Figure 4-13. Pressure varies inversely with the volume of a gas. What is the pressure when the same number of molecules of gas is confined in a volume of $\frac{1}{4}$ ft³?

[12] Heimler and Price, p. 71.

Figure 3–4[13] shows diagramatically the classification of matter.

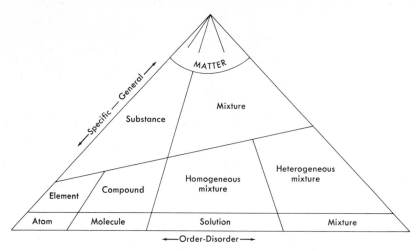

FIGURE 3-4. This pyramid classifies matter in two ways: from general terms to specific terms, and from pure ordered substances to increasingly disordered mixtures.

Diagrammatic representation of the classification of matter.

Students should be able to outline the classification which is also described in the printed text.

Matter
  Substance
    Element
      Atom
    Compound
      Molecule
  Mixture
    Homogeneous mixture
      Solution
    Heterogeneous mixture
      Mixture

Concept also shown regarding the relationship of order ↔ disorder, specific ↔ general

7. Reading for Exact Meaning

This involves noting main ideas and supporting details, and seeing organization. It is basic to comprehension and is a prerequisite to the skills of forming conclusions, inferring, and weighing evidence. One approach to teaching these skills requires that the student be able to recognize and analyze types of scientific writing. Nila Banton Smith suggests that these types include classification, problem solving,

[13] Smoot et al, p. 46.

statement of fact and information, and cause and effect.[14] These are basic patterns, and much scientific writing does not clearly follow the patterns. They may be used in combination and the student may be confused as he tries to fit the pattern to the content. Consequently, the basic techniques we must help the science student to acquire are:

1. to develop the basic vocabulary and the concepts it represents,
2. to be alert to the author's organization through the use of topical headings,
3. to read for specific purposes,
4. to know how to apply the steps of problem-solving,
5. to know how to use graphic aids, and
6. to note the interrelationships of items of information—organization of data which include the skills of reading for the main idea, for sequence or outline, and for details.

The following paragraphs from science texts illustrate typical patterns and the applications the student needs to make of the basic techniques.

Paragraph of Explanation and relationships with example

Time, distance, and velocity are related in the equation:

$$d = vt$$

} ⟶ Main idea

In this equation, d represents distance, v represents velocity, and t represents time.

} ⟶ Explanation

①The distance, d, varies directly as the velocity, v, and as the time, t. If v or t is increased in the equation, the product, d, also increases.②However, v and t vary inversely. If v is doubled, t must be halved if the product of the two is to remain the same.

} ⟶ 2 Relationships

For example, if the distance is 120 miles and the average speed is 40 mi/hr, the time required is 3 hours. If the speed is doubled to 80 mi/hr, the time must be halved to 1½ hours for the distance to remain 120 miles. Suppose the time is increased to 6 hours; how is the speed changed for the distance to remain 120 miles?[15]

} ⟶ Example

The paragraph can be analyzed and charted thusly:

Time, distance, velocity formula: d=vt

1. d.
2. v.
3. t.

---

[14] Nila Banton Smith, "Reading in Subject Matter Fields," *Educational Leadership* XXII (March 1965): 382–385.

[15] Heimler and Price, p. 70.

Relationship of d, v, and t.
1. d. is dependent upon v and t,
    d. is increased, if v. and t. are increased.
2. v. is increased, t. is decreased if d. is the same and if t. is increased,
    v. is decreased if d. is the same.

Paragraph of Problem-solving	Does a force always produce motion? Push down on your desk top as hard as you can. Attempt to lift yourself by pulling upwards on your shoes.	Problem / Gathering evidence
	Through the action of your muscles, you can exert a force on objects around you. In some cases when you exert a force,	Findings
Main idea is the answer to the problem	little or no motion occurs. For a force to produce motion, the force must be large enough to overcome any resistance from the object. Resistance is any opposition which slows down or prevents motion.[16]	Conclusion / Concept basic to conclusion

Chemistry

Introductory paragraph
Reference made to
objects in students'
experiential background

3 MATTER

The world around us is filled with objects of many kinds: people, chairs, books, trees, quartz crystals, lumps of sugar, ice cubes, drinking glasses, door knobs, and an endless number of other familiar objects. Each of these objects may be characterized by its size, shape, use, color, and texture; by its physical attributes. Many diverse objects have certain important things in common. For example, a tree and a chair are both made of wood. Millions of other objects with different shapes and different purposes may also be made of wood. The word _material_ is used in referring to a specific kind of matter (such as wood). Materials which are familiar to us in the everyday world are wood, steel, copper, sugar, salt, nickel, marble, concrete, milk, etc.

42

---

[16] Heimler and Price, p. 5.

CLASSIFICATION

Paragraph of Concept development— definition: homogeneous materials phase substances

3:1 Homogeneous Materials

A homogeneous material is one which is the <u>same throughout.</u> If you break it up into smaller pieces each small piece has the same properties as every other small piece. If you examine one of the pieces under a microscope, it is impossible to distinguish one part as being a different material from any other part. Examples of homogeneous materials are: sugar, salt, sea water, quartz, window glass, etc. <u>Any sample of homogeneous material</u> is referred to as a *phase.* Every sample of a homogeneous material is a single phase. Sometimes we can actually distinguish between different phases of the same homogeneous material, for example, ice and water. Some homogeneous materials like pure salt, pure sugar, pure water, or pure sulfur <u>always have the same composition.</u> Such materials are referred to as *substances.*

Graphic aid: diagram to show classification

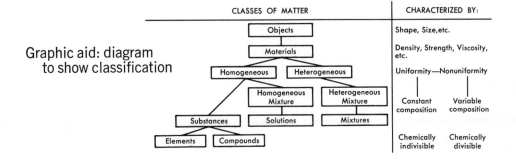

FIGURE 3–1. Both heterogeneous materials and solutions are mixtures of substances.

Paragraph of Classification Definitions: elements compounds

According to the atomic theory, matter is composed of minute particles called atoms. <u>Substances</u> may be divided into <u>two classes.</u> Substances composed of <u>only one kind of atom</u> are called *elements.* Examples are: sulfur, oxygen, hydrogen, nitrogen, copper, gold, and chlorine. If the particles of a substance are <u>composed of more than one kind of atom</u>, the <u>substance is called a</u> *compound.* The atoms in the particles of compounds are always bound together in definite ratios. Chemistry is a study of substances. The composition of the particles in a compound may be determined by a

Restatement of former concepts: Substances Elements Compounds

process called chemical analysis. Chemistry is sometimes defined as the science of substances and of the processes by which substances may be transformed into still other substances. Homogeneous materials which always have the same composition are called substances.

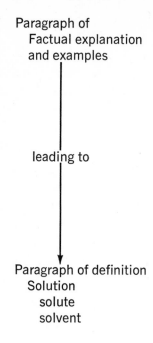

Paragraph of
  Factual explanation
  and examples

leading to

Paragraph of definition
  Solution
    solute
    solvent

Other homogeneous materials such as sea water, window glass, and gold-silver alloys, have a variable composition. If we put a small quantity of pure salt into pure water and let it stand, we get a homogeneous material. If we add a larger quantity of pure salt to the same amount of pure water we again get a homogeneous material but the composition of this material is different from the first. The second material is homogeneous but it contains more salt in an equal volume of water. Such a homogeneous material is called a *solution*. For example, we may add 5, 10, or 15 grams of salt to 100 grams of water and in all cases the resulting material is homogeneous. A solution may be defined as a single phase which may have a variable composition. Solutions are not necessarily liquid. Air is a homogeneous material composed of nitrogen, oxygen, and smaller quantities of other gases. Window glass and silver-gold alloy may also have a variety of compositions, yet each sample is homogeneous. All of these materials are examples of solutions.

A solution is generally thought of as consisting of a *solute*, or dissolved material, in a *solvent*, or dissolving material. The solute is dispersed throughout the solvent in such small particles (of molecular or smaller size) that the solution appears uniform even under the most powerful optical microscope. Since the dispersion of particles appears to be completely uniform, solutions are classified as homogeneous materials.

3:2 Heterogeneous Materials

Most of the materials which we can see around us can be distinguished either with the naked eye or the microscope as consisting of two or more materials which are distinct from each other. Such non-uniform materials are said to be *heterogeneous*. Wood, granite, concrete, and milk, are examples. It is usually possible with the naked eye to see that granite is composed of at least three minerals: quartz, biotite, and feldspar. If a specimen of granite is crushed so that the particles are the size of fine sand, it is possible to pick out the quartz and separate it mechanically from the biotite and feldspar. Milk normally appears to be homogeneous but under the microscope particles of various kinds can be seen suspended in water. Milk is not a solution; it is a heterogeneous mixture. One type of particle (in this instance, globules of fat), can be separated from the other particles of milk by a device called a centrifuge or cream separator.[17]

Activities to help students develop these comprehension skills include:
Reading for the Main Idea
  A. Express the purpose of an experiment in one or two compact sentences.
  B. Express the finding of an experiment in one sentence.
  C. Express the utility of this finding in one sentence.
  D. Find the author's statement of the purpose of an experiment.
  E. Find the main idea in a number of different kinds of paragraphs.
  F. Write a paragraph containing a main idea. Give the paragraph to another person who must find the main idea.

[17] Smoot et al., pp. 42–44.

Reading for Sequence or Outline

    A.   Note the purpose of the experiment, and as you read, anticipate what will be done; see how the steps are related to the purpose.

    B.   Note the steps you must take to carry out an experiment. Translate the author's words carefully into your own in a list of things to be done. Read the list you have made to see why each step is necessary, noting especially the order in which the steps occur.

    C.   List the chain of events leading to a scientific discovery.

    D.   Number the steps in the life cycle of an insect or animal. Try to see the relationship of one step to another. If a title for each of these stages is not given, write in the margin a title for each. Underline or write the important characteristics of each state. Close the book and try to enumerate the states; open the book and compare; repeat if necessary.

Reading for Details

    A.   In scientific definitions and laws, notice the qualifying words: the descriptive words, the phrases that narrow the application of the law or the scope of the thing defined. Read the definition carefully for the general meaning and look up any words that trouble you. Put the definition into your own words.

    B.   Read additional material which gives the function of the thing referred to, and tells for what uses it is good or bad. Make some special note of the definition, underlining it, writing the word and its definition in the margin, putting the word with a statement of its characteristics and its functions into a vocabulary notebook.

    C.   Read through the explanation of the derivation of the formula. See whether you can follow the reasoning that leads to its final form. Note the examples and read the text to find out to what kind of situation the formula is appropriate. Work a problem through to experience the effectiveness of the formula. Notice what precautions must be taken in the use of the formula.

    D.   In reading an experiment, notice the kinds of words that suggest the introduction of a new step: *then, to this, add,* etc.

    E.   Number the steps as they are given.

    F.   Underline or write down the important words of each step. Reread each step underlined and try to visualize it or draw a diagram of it. Try to see the relationship of each step to the next and of each to the purpose of the experiment. Ask yourself "Why do we do this?" and "Why does this step come here instead of sooner or later?"

    G.   Close the book and try to enumerate the steps and their details; open the book and compare.

    H.   In reading about the life of a scientist, be sure you know the time he lived, his country, the field to which he contributed. Try to recall in what connection you have ever heard of him. Note the words (*then, his chief contribution,* etc.), or the forms (new paragraph) that introduce new steps in his life. Underline or write the important events in his life. Number them. In the margin give a name to each discovery or event.

I. Note the methods that he used in his studies, if those methods are important. For each discovery notice what the author has to say about its value or significance to scientific thought and to our lives. Try to think of ways in which each of the scientist's discoveries has affected your thinking or your life.

J. Close the book and enumerate the events or discoveries and give the important details of each; open the book and compare.

K. In material that has too many facts for you to remember, decide how many things you can remember. Notice the ways in which the author indicates, if he does, the relative importance of these facts:
   1. By giving more space to the discussion of one fact than to another.
   2. By the use of introductory remarks; *above all, pre-eminent, the chief factor,* or *probably the most crucial.*
   3. By organization, such as paragraphs in which a big fact is illustrated or supported by a lot of little facts or where marginal headings are used to point out the big facts.
   4. By questions at the beginning or end of the chapter to call attention to the most important facts.
   5. By a list of important words at the end of the chapter.
   6. By a summary at the end of the chapter or section.
   7. By the use of italics.
   8. By pictures or other illustrative material.

   Otherwise, note for yourself the relationships among the facts and choose the key facts among these. Compare the facts in the text with the kind the teacher usually requires in his questions in class, in his tests, in his assignments.

8. Reading Directions Accurately

This is not only a skill but is also a pattern of writing when it is used to direct a student in the conduct of an experiment. When reading directions the student will need to be certain he knows the meaning of all of the words used and that he is able to distinguish one step from another. He may need to be alerted to structure words such as *next, after, first,* and so on, which indicate the steps. In reading directions the following procedure is suggested:

1. Read the entire set of directions to get an overview of the procedure. At this time the student should obtain clarification of any words he does not know.
2. Read the directions to note the equipment needed and collect it.
3. Read each step of the directions and proceed as indicated.
4. Read the step again to check whether the procedure was carried out correctly.
5. Repeat items 3 and 4 as many times as there are steps to be followed.
6. Upon completion of the directions, look them over once again as a final check.

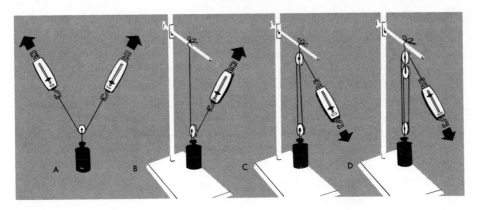

Paragraph of
  following directions
Help students to get
  overview.
Have students
  note steps.

Part 1 { EXPERIMENT.   *A pulley may be used to lift objects: (1) Lift a 100 g weight with a spring balance and observe the reading of the balance. Next, run a piece of string 2 ft long through a single pulley. Attach each end of the string separately to a spring balance as shown in A above. Attach a weight to the pulley. Lift the weight by holding the spring balances and record the reading on each balance. (2) Arrange pulleys as shown in diagrams B and C above. Find the force needed to lift the weight. The force is the reading on the spring balance.*

Part 2 { *How does the number of supporting strings affect the force needed to lift a weight? Predict the force needed to lift the*

Part 3 { *weight in D above.*[18]

9. Evaluating, Drawing Conclusions, Making Judgments

Though there is much factual data a student must acquire in science, he must go beyond the mere acquisition and be able to make judgments about it, and draw conclusions from evidence. Some examples of techniques:

1. Have the students note the structures of various living organisms and the characteristics of their environments. Show the indication of *cause and effect:* environmental conditions as the cause of the structural characteristics.

2. Have the students *compare and contrast* characteristics of two or more kinds of living organisms or inanimates.

3. Have the students speculate as to the effects of specific conditions, either real or fanciful. In an experiment the students may be asked to *make a judgment* of what will happen under a specific set of conditions. The experiment can then be conducted to show the validity of the judgment. Or, the students may be asked to predict what would happen if the polar ice caps were to melt in the next 50 years.

4. Assist students in the ability to *suspend judgment*. For example, if an experimental finding appears to be contrary to a belief of long standing and apparent logic, have the students plan to gain further evidence, i.e., from reading from authoritative sources and by conducting the experiment again.

[18] Heimler and Price, p. 5.

10. Applying Data from Reading to Practical Problems

One of the goals of reading instruction is the ability to read creatively, which means, in part, applying information from books to practical problems and life situations.

Suggested techniques to encourage this application might include:

1. Relate an experience you have had with a principle or an object discussed either in your science text or in class.
2. Apply the results of an experiment to various areas of life. Show how a specific occupation or people in general are affected by the results. Explain how it changes the way things are done.
3. From descriptions of various plants and animals, determine their major characteristics—where they live, what they eat, what their role is in the earth's ecosystem.
4. As you read about the conditions needed for life, relate the information to plants and animals and determine if all of the conditions are needed for each species.
5. Whenever a scientific law or principle is cited in your science text, think of at least two applications.

SUGGESTIONS OF PROCEDURE

Reading skills can be fused with science content through various procedures. These include fusing skills with scientific method, daily lessons, the science unit plan, and wide reading.

Fusing Reading Skills with Steps of Scientific Method

The scientific method and the reading skills must always be associated in the student's mind with some subject matter. The subject matter becomes the medium in which to practice using the tools of inquiry and information acquisition.

Shepherd has listed the steps of the scientific method and the reading skills pertinent to each.

> The first step of the scientific method is to define the problem to show that it has limits, is specific, and can be investigated. The basic reading skill needed here would relate directly to the vocabulary of science. An adequate background in scientific vocabulary as well as precision in the use of such terms are both requirements to be met if the student is to state his problem with accuracy and definiteness.
>
> The next step is collecting evidence that bears upon the problem. The skills of reading that are related to his step of problem solving are (a) those needed for locating information in printed sources (using various parts of a book and many different sources), and (b) those needed for getting the literal understanding of the reading material (understanding scientific vocabulary, symbols, and formulas; interpreting graphic aids; reading directions accurately; noting main ideas, their supporting details, and the sequence or organization of main topics).

Setting up hypotheses is the third step. In setting up possible solutions to the problem, the pertinency and relative importance of the individual data that have been collected must be determined. Basic relationships between the data must be perceived. (Steps 3, 4, and 5 of the scientific method involve critical thinking and critical reading. They require an interpretation of the facts. The validity of the interpretation depends upon the ability to evaluate science materials and to draw conclusions.)

The fourth step is selecting the most likely hypothesis and testing it. Selecting and testing the most likely hypothesis involves substantiating all data, organizing the data into the logical sequence, and determining the adequacy of the selected hypothesis by relating it to the problem.

The fifth step, drawing conclusions, requires the student to compare the consistency of the conclusion with the data and the problem. Judging the significance of a finding and seeing the relationships of it to various phenomena point up the use of such interpretative reading skills in science.

Finally, the sixth step is applying scientific data to practical situations. Even though "applying scientific data to practical situations" is not a step of the scientific method, the ability to think of practical applications is of such importance that instruction in the skill is generally included in any problem solving unit.[19]

In each of the steps of the scientific method, the student must ask questions. This is akin to and in some cases the same as formulating questions before reading. These are purpose questions pinpointing information which must be found. The student will ask himself such guide questions as: What is to be found or proven? What outcomes are to be anticipated? What facts are known? What other facts are needed? How will the solution be derived? What are the steps? What equipment is needed? What numerical quantities are to be or can be used to solve the problems? What do the findings imply? Are they reasonable? How can they be applied? What other problems have been discerned? What conclusions can be made? Do these coincide with the tentative solutions suggested at the time that the problem was defined?

The Science Project

The science projects provide the student with the opportunity to use his imagination to find out some information of interest to him. It can thereby enlarge the student's view of the uses of science. Projects help in many ways. First, they enable the student to seek further information and understandings. Second, they can help to develop student interest. Third, they provide a practical application of the scientific process and thereby help to inculcate the process as a means of investigating a problem. Fourth, they provide further application of the reading skills as applied to scientific information.

When you help your students in planning a science project, help them to consider all of the steps from the beginning to its final completion. Perhaps they will find a listing of Do's and Don't's helpful as types of guidelines.

---

[19] David L. Shepherd, "Reading and Science: Problems Peculiar to the Area," in *Fusing Reading Skills and Content,* ed. H. Alan Robinson and Ellen Lamar Thomas (Newark, Delaware: International Reading Association, 1969), pp. 151–161.

Certainly you will know the reading study skills they will need to use as they search for existing knowledge from printed sources. You must provide whatever instructions would be needed in any of the skills of science reading and research reading which your students need for competence.

The Unit Plan

The Unit Plan encompasses the study of a topic which may cover from one to several weeks in which many individual lessons are taught. It follows the basic structure of the individual lesson with preparation for reading, reading for specific purposes, discussion and experimentation, rereading for further understanding of both content and skill and finally culmination in an activity.

A suggested science unit of approximately one week follows:

UNIT IV.   How does Weather Affect Your Everyday Living?

Problem	What are the physical forces that produce the climate of a place? What are some of the elements of climate?
Aims (These can also be stated in the form of behavioral objectives)	To show pupils that the same physical forces that control the weather produce the climate of that place. To help pupils form an awareness of the great variety of climates on the earth. To assist pupils in determining how climates modify the activities of people living in them.
Method	Discussion-Demonstration

Procedure

   I. Readiness:
      A. Review
          1. Types of climates discussed in previous lesson.
          2. Demonstrations on condensation and evaporation (Re-do experiment if necessary).
      B. Source Materials
          1. Read short stories or selections from Walt Disney's work pertaining to weather.
          2. Use films (if available) depicting: occupations, recreation, houses, and clothing of people in various geographical regions. Discuss.
      C. Questions
          1. What type of climate do we live in?
          2. Why do you think we have the three types of climate? Make a list of factors that cause climates to vary from each other. (Record list on board.)

  II. Concept Development—Understandings
      A. The normal run of weather conditions over a long period of time denotes climate.

B. Physical forces that influence weather produce the climate of an area.
C. The heat of the earth comes from the sun.
D. Land and water absorb this heat.
E. Weather and climate depend on the condition of the air.
F. Living things are prepared to meet climatic conditions.

III. Vocabulary
　　　Evaporation
　　　　relative humidity—moisture
　　　　water vapor
　　　　saturated
　　　Condensation
　　　　dew
　　　　fog
　　　　frost
　　　Mountains
　　　　altitude
　　　Wind
　　　　adaptation

IV. Establishing Purposes for Reading
　　(Solicit questions from students if possible)
　　A. What happens when warm moisture-filled air comes into contact with cool air?
　　B. Is the air cooler on a mountain than on a flat plain or valley?
　　C. How does the moisture get into the air?
　　D. How does the air lose its moisture?
　　E. Skim page _____ to find in what region most people live. Why?

V. Silent Reading
　　(Reading to find answers to specific questions in Part IV.)

VI. Oral Discussion
　　(Discussion of purpose questions)

VII. Re-reading (Silent or oral)
　　(For clarification or critical examination of questions and discussion)

VIII. Developing Deeper Comprehension—*Demonstration*
　　Demonstration I-Condensation
　　　Problem: What causes water to change?
　　　Materials: One jar and cover (top); water
　　　Procedure: Pour a small amount of water, about one-fourth inch deep, into the jar. Place cover on jar. Set the jar in the sunshine. Let stand for one-half hour or more.
　　　Results: A misty film inside, on the side of the jar. There are several large drops of water hanging down from the cover. What caused the misty film and the water drops to form on the surface?

Demonstration II

Problem: What happens when warm air comes into sudden contact with cool air?

Materials: clean dry glass; ice; water; colored ink

Procedure: Fill a clean dry glass with ice water and add a few drops of colored ink. Wait for several minutes after filling the glass with ice and water; examine the outside of the glass.

Results: The outside of the glass is not dry. Why? When air is cooled, does it hold more or less moisture?

Repeat same experiment on humid days and on dry days. What are your results? Does the moisture in the air differ on different days?

Demonstration III—Relative Humidity

Problem: Does temperature affect humidity?

Materials: Sponge; water; pan

Procedure: Place a dry sponge (a sponge that has been heated in the oven for some time so that it will have no dampness) in a pan of water. Wet the sponge only enough to hold the water without dripping.

Results: The soaked sponge has 100% (or all) the water it will hold. What happens if more water is added to the top of the sponge? Help the students to draw the following conclusion: At any given temperature the air will hold a certain amount of water and no more, just as a sponge reaches a point at which it will hold no more water without dripping.

IX. Related Activities
1. Plan a bulletin board of science pictures and reports on weather and climate.
2. Help pupils to plan a science quiz by using various concepts and vocabulary words.
3. Encourage students to find out the average climatic conditions of their community and compare it with nearby communities.

X. Assignment:

Have students pass in a list (with illustrations) of ways in which water gets into the air.

Some students might want to do other demonstrations showing the processes of condensation and evaporation. (Water coming out of the air and water going into the air)

With each experiment it is suggested that the teacher write on the board, in vocabulary terms familiar to the pupils, step-by-step observations and results.

WIDE READING IN SCIENCE

Science is generally viewed as a subject which requires intensive reading of relatively small quantities of material. Yet wide reading in science is as beneficial to the student as in other disciplines in which large quantities of reading are required. Wide reading often helps to foster a student's interest in areas of science, and is valuable for clarification of concepts, principles and generalizations in science for the student. It thereby supplements the textbook and enriches the informational base of the subject. It helps also in the acquisition of skills and techniques necessary for gaining further scientific information with understanding. It is important to realize that much information, even in science, is gathered and clarified through reading. It is not possible to teach all scientific understandings efficiently and fully through observation and experimentation. Students should be guided to realize that the most eminent scientists gain much information through printed material.

However, high school science students do little outside reading, especially in science. Walberg found from his study of high school physics students, notwithstanding the high mental ability and educational aspirations, that a quarter of them did not read much nonfiction. He states further that a little less than 40% of the boys and 58% of the girls did not care to read technical or professional books. Many of the students are not interested in either academic or nonacademic reading or study.[20] Reasons for such attitudes may be many—we do not know why many of the students regard scientific reading negatively. However, teachers can foster it by enthusiasm, by adequate materials and by time spent on it—even in today's crowded curriculum.

Wide reading materials in science at the secondary level range from technically written references and journals to trade books, magazines and newspapers which are usually written in a nontechnical style, to science fiction. Pamphlets and brochures published by various industries as well as publications of many governmental agencies are also excellent sources of scientific background for students.

SUGGESTED QUESTIONS AND PROBLEMS TO BE CONSIDERED IN REFERENCE TO YOUR OWN CLASSROOM

List A (For readers who are training to be teachers)

1. Select paragraphs from science textbooks and analyze them to determine their structure and their use of structure words.
2. Devise or use behavioral objectives for your lesson procedures. Either cite the reading skill needed for each behavioral objective in science or state the skills as behavioral objectives.
3. Develop a tentative list of Do's and Don't's for a science project.
4. Plan in your lesson procedures how you will provide time and opportunity to foster wide reading.

List B (For readers who are teaching)

1. Review your textbook(s) thoroughly and note the study aids for your students. Plan to alert them to these aids and to teach their uses.

---

[20] Herbert J. Walberg, "Reading and Study Habits of High School Physics Students," *Journal of Reading* XI (February 1968): 327–332, 383–389.

2. In the next reading assignment, determine how the student can best organize his notes from the material: outline, chart, table, comparison and contrasting columns, diagrams, graphs, etc.

3. Consult with your school librarian and compile a bibliography of reference material for your science class. For each major unit prepare a bibliography of extended readings.

4. Throughout the school year make a list of the Greek and Latin roots used in your science vocabulary.

5. Evolve with your students a tentative list of Do's and Don't's for a science project.

CHAPTER ELEVEN

Applying the Reading Skills to Mathematics

Mathematics may be viewed as being comprised of two languages. One is the language of word symbols which are part of the technical vocabulary of the discipline as well as the peculiar usage of common words. The other is the language of the mathematical symbols which are also technical. The symbolization of mathematics may be simple or highly complex. The student will find that distinct mathematics symbols represent words or even phrases that indicate relationship or process. For instance, = means "is equal to," and embodies the idea of equality, a basic but simple symbol. A more complex symbol is $\dfrac{(\sqrt{2} - 3)^2}{(\sqrt{2} + 3)^2}$ which, if written in words would be "the square root of 2 minus 3 squared divided by the square root of 2 plus 3 squared." Mathematics symbols are in effect another language. Both the words and the symbols label concepts and ideas in mathematics.

The reading of mathematics involves the student's ability to read two languages and to translate from one to the other. Lerch has pointed out that English words are used in explanations, giving directions, descriptions, and in word problems. Mathematical signs are also used, he says, in much the same way in explanations, illustrations, examples, and descriptions. Student competence in both languages is needed if the objective of mathematics is to be achieved.[1]

---

[1] Harold H. Lerch, "Improving Reading in the Language of Mathematics—Grades 7–12," in *Improving Reading in Secondary Schools: Selected Readings,* ed. Lawrence E. Hafner (New York: The Macmillan Company, 1967), p. 345.

THE OBJECTIVES OF MATHEMATICS

There are three major objectives of the various fields of mathematics. Each relies upon the student's understanding of the language of mathematics. Each involves the various uses of language—speaking, listening, reading and writing.

The first objective is to enable the student to understand and be conversant with the concepts, ideas and meanings of mathematics. The accomplishment of this objective is dependent upon the mastery of vocabulary—both the English words and the mathematics symbols. In mathematics the student explores, hears, discusses, experiments with, talks about, and explains as he develops the concepts.

This leads us to the next major objective. The student should learn to reason, a skill which can be developed only after the concepts are grasped. Word problems require reasoning. Reasoning is the rearrangement of known facts to derive a new relationship. Specifically, the student needs to be able to recognize the essential characteristics of a problem situation as well as to test a hypothesis and evaluate conclusions. It involves using what is known in a problem to find what is unknown.

The third major objective relies upon the ability to reason. The student must know how to compute and estimate. This involves the processes of mathematics. The student should become competent in such processes as (1) the fundamental operations with integers and fractions and their generalizations to signed numbers and literal numbers, (2) the use of computational tables, (3) making and interpreting measurements, (4) working with approximate data, (5) constructing and interpreting simple statistical and functional graphs, (6) making geometric constructions and simple scale drawings, and (7) using simple formulas and equations. If the concepts are established, the student should also know the reasons for the form of the process—why it functions the way it does.

These three objectives are designed to have the student become independent with mathematics concepts and processes. Call and Wiggin pointed up the need for reading instruction in mathematics classes. They conducted a study to determine whether there is a correlation between a student's ability to solve word problems in second year algebra and the presence or absence of special reading instruction. The results, they said, indicated that the students receiving reading instruction in their classes did better in problem-solving than those who did not. They made the following inferences:

1. There is some merit in teaching special reading skills for the solution of mathematical problems.
2. Even very good readers, as measured by the Cooperative Reading Tests, have difficulty in the interpretation of the kind of reading found in word problems.
3. Part of the difficulty which teachers encounter in the teaching of mathematics comes from a special kind of reading disability which does not appear on standard measuring instruments.
4. Part of the difficulty which teachers encounter in the teaching of mathematics is that they are not equipped to teach reading.

5. If by teaching reading, instead of mathematics, we get better results, it seems reasonable to infer that the competent mathematics teacher might get considerably better results if he were trained to teach reading of the kind encountered in mathematics.[2]

If these inferences are correct what then are the skills of reading as they apply to mathematics? What kind of writing will the student be asked to comprehend? What skills must he develop?

Reading material in mathematics is concise, terse, intense, to the point and specific. It requires analysis, the recognition of ideas and the relationships among them. Of special concern is the vocabulary of mathematical reading in which precision of meaning is required. The concepts represented by the vocabulary are built sequentially, one upon the other. Another concern is the use of symbols which in a sense is another form of vocabulary. Basic to the student's understanding of mathematical reading are two considerations. One is the student's knowledge of how to attack the reading—the strategies to use which are determined by the nature of the material and the student's purpose. The other is the student's command of the mathematical concepts.

Much emphasis today is placed upon the student's understanding of concepts and the reasons for and analysis of the processes. This emphasis has resulted in straight-forward expository writing in textbooks. It is expected that the student will read to understand prior to working examples and problems. In fact, there are two specific types of writing in mathematics textbooks today: explanation of concepts for understanding and word problems. Examples of each type of writing are found on pp. 254–257. Both types of writing require student competence in gaining ideas from the printed page. And as Hartung has pointed out,

> The ideas (of mathematics) are all abstract from the beginning. Mathematical ideas cannot be seen, or heard, or touched. They have no color, or weight, or size or texture. They are of the mind . . . Merely pronouncing the words and naming the signs is not enough. They must communicate meaning to him.[3]

The student, then, needs training in a number of skills which are basic to his ability to use the ideas of mathematics. (1) He needs to be able to solve problems— to know what he has, to rely on the results obtained, and to know how to use them. (2) He needs to be able to check answers and verify results. (3) He must acquire the ability to make intelligent estimates. (4) He must be able to interpret quantitative data. (5) He must recognize and interpret relationships. (6) He must acquire the ability to make and interpret generalizations. And finally, (7) the student must be able to think in symbolic language. Whatever the grade level, the instructional

---

[2] Russell J. Call and Neal A. Wiggin, "Reading and Mathematics," *Mathematics Teacher* LIX (February, 1966): 149–151.

[3] Maurice L. Hartung, "Methods and Materials for Teaching Reading in Mathematics," in *Sequential Development of Reading Abilities,* ed. Helen M. Robinson, Supplementary Educational Monographs #90 (Chicago: University of Chicago Press, 1960), p. 142.

EXPLANATION OF A CONCEPT
Teacher's edition (Marginal notes
   are suggestions to teachers)

8:3   MONOMIAL FACTORS   See T.G.

Let us turn our attention from numbers to algebraic expressions that represent numbers. You have found many *products* in earlier chapters. You will recall that the basis for multiplication of poly-   Stress
nomials is the Distributive Property of Numbers.

Note difference between multiplication
   and factoring

$$\textit{Multiplication}$$
$$a(b + c) \xrightarrow{\hspace{2cm}} ab + ac$$
$$\xleftarrow{\hspace{2cm}}$$
$$\textit{Factoring}$$

Paragraph giving factoring
   concept ending in definition

The arrows indicate that the property is reversible, that is, the Symmetry Property applies. If we are given an expression in the form of the left member, we can carry out the operation of multiplication according to the Distributive Property and express the product as two terms. We sometimes call this operation "removing parentheses." It is also possible to use the Distributive Property when we are given an expression in the form of the right member. In this case there must be a common factor, that is, an exact divisor, in each term. If the equation is read from right to left we can remove, or "factor," the common factor, and express the result as a product. Factoring is a process of renaming a number or algebraic expression   Note: This is the mean-
as the product of two or more numbers or expressions. In the expres-   ing of factoring.
sion $a(b + c)$, a is a factor and so is $(b + c)$.

Review—with most students such
   review should be directed
   by the teacher in class.

A review of multiplication and division of polynomials (Sections 4:4, 4:5) is desirable at this time. This will help you develop speed and accuracy in performing these operations. The Laws of Exponents will also be required. In this list of exercises you should do   Stress
as much of the work mentally as you can.

Former concepts used.
Teacher will need to insure student understanding of them.

Concrete illustrations: Should be explained
and worked by Teacher and students
in class.

As we have shown, the Distributive Property enables us to factor certain algebraic expressions. Monomials are usually considered factored because the single term involves only products. For example, $10ax^2$ is the product of 10, a, and x^2, each of which is a factor. If a prime factorization is desired, we can write $10ax^2$ in the form $2 \cdot 5 \cdot a \cdot x \cdot x$. This is not ordinarily needed, however.

Factoring is clearly related to division. If one number or algebraic expression, N, is divided by another number or algebraic expression, D, it gives a quotient, Q. Then, according to the definition of division, we have the relation

$$\frac{N}{D} = Q, \text{ if and only if } N = D \cdot Q$$

which means $\frac{N}{D} = Q$ implies $N = D \cdot Q$ and $N = D \cdot Q$ implies $\frac{N}{D} = Q$. We say that D and Q are factors of N.

Suppose that N is the binomial $8x^2 - 12x$. Let us divide this expression by the common factor 2.

$$\frac{8x^2 - 12x}{2} = 4x^2 - 6x$$

Therefore, $8x^2 - 12x = 2(4x^2 - 6x)$, where 2 and $(4x^2 - 6x)$ are factors of $8x^2 - 12x$.

First application

Can $8x^2 - 12x$ be factored in other ways? Check these factorizations by using the Distributive Property.

Ask the students to do this.

$$4(2x^2 + 3x); \quad x(8x - 12); \quad 2x(4x - 6); \quad 4x(2x - 3)$$

We say that a polynomial has been completely factored if each of the factors is *prime*. The binomial $2x - 3$ is prime if we restrict ourselves to integers as coefficients. No polynomial would be prime, however, unless we place such a restriction upon the factors. For instance, we could factor $2x - 3$ into $2(x - \frac{3}{2})$ or $\frac{1}{3}(6x - 9)$, and so on indefinitely. It is understood that in complete factoring the greatest common factor is to be removed, even if it is not a prime number. In the example $8x^2 - 12x$, complete factoring gives us $4x(2x - 3)$. Although x might be replaced by a real number that would enable us to factor further, we consider the expression $4x(2x - 3)$ as a prime factorization.

Vocabulary that is assumed to be known.

Further explanation

Note: This is sometimes called G.C.F. and is defined to be the product of all prime common factors of two or more numbers or polynomials.

▶EXAMPLE: Factor completely $12a^3 - 18a^2 + 3a$.

Solution: The number 3 is the only common factor of the coefficients, and a^1 is the highest power of a that occurs in *each* term. Therefore the expression can be divided by $3a$ and written in factored form.

Illustration 4

$$3a(4a^2 - 6a + 1)$$

---

[4] Glen D. Vannatta, A. Wilson Goodwin, and F. Joe Crosswhite (Consultant), *Algebra One: Teacher's Guide and Solutions Manual* (Columbus, Ohio: Charles E. Merrill Publishing Company, 1970), pp. 275 and 277.

WORD PROBLEMS

Directions to
students of
procedure in
solving problems,
Problem must be
read several
times.

4:4   Using Mathematical Sentences

We have seen that we may translate many English sentences to mathematical sentences. Often such a translation is helpful in solving problems. For example, consider the following problem:

1st reading
Overview

Bill and Frank drove to the beach for some surfing. Frank was certain that he had $4.20 with him when he left home. Bill forgot the exact amount he had with him. Frank spent $.60 more than Bill, who spent all of his money, and together the boys spent $6.00. How much money did Bill take with him? How much money did Frank have left after the trip?

Here we have several English sentences which can be translated to mathematical sentences. Read the paragraph carefully. Pick out the sentences or phrases which include mathematical information.

2nd reading
What is given

Frank was certain that he had $4.20 with him . . .
Frank spent $.60 more than Bill . . .
Bill . . . spent all of his money.
. . . together the boys spent $6.00.

3rd reading
What is asked

There are two questions to answer. What are they? Consider them one at a time. Let us try to answer the first one: How much money did Bill take with him?

Let x represent the amount of money which Bill took with him. Since Bill had no money left when he returned home, he must have spent x dollars or the same amount of money which he took with him.

General vocabulary———►Frank spent $.60 *more* than Bill. This implies *addition*. Frank spent
indicating direction $x + \$.60$. They spent $6.00 altogether. Thus,
in process.

Bills' money	+	Frank's money	=	Amount spent by both boys
x	+	$(x + .60)$	=	6.00

Simplify the left member of the equation:

Solving the
problem.

$$x + x + .60 = 6.00$$
$$2x + .60 = 6.00$$

May involve
additional reading
of problem.

Eliminate the quantity .60 from the left member by subtracting .60 from both members:

$$2x + .60 - .60 = 6.00 - .60$$
$$2x = 5.40$$

Divide each member by 2:

$$\frac{(2x)}{2} = \frac{(5.40)}{2}$$
$$x = 2.70$$

Since x represented the amount of money which Bill took with him, we know that Bill had $2.70.

Let us consider the second question: How much money did Frank have left after the trip?

Frank spent $.60 more than Bill, and Bill spent $2.70. Therefore, Frank spent $2.70 + $.60. How much did he have with him when he left home? How much did he have left after the trip? $ .90
$4.20

Encourage students to
write out these
sentences to clearly
identify what the
variable represents.

Exercises

Translate the following English sentences to mathematical sentences and determine the solution set for each.

1. Charles is 4 years <u>older than</u> his brother Dave. The sum of their ages is 24. How old is Dave? (*Hint:* <u>Let x represent Dave's age. Then Charles' age is x + _?4._</u>) $x + x + 4 = 24$; $x = 10$

2. The <u>difference</u> in age between Keith and his younger brother Robert is 10 years. The sum of their ages is 18 years. How old is Robert? (*Hint:* Represent Keith's age by x. Then Robert's age is $x -$ _?10._) $x + x - 10 = 18$ $x = 4$

3. Richard is now 14. Four years from now he will be <u>twice as old</u> as his sister. How old is Richard's sister now? (*Hint:* Let x represent the age of Richard's sister now.) $2 (x + 4) = 18$; $x = 5$ [5]

Vocabulary indicates relationship and process:

older than	— relationship
sum	— addition
difference	— subtraction
twice	— multiplication

---

[5] Eugene P. Smith, et al., *Discoveries in Modern Mathematics, Course 2: Teacher's Annotated Edition* (Columbus, Ohio: Charles E. Merrill Publishing Company, 1968), pp. 124–125.

emphasis in mathematics must be directed toward an appropriate comprehension of basic concepts, appreciation of significant meanings, development of desirable attitudes, efficiency in making sound applications, and confidence in shaping intelligent and independent interpretations as well as toward proficiency in fundamental skills.

READING SKILLS PERTINENT TO MATHEMATICS

The fundamental charge to the mathematics teacher is to teach students the mathematical concepts so that they can develop competence in the mathematical processes. The teacher's responsibility is thereby twofold. He must teach students how to read mathematical materials as well as teaching them the concepts and their applications. The student will be better able to understand and gain a mastery of the mathematics if he is able to understand the textbook and related materials. In order to teach the reading of mathematics, the teacher must first know the basic concepts and generalizations of the subject. Second, he must be familiar with the skills of reading as they relate to mathematics. Finally, he must know how to relate instruction of the skills to the mathematics content—how to fuse the subject matter and the skills of attaining it.

The first prerequisite is not the subject of this book. It is assumed here that you are trained and competent in mathematics.

The reading skills as they apply to mathematics are:
1. Intense reading of the succinct language of mathematics material.
2. Understanding the vocabulary which includes technical terms, words labeling processes, general words with a mathematical meaning, and general words.
3. Interpreting mathematical symbols which are extensions or a shorthand of mathematical terms.
4. Analyzing statistical reports such as tax and financial data.
5. Solving word problems by using the necessary analytical and computational steps.
6. Analyzing and interpreting pictorial and graphic representations.
7. Relating previous information to what is currently being read.
8. Following directions.

Reading for a Purpose

Mathematics material requires methodical and slow word-by-word reading. Often, as with word problems, repeated readings are required, each with a different purpose. Your responsibility is to assist the students in making a habit of establishing purposes. You will need as well to assist the student in the delineation of each purpose. The purposes tend to be more specific in the mathematics than in narrative and expository material. The purposes in problem reading are intrinsic to each step of problem solving or specific to the sequence and orderliness of a process in explanatory passages.

Vocabulary

There is a heavy load of vocabulary in mathematics. Often the lack of vocabulary is the major barrier to the student in communication and thought about the mathematical processes and understandings. In the study of mathematical vocabulary two aspects of it need to be explained to the students. One aspect is the conceptual foundation of the terms. The student must have the conceptual background if he is to understand and not learn his mathematics by rote. Mathematical understandings are also cumulative—one builds on the concept which preceded it. The second aspect is the recognition of the words. This may involve assistance in syllabication, and structural analysis of prefixes, roots, and suffixes.

In mathematics there are four kinds of vocabulary words, any of which can cause difficulty. The first type is the technical word peculiar to some area of the mathematics. For example, *sine* and *cosine* in trigonometry; *polynomials, linear equations* in algebra; and *isosceles, arc,* and *polyhedron* in geometry. The second type is the general word in our language which has a mathematical meaning such as *prime, natural, radical, exponent, square,* etc. A third type is the word which signals a mathematical process. This includes such words as *subtract, times, multiply, difference, column.* Many of these also have other meanings in general language usage. Finally, the fourth type is the general word which can determine a student's comprehension. Such words as *before, of, compare, increase, least,* are examples.

In developing the concepts of the vocabulary terms, you may well start with concrete objects or situations which are known to the student. You begin at the experiential base of the student's knowledge, widening it as necessary, to provide the foundation for the concept.

For example, draw diagrams on the blackboard to show graphically the sine and cosine:

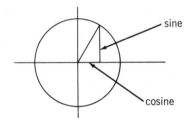

Use a practical problem to show the use of the functions of sine and cosine. With *polynomial,* break the word into its parts: poly—many, and nomial—pertaining to number. Then illustrate alegbraically what the polynomial is. Or with the word *arc,* show what an arc of light, made with a flashlight would be. Draw a diagram showing it as part of a circle. In short, present the words through actual non-mathematical experiences the students would know, investigate the derivations of the terms and note how the root meaning applies, show the concept diagramatically, or relate the term to former mathematics knowledge. You may think that such procedures are too elemental, but independent facility comes only as all are able to apply the knowledge concretely to their existing fund of knowledge. This is important if independent student functioning is to be acquired rather than the rote manipulation of process. Then, the student should talk about the experiences—the situations which illustrate the concept—to evolve the interrelationships and significance. Also, a feeling of familiarity that comes from and aids understanding develops as the student uses language to internalize the understandings. Next, you will introduce the appropriate symbols used in mathematics that represent the concept. Finally, the students must be given opportunities to apply the concept to practical and theoretical situations. Adequate practice must be provided to allow the student to feel completely masterful with the concept.

Though vocabulary knowledge and usage may properly begin at the oral discussion stage, the goal is for the student to become independent in his use and analysis. He must become able to read written statements in mathematics and comprehend the thought. Reading, of course, also helps the student to further establish and clarify the mathematical concepts which the teacher helped him to acquire initially through concrete experiences.

INTERPRETING SYMBOLS

Symbols and signs in mathematics are a type of vocabulary. They should be developed sequentially and meaningfully—usually at the time when the concept related to them is developed. You should not assume that the student knows the symbol. Whenever an example is worked by the student, you should question him about the meaning and use of the symbols, clarifying as necessary. In this way gaps in understanding or misinformation can be noted and filled in or corrected.

Analyzing Statistical Reports (tables, formulas, equations)

This material is often tabular and may include statistical equations and formulas. If the concepts represented in the material are understood, the following steps, engaged in by teacher and student together, can aid in understanding:
1.   Read and understand the statement that tells what the table represents.
2.   Study each vertical column of items and read the headings for them to see what they represent.
3.   Study the vertical column(s) thoroughly to compare and/or draw conclusions.
See p. 261 for an example.

In order to deal with formulas and equations, the student must acquire the concept that each formula and equation is a sentence in mathematical shorthand. In fact, some textbooks call equations in algebra *algebraic sentences*. Therefore, a first step might be to have the student write the formula and equation in a sentence (or state it orally in class). It represents a sentence with a subject and a predicate. The operational symbols ($+$, $=$, $-$, $\div$, and $\times$) represent verbs. Next, have the student retranslate the formula or equation into mathematical symbols. Or, if the formula is given in a sentence in the text, as in word problems, have the student start by

Explanation to students
showing how the table
should be read.

The table below shows how your money would grow if you were receiving 5% interest. The first column shows the number of years your $100 was in the bank. The second column shows how it would grow at simple interest, with $5 added each year and no interest on the previous interest. The third column shows how it would grow at compound interest, with interest paid on the previous interest you have earned.

Discuss the chart
with students. Help
them to learn how to
read and interpret it.

At this rate, investment doubles in less
than 15 years at
compound interest.
This takes 20 years
at simple interest.

How $100 Grows at 5% Interest		
Years	With Simple Interest	With Compound Interest
1	$105.00	$105.00
2	110.00	110.25
3	115.00	115.76
4	120.00	121.55
5	125.00	127.63
6	130.00	134.01
7	135.00	140.71
8	140.00	147.75
9	145.00	155.14
10	150.00	162.90
11	155.00	171.05
12	160.00	179.60
13	165.00	188.58
14	170.00	198.01
15	175.00	207.91
16	180.00	218.31
17	185.00	229.23
18	190.00	240.69
19	195.00	252.72
20	200.00	265.36

[6]

[6] Smith, et al, p. 312.

translating it into its mathematical equivalent. The following formula was written in a textbook:

$$(a + b)^2 \qquad\qquad =$$

The square of the sum of two numbers equals
verb

$$a^2 \qquad\qquad + \qquad\qquad 2ab$$

the square of the first number plus twice the product of the numbers,
structure word

$$+ \qquad\qquad b^2$$

plus the square of the second number.
structure word

Algebraic form: $(a + b)^2 = a^2 + 2ab + b^2$

In such intensive detailed reading you can help your students by analyzing the written version of the formula as shown, indicating to the students the basic parts of the sentence and the function of the process and structure words. Then have them place all known number values for the letters. At this point, the student is ready to solve the formula or equation mathematically.

Solving Word Problems

The student's grasp of the concepts and his understanding of the way he should read mathematics becomes very apparent as he reads written problems. A specific series of steps are necessary as a guide to the student's reasoning and purposeful reading of the problem. They are:

1. *Read* it slowly and carefully. Picture the scene of the problem in your mind.
2. *Re-read* the last sentence—decide what is asked.
3. *Re-read* the entire problem—determine the facts given to work with.
4. Decide the process to use.
5. Estimate the answer—judge reasonableness of estimate.

For example, these steps would be followed for the following problem:

Mr. Stone bought a new sewing machine for his wife. The store asked him to make a down payment of 20%. If the cost of the machine was $160.00, how much was the down payment?

1. The situation: Mr. Stone is buying his wife a sewing machine and he must make a specified down payment.
2. What is asked: How much is the down payment?
3. Facts given: The sewing machine cost—$160.00
   Down payment must be 20%
4. Process: Multiplication to compute the size of the down payment.

5.   Estimate: A little more than $30.00
                         (20% of 100 is 20.00; 20% of 50 is 10.00)
6.   Compute the problem: 20% of 160
      Some suggestions for overcoming difficulties in reading problems are:
1.   Have many exercises in vocabulary study.
      a.   Finding meanings
      b.   Matching words with objects
      c.   Grouping words that relate to the same process i.e., *plus, sum, and, longer
            than* relate to addition
      d.   Classifying and identifying words and concepts i.e., *radius, diameter, cir-
            cumference, arc* refer to circle
      e.   Dramatizing concepts such as buying and selling
2.   Have students determine unfamiliar word(s) or expression(s) in a problem.
3.   Begin with an easy problem and have students state what the numbers in the
      problem stand for.
4.   Help the students to visualize the problem situation. Can they describe the sit-
      uation presented in the problem without using the quantities cited?
5.   Have the students read many different types of problems, i.e.,
      a.   One-step problems—If 18 inches of ribbon are needed to tie one diploma,
            how many inches will be needed to tie all the diplomas for a graduating
            class of 106?
      b.   Two-step problems—Martin's Department Store was having a 98¢ sale.
            Danny's mother bought three tee shirts at 98¢ each, five pairs of socks at
            98¢ a pair, and six towels at 98¢ each. How much did she spend altogether
            (not including tax)?
            (1)   Find total cost of each type of item;
            (2)   Find total cost of all items together.
      c.   Problems with hidden questions—A telephone pole 57 feet long fell
            straight across a road. If 2⅓ feet were on one side of the road and 14¾
            feet were on the other side of the road, how wide was the road? Hidden
            question: How many feet of the pole were not on the road?
            (A two step problem)
      d.   Problems without numbers—What unit of measure would you use to
            measure the area of this page in your book? The area of New York City?
            The area of your classroom floor?
      e.   Problems with irrelevant facts—Tim liked to sit at the street corner and
            count cars. During *a half hour period* 38 station wagons, 97 sedans, 18
            convertibles, and 46 sports cars passed by. How many cars were there in
            all?[7] (A one step problem)
6.   Have the students in class discussion *talk through* the problem to determine
      everything the problem does and why.

---

[7] Eugene P. Smith, George A. Calder, William G. Mehl, and Dean S. Rasmussen, *Discoveries in Modern Mathematics, Book I* (Columbus, Ohio: Chas. E. Merrill Publishing Company, 1968) pp. 63, 75, 191, 361, 57.

7. Have the students solve problems orally and use, when possible, classroom situations.
8. Have students make up and read problems related to their own activities.
9. Have the students keep a chart throughout the year on which they record all of the words used to indicate the use of a specific symbol or process. For instance, for the symbol = such words as *equals, is equal to, the same as,* would be noted. The chart would look similar to this:

=	×	+	÷	−
is	times	add	divide	minus
equal	multiply	plus	ratio	less than

Interpreting Pictorial and Graphic Representations

Students are taught in mathematics to construct graphs to show visually the results of division, mathematical growth, gain, etc. Graphs of various types—bar, line, circle—are used to enable the reader to see quickly results from which conclusions can be drawn. They are, also, a type of reading material. The students should be guided to read graphs by:
1. Reading the phrase beneath the graph so that they will know what it is supposed to picture;
2. Reading the numbers at the left of the graph so that they can analyze and note what is being measured;
3. Reading the letters at the bottom so that they can analyze and note the quantity or units of measurement;
4. Noting the name and amount of the fractional part of each section. If the graph is a pictograph, they will need to be able to use the key to translate each picture into numbers.

Sample graphs can be found on pp. 265–269.

Relating Previous Information to What is Currently Being Read

In perhaps no other discipline is it so important for the student to be able to relate new concepts to previously learned and supportive concepts. You will always need to help the student realize the development of information within the subject. This can be started at the beginning of the school year when the overview of the course is presented. Many textbooks include a review of essential concepts in the first chapters. This must further be done throughout the year as new concepts are introduced. When new concepts are introduced, you should make sure that the students are in full understanding of the previous ones. Students themselves should be asked to determine the previous understandings in a newly met concept. Another effective practice is to have the students see the order of development within a chapter. For example, the preview section of a chapter entitled "Operations with Polynomials" indicates to the student the understandings they should have acquired before the study of the chapter. (See p. 270.)

Enrich concept of plotting on a coordinate grid
by a comparison to plotting on a map—
a place or ship's position using longitude
and lattitude as coordinates.

Here is a coordinate grid that has each quarter section or *quadrant* labeled by a Roman numeral. Notice that the quadrants are numbered in counterclockwise order.

Vocabulary that
should be
known.

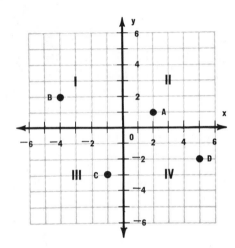

Observe point *A* in quadrant I. How many units is it to the right of the *y*-axis? How far is it above the *x*-axis? The distance from the *y*-axis is always described first or before the distance from the *x*-axis. Thus we would say that point *A* represents $x = 2$, $y = 1$, or the *coordinates* of *A* are $(2, 1)$. Similarly, the coordinates of point *B* are $(^-4, 2)$. What are the coordinates of point *C*? What are the coordinates of point *D*? The process of locating a point on a coordinate plane is called **plotting** the point.

Exercises

Draw a pair of coordinate axes and locate the following points. Label each point with its coordinates.

1. $(3, 3)$	**3.** $(^-2, 1)$	**5.** $(4, ^-2)$	**7.** $(^-3, ^-1)$	**9.** $(5, 2)$
2. $(4, 5)$	**4.** $(1, ^-3)$	**6.** $(^-5, ^-2)$	**8.** $(^-3, 6)$	**10.** $(^-1, ^-4)$[8]

---

[8] Smith, et al., p. 140.

Tom is a member of the school basketball team and he has been keeping a record of the number of field goals he has made in each game. Here is Tom's record for the first nine games represented by a bar graph:

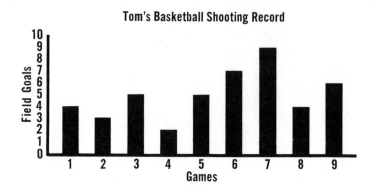

Tom's Basketball Shooting Record

↓Explanation to student

The vertical number line along the side of the graph is called the *scale*, which shows how many field goals each bar represents. The labels along the bottom of the graph tell which game each bar represents.

Exercises (to check and extend students' understanding).

1. How many field goals did Tom make in the first game?

2. In which game did he make the least number of field goals?

3. In which game did he make the most field goals?

4. In which sets of games did Tom make the same number of field goals?

5. Does the graph in general show improvement or decline in completed field goals as the season progressed?

6. What is the total number of field goals Tom made in the first five games? In the last five games?

7. **a.** Find the *arithmetic mean* of the number of field goals he made for all nine games.
   b. Find the *median* number of field goals for all nine games.

8. Can you think of a reason why Tom's scale (0 to 10) ends with the number 10? Why didn't he end it with the number 8? Why does the scale begin with 0?

9. What is the title of this graph?

10. Do the bars in the graph run horizontally or vertically?

11. Why are there no fractional parts represented in this graph?

Exercises

Study the information which is presented in the following circle graph. Use the information in the graph to answer Exercises 1-6.

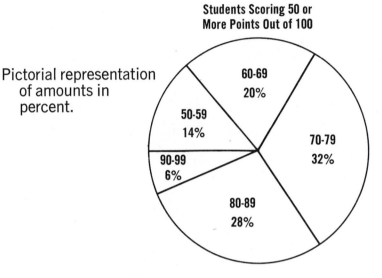

Pictorial representation of amounts in percent.

Students Scoring 50 or More Points Out of 100

60-69 20%
50-59 14%
90-99 6%
80-89 28%
70-79 32%

1. If 120 students took the test, and all scored 50 or more points, how many students scored between 59 and 70 points on the test?

2. What percent of the total number of students scored below 80?

3. Does the graph show that anyone received a score of 100%?

4. According to the appearance of the graph, which two score ranges included approximately the same number of students?

5. How many students scored better than 69 points, but less than 90 points?

6. Which two groups together have the same percentage as the 60-69 group?

7. David stood at a busy highway intersection and counted the number of automobiles which were painted white, red, blue, and green for a period of one hour. His research provided him with the following data:

White Automobiles	270
Red Automobiles	45
Blue Automobiles	108
Green Automobiles	27

Construct a circle graph to show the results of David's research.

12:8   Broken Line Graphs

Broken line graphs are useful for pointing out changes in data over a period of time or changes brought on by varying conditions. In a broken line graph, line segments are used to connect the points which represent the given data. In some line graphs, these line segments are drawn only to guide the eye and to indicate the rate of change. In other line graphs, the connecting lines can be used to guess information which was not given.

The broken line graph below records the number of rainy days for each month of the school year in a particular city. The dots represent the number of rainy days in a given month. The lines help to show the amount of increase or decrease in rainy days from month to month. Note that there are two scales on a line graph: one on the horizontal axis and one on the vertical axis.

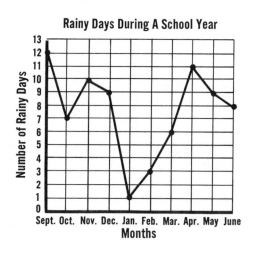

Rainy Days During A School Year

_____   General

~~~~~~~~~~   Explanation to student

----------   Specific

12:10   Histograms

At the beginning of this chapter you organized data to find measures of central tendency. Sometimes it is useful to know how frequently a particular score, weight, height, or other kind of numerical event occurs within a set of data. One way of presenting such data is by a *frequency table* or *frequency distribution.* A *tally* or count is kept of the number of times each "score" appears in the data.

Explanation

New
vocabulary

Example: Mr. Kelley's mathematics students made the following scores on a test: 90, 85, 85, 95, 85, 80, 75, 65, 80, 75, 85, 95, 100, 85, 90, 80, 80, 65, 75, 90, 85, 100, 85, 95, 90, 80, 75, 80, 85, 90, 80, 75.

Mr. Kelley recorded the information on a distribution table, marking a tally mark in the appropriate line for each score.

Score	Tally	Frequency
100	//	2
95	///	3
90	̷H̷H̷	5
85	̷H̷H̷ ///	8
80	̷H̷H̷ //	7
75	̷H̷H̷	5
70		0
65	//	2

Areas of Four National Parks

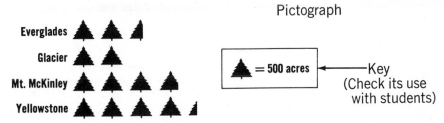

Pictograph

Everglades

Glacier

Mt. McKinley

Yellowstone

▲ = 500 acres ◄—— Key
(Check its use
with students)

11. Which park has the largest area represented?

12. What is the approximate area of Everglades National Park?

13. How does the size of Mt. McKinley National Park compare with the size of Glacier National Park?

14. How many symbols would represent an area of 1,500 acres?

15. The area of the Olympic National Park in Washington is 889 acres. Make a sketch on your paper using the symbol from the graph to represent this fact.[9]

---

[9] Eugene P. Smith, et al., *Discoveries in Modern Mathematics, Course One: Teacher's Guide and Annotated Edition* (Columbus, Ohio: Charles E. Merrill Publishing Company, 1968), pp. 422, 432, 433, 439, 442.

Operations with Polynomials **4**

4:1   PREVIEW

Before you could solve practical problems in arithmetic, you had } #1. Former
to be able to perform the <u>fundamental operations with numbers.</u> } knowledge
You needed to know the <u>addition combinations</u> before you could→ a
find the total cost of a number of items. You needed to know how
to <u>multiply</u> accurately before you could find the cost of several→ b
pounds of a commodity at a given price per pound. Before you could
work problems containing <u>fractions and decimals,</u> you had to learn→ c
the <u>operations</u> with those special types of numbers.

In algebra, we shall be dealing largely with polynomials. You   New material to
must learn to perform the basic operations with polynomials before   be learned
you can use them in practical applications. You already have an
understanding of the <u>properties of the set of rational numbers and</u>→ #2. Former
the <u>operations with monomials.</u> This knowledge should help you in   knowledge
learning to handle polynomials. Check yourself to be sure that you
remember and can use the rules of operations with rational numbers
and the laws of exponents. You must know these principles in order
to combine monomials by addition, subtraction, multiplication, and
division.

Remember that a polynomial is an algebraic expression made up
of sums and products of variables and constants. A polynomial in
one variable is an expression like $3x^2 - 2x + 1$, $4x + 3$, or $3x^4$.
The general form is $ax^n + bx^{n-1} + \cdots + k$, where a, b, $\cdots k$ are   Introductory
constants and n is a non-negative integer. You will learn how to add   statement
and subtract polynomials with two or more terms by combining like
terms. Later in this chapter you will multiply and divide polynomials by procedures similar to those used in arithmetic. When   New material
you have mastered the basic operations with polynomials, you will   to be learned.
use your knowledge to solve algebraic sentences and other problems
in algebra.[10]

Knowing that they will be dealing with *operations,* the students may be able
to anticipate some of the major sections of the chapter. As they would note the organization, the following headings would be listed:

> Addition of polynomials
> Subtraction of polynomials
> Multiplication of polynomials
> Division of polynomials

---

[10] Vannatta, et al., pp. 138–139.

Sentences with polynomials
Sentences with fractions

Following Directions

Following directions is considered to be as important in mathematics as it is in science. Directions require a highly intensive reading and the student will need to follow these steps:

1. Read the directions completely and carefully to get an overview of the total scope.
2. Read just one direction at a time very carefully (if need be, word by word).
3. Think about each direction and be sure that the exactness is understood. If not, reread the direction.
4. Carry out the directions.

THE RETARDED READER IN THE MATHEMATICS CLASS

The concept load and the intensiveness of mathematical writing can readily spell defeat for the retarded reader. It is desirable, of course, for the retarded reader to get assistance in the skills of reading in specific remedial settings, and many do. However, the mathematics teacher will still find the student in his class as the remedial help is being extended. Therefore, he is faced with the need to vary his instructional techniques and procedures in order to insure as much student success as possible.

One of the most important measures you can employ is to build the student's background by a program of readiness before each new concept. In the readiness period, you may do any or several of the following:

1. Inventory the student's mastery of the skills to determine the gaps and specific points of difficulty that need to be corrected. Then teach to these.
2. Use a sequential question and answer technique to lead the student to the concept or process. Guide his reasoning in minute steps to the desired understanding.
3. As each new understanding is evolved, and as each old one is reviewed, write the appropriate word or term on the blackboard. Focus attention upon it. Underline the word to indicate the syllables.
4. Use discussion to elicit questions from the students as well as experiences they have had which involve the concept or process. Guide the students in the use of the words.
5. Review frequently and show the interrelationship of understandings.
6. Use concrete materials and illustrations wherever possible.
7. Review the use of mathematical symbols and their meaning as they are required.
8. Find easier materials if possible.
9. Rewrite explanations and problems. One technique may be to explain a concept and then have the students evolve an explanation in their own words which can then be typed and presented to them as a supplement to their textbook.

WIDE READING

Extensive outside reading is not usually considered in the teaching of mathematics. Yet such reading can do much to develop interest and increase mastery of understandings and concepts. The textbook in mathematics can be stifling whereas wider reading can be enriching as a supplement. Students can read to see how various mathematical concepts are used in chemistry, physics, history, industrial arts and home economics. Teachers can coordinate their efforts in this direction also, which will help the student to note the uses of the concepts he is learning. Wide reading will help the student to see the relationship of his mathematics to industry and science. It will lead to a deeper appreciation of math in our culture.

Both classroom libraries and the school library should be well stocked with books relating to mathematics—special areas of mathematics, biographies of mathematicians, mathematical teasers, special applications of mathematical theory, and so on. Austin maintains that

> Teachers who wish to achieve the objective of wide reading in mathematics will plan their work to include the following steps: (1) Review the mathematics courses to find places where time may be saved from content without neglecting the essentials; (2) Select a few topics in connection with which wide reading may be done; i.e., a bibliography including the history of a topic, biographies of mathematicians, and more extended writings or articles related to certain topics or units in the texts; (3) Locate these references, examine and evaluate them, and distribute them to the pupils; (4) Give the pupils time to use these materials and time to discuss the ideas they have gained.[11]

See Appendix I for a sample bibliography from a mathematics textbook.

LESSON PROCEDURES

The Directed Reading Activity class procedure as applied to mathematics includes the following steps:
1. Readiness—This beginning step of the lesson is designed to enable the student to accomplish the objective of the lesson. The teacher will
   a. explore, and supplement where necessary, the student background necessary for the understanding or concept to be developed in the lesson,
   b. introduce the new terms and vocabulary which may consist of both general words and technical ones, and
   c. set purposes with the students for the tasks to be accomplished.
2. Guided silent reading pertinent to the purposes or problems of the lesson.
3. Discussion of the reading material, either explanation of a process or a problem, to probe and aid student understanding. You may use different types of questions (fact, vocabulary, inference, step of problem solving, relationship)

---

[11] Mary C. Austin, "Improving Comprehension of Mathematics," in *Reading in the Secondary Schools,* ed. M. Jerry Weiss (New York: The Odyssey Press, Inc., 1961), pp. 391–396.

to assist the students in their logical thought and understanding. Specific mathematical problems and exercises may be used to apply the conceptual and explanatory material.

4. Rereading which may be silent or oral and is done as the need arises to determine a specific fact or consideration. Such need may arise from the problems and exercises, indicating the student's grasp of the material.
5. Application in which the student practices, independently or with individual teacher help, by applying the process to specific problems.

When students have been taught the theoretical concepts and the lesson is now concerned with the application through the computation of verbal problems, you will note that an effective procedure is a union of the standard steps of a reading lesson and the steps of problem solving.

1. The preparation for reading and understanding would have been completed in the explanation and discussion of the conceptual processes.
2. Have the student read the problem. For example, "The perimeter of a triangle is 62 inches. The second side is 4 inches longer than the first and the remaining side is 6 inches less than the second. Find the lengths of the three sides."
3. Develop comprehension. Have the student visualize the situation of the problem. Clarify vocabulary as necessary. In this instance clarify the words, *perimeter, than, less than* (Note that *than* means "as compared to").
4. Rereading—read to find what is asked for and what is given. Determine the process in this case, the mathematical equation or sentence: $X+(X+4)+(X+4-6) = 62$.
5. Compute the problem. Check it against the facts given in the problem.
6. Follow up. Application of procedure to other problems following steps 2–5 inclusively.

The discipline of mathematics has a dual language which is inextricably interwoven. To understand either the language symbols or the mathematical symbols as they apply to mathematics, the student must be able to use both sets of symbols. These symbols which label the mathematical concepts are best taught by the mathematics teacher since he is the one who is expert in the discipline. For the student to become independent in his study and reading of mathematics materials, he must become competent in the languages of mathematics. This is best accomplished in the classes where the mathematics processes, concepts, and relationships are taught.

SUGGESTED QUESTIONS AND PROBLEMS TO BE CONSIDERED IN REFERENCE TO YOUR OWN CLASSROOM

List A (For readers who are training to be teachers)

1. Review a mathematics textbook and list
   a. the technical vocabulary

    b. the general words used with mathematical meaning

    c. words that indicate process

    d. general words (often of just one or two syllables, i.e., *than*) that may indicate relationship or degree.

2. Before you plan to teach a formula, analyze the verbal form of it, noting the meaning units, words indicating process and relationship. •

3. For each major topic in a specific mathematics class, determine practical applications to help students realize the relevance.

4. For each topic, determine the prior knowledge the student should know so that he will realize the cumulative nature of mathematics.

5. Consult with the school librarian and prepare a bibliography of related mathematics materials for supplementary and enrichment use.

6. Analyze verbal problems for words which indicate process and relationship.

List B (For readers who are teaching)

1. Analyze the printed material in your mathematics textbook and note for each assignment the vocabulary that would be technical, general words used with a specialized mathematical meaning and words indicating process.

2. Use a class assignment and determine how you can help your students realize the practical application of the information.

3. Poll your students for reasons why they think verbal problems are difficult. List the reasons and evolve with them appropriate techniques for overcoming the difficulties.

4. Analyze the mathematics textbook with your students to determine the patterns of writing.

5. As you plan to teach a new mathematical concept, determine the steps you would employ to introduce and to clarify the concept.

A Sample Bibliography from a Mathematics Textbook

*ABBOTT, EDWIN A. *Flatland: A Romance of Many Dimensions*. New York: Barnes and Noble, 1964

ADLER, IRVING. *The New Mathematics*. New York: John Day Co., 1958

BELL, ERIC T. *Men of Mathematics*. New York: Simon and Schuster, 1937 (paperback edition, 1961)

*BENDICK, JEANNE, and LEVIN, MARCIA. *Take a Number*. New York: Whittlesey House, McGraw Hill Book Co., 1961

*BERGAMINI, DAVID, and the editors of *Life*. *Mathematics*. New York: *Life* Science Library, *Time,* Inc., 1963.

BURGER, DIONYS. *Sphereland: A Fantasy about Curved Spaces and an Expanding Universe*, trans. by Cornelie J. Rheinboldt. New York: Crowell, 1965

*GARDNER, MARTIN. *Mathematical Puzzles*. New York: Thomas Y. Crowell Co., 1961

*GARDNER, MARTIN. *New Mathematical Diversions from the Scientific American*. New York: Simon and Schuster, 1966

*GARDNER, MARTIN. *The Scientific American Book of Mathematical Puzzles and Diversions*. New York: Simon and Schuster, 1959

*GILLES, WILLIAM F. *The Magic and Oddities of Numbers*. New York: Vantage Press, 1953

*GLENN, WILLIAM H. and JOHNSON, DONOVAN A. *Invitation to Mathematics*. Garden City, N.Y.: Doubleday, 1962

---

* Titles marked with an asterisk are especially suitable for student reference.

*GLENN, WILLIAM H. and JOHNSON, DONOVAN A. *The Pythagorean Theorem.* St. Louis: Webster Publishing Co., 1960

*HOGBEN, LANCELOT. *The Wonderful World of Mathematics.* Garden City, N.Y.: Doubleday, 1955

HOOPER, ALFRED. *Makers of Mathematics.* New York: Vintage Books.

*KASNER, EDWARD and NEWMAN, JAMES. *Mathematics and the Imagination.* New York: Simon and Schuster, 1940

*MENNINGER, K. W. *Mathematics in Your World.* New York: Viking Press, Inc., 1962

MEYER, JEROME SYDNEY. *Fun With Mathematics.* Cleveland, Ohio: World Publishing Co., 1952

MEYER, JEROME SYDNEY and HANLON, STUART. *Fun with the New Math.* New York: Hawthorne Books, Inc., 1966

NATIONAL COUNCIL OF TEACHERS OF MATHEMATICS. *Enrichment Mathematics for the Grades.* Twenty-seventh Yearbook. Washington, D.C.: National Council of Teachers of Mathematics, 1962

NATIONAL COUNCIL OF TEACHERS OF MATHEMATICS. *The Growth of Mathematical Ideas, Grades K-12.* Twenty-fourth Yearbook. Ed. by Phillip S. Jones. Washington, D.C.: National Council of Teachers of Mathematics, 1959

NATIONAL COUNCIL OF TEACHERS OF MATHEMATICS. *Topics in Mathematics for Elementary School Teachers.* Twenty-ninth Yearbook. Washington, D.C.: National Council of Teachers of Mathematics, 1964

NEWMAN, JAMES R. *The World of Mathematics.* New York: Simon and Schuster, 1956

*NORTON, M. SCOTT. *Finite Mathematical Systems.* St. Louis: Webster Publishing Co., 1963

OSBORN, R., DEVAULT, M. V., BOYD, C. C. and HOUSTON, W. R. *Extending Mathematics Understanding.* Columbus, Ohio: Charles E. Merrill Publishing Co., 1961

*PECK, LYMAN C. *Secret Codes, Remainder Arithmetic and Matrices.* Washington, D.C.: National Council of Teachers of Mathematics, 1961

SAWYER, W. W. *Mathematicians' Delight.* Baltimore, Md.: Penguin Books, Inc., 1943

SAWYER, W. W. *Vision in Elementary Mathematics.* Baltimore, Md.: Penguin Books, Inc.

SMITH, DAVID EUGENE. *History of Mathematics.* New York: Dover Publications, Inc., 1957

SPRECKLEMEYER, RICHARD. *The Integers.* Boston: D. C. Heath and Co., 1964

VALENS, EVANS G. *The Number of Things: Pythagoras, Geometry, and Humming Strings.* New York: E. P. Dutton and Co., Inc., 1964

YARNELLE, JOHN E. *Finite Mathematical Structures.* Boston: D. C. Heath and Co., 1964

---

* Titles marked with an asterisk are especially suitable for student reference.

Bibliography taken from Eugene P. Smith, et al., *Discoveries in Modern Mathematics: Course 2* (Columbus, Ohio: Charles E. Merrill Publishing Company, 1968), Teachers Manual Insert pp. 31–32.

CHAPTER TWELVE

Applying the Reading Skills to Other Areas

A major premise of this book is that the reading skills have a specific application to each content area. The premise holds for each of the subjects in the high school as well as the basic disciplines—English, social studies, science, mathematics. In this chapter there will be suggested adaptations to business education, the vocational subjects (industrial arts and home economics), foreign language, art, music, and physical education.

BUSINESS EDUCATION

Business education encompasses a cross-section of the student body and the adaptation of all of the reading skills found in the other disciplines. The students who enroll in business courses range from the potential dropout to the college-bound—from unmotivated potential failures who may be disabled in reading to the student who is motivated and competent. Many business education classes therefore have a wide range of reading levels, sometimes from a third grade level to the college level—an eight to ten year spread. In subject matter business education courses range from those of a social studies nature such as business law, to those of a mathematical nature such as bookkeeping and accounting.

In one comprehensive suburban-urban high school a listing was made of the courses in the business department. The nature of each course was identified with one of the four major disciplines and the reading skills pertinent to each course were listed. The chart served as a graphic representation of the reading tasks required for each course as well as for the department in general. See p. 278.

RELATED SUBJECT TYPE	SUBJECT	Proof and Copy Reading	Reading Verbal Problems	Relationships: Formulas	Reading Pictures, Graphs	Applying Theory	Following Directions	Researching	Dr. Concl., Crit. Rdng.	Seeing Organization	Supporting Details	Noting Main Idea	Vocabulary: Special Symbols	Vocabulary: General	Vocabulary: Technical	Using Parts of Book	Reading-Study Technique	Reading for Purpose
Mathematics	Bookkeeping I		✓	✓	✓	✓	✓	✓	✓	✓	✓	✓	✓	✓	✓	✓	✓	✓
Mathematics	Bookkeeping II		✓	✓	✓	✓	✓	✓	✓	✓	✓	✓	✓	✓	✓	✓	✓	✓
Mathematics	Business Arithmetic		✓	✓	✓	✓	✓		✓	✓	✓	✓	✓	✓	✓	✓	✓	✓
Mathematics	Clerical Mathematics		✓	✓	✓	✓	✓		✓	✓	✓	✓	✓	✓	✓	✓	✓	✓
English/Science	Clerical Typing	✓				✓	✓				✓			✓	✓			
Science, gen'l.	Everyday Business		✓		✓	✓	✓	✓	✓	✓	✓	✓		✓	✓	✓	✓	✓
Science, gen'l.	Introduction to Business		✓		✓	✓	✓	✓	✓	✓	✓	✓		✓	✓	✓	✓	✓
Mathematics	Nurses Mathematics		✓	✓	✓	✓	✓	✓	✓	✓	✓	✓	✓	✓	✓	✓	✓	✓
Science	Office Machines				✓		✓		✓	✓	✓			✓			✓	✓
Science	Office Practice I						✓		✓	✓	✓	✓		✓			✓	✓
Science	Office Practice II						✓		✓	✓	✓	✓		✓			✓	✓
Soc. Studies	Personal Law				✓	✓		✓	✓	✓	✓	✓		✓	✓	✓	✓	✓
Science/Math.	Record Keeping				✓	✓	✓		✓	✓	✓	✓		✓	✓	✓	✓	✓
Soc. St./Math.	Retailing I		✓	✓	✓	✓	✓	✓	✓	✓	✓	✓	✓	✓	✓	✓	✓	✓
Soc. St./Math.	Retailing II			✓	✓	✓	✓	✓	✓	✓	✓	✓	✓	✓	✓	✓	✓	✓
Science	Secretarial Practice			✓		✓	✓	✓	✓	✓	✓	✓		✓	✓	✓	✓	✓
English	Shorthand I				✓	✓	✓						✓	✓	✓	✓	✓	✓
English	Shorthand II and Transcription				✓	✓	✓						✓	✓	✓	✓	✓	✓
English	Stenoscript				✓	✓	✓						✓	✓	✓	✓	✓	✓
English/Science	Typewriting I						✓			✓	✓	✓		✓	✓	✓	✓	✓
English/Science	Typewriting—personal						✓			✓	✓	✓		✓	✓	✓	✓	✓
Soc. Studies	Business Law				✓	✓	✓	✓	✓	✓	✓	✓		✓	✓	✓	✓	✓

As he is engaged in different courses in the department, the business educa-tion student is required to be highly flexible in his application of the reading skills. He needs to adjust to the demands of each type of course.

A quick glance at the chart will show that the courses offered under the de-partment of business education relate in type and hence in pertinent skills to various other disciplines. A closer look shows that each course in the department is differ-ent in its requirements. Therefore the business education teacher has a formidable requirement for flexibility in order to help the students with the varied types of courses offered. (In using this book, the business education teacher will need to refer to the chapters dealing with English, Social Studies, Science, and Mathematics, as appropriate.)

Additional Suggestions for Classroom Procedure

Anderson has pointed out that the business teacher should be capable of de-veloping his own skills in teaching students how to read the books and other ma-terials in his courses. The teacher can do this by (1) thinking through the processes that he went through in learning a specific concept, (2) a careful analysis of the reading materials to be used, and (3) an analysis of how the students read and study the materials.[1]
These three suggestions can be implemented by specific classroom practices:

1. Conduct a diagnostic analysis of possible learning difficulties in the read-ing of business materials.
2. Be alert to the trouble spots and vocabulary difficulties of the students and make efforts to clarify the difficulties for them.
3. Review the basic essentials relating to the new concepts to be presented. This is a basic part of the first step of an effective reading lesson.
4. Present new concepts and develop them by factual information. This be-gins when the students are getting ready to read a selection. Various audio-visual aids, demonstrations, and concrete illustrations may be used to present the new concept prior to the abstract statement of it.
5. The adaption of new learnings to practical application and use is neces-sary if the student is to be aware of the relevance of his learning.
6. Review assignments and relate them to past learning, and further develop concepts, giving explanations where needed and citing practical examples.
7. Guide students in what to read for in new assignments.
8. Provide for some supervised study when you can assist individuals and small groups with specific difficulties.

Vocabulary is a major problem in business education as in any discipline. The basic techniques of vocabulary development apply. You are concerned with two kinds of vocabulary, specific technical words and common words with special meanings. For example, *bulk sale, forged indorsement,* and *warranty deed* would be classified as technical terms while *credit, statement,* and *capital* are words in common usage, but with special meaning in business courses. Students learn words best when they can associate them with experiences. You may need to probe for

---

[1] Bernice Anderson, "Business Teacher: Are You Prepared to Teach Reading?" *Business Education Forum* 26, No. 1 (October, 1971): 3–4.

experiences the student has had or provide experiences relevant to the words being studied. It would be wise to analyze the reading material for both technical words and special common words and from such a listing insure that the students learn their spelling and meaning. Avoid confusion by being consistent in vocabulary usage. Or, if two or more terms such as "charge sales" and "sales on credit" are used, the student should be alerted to the synonymous meaning. Study guides can be used to alert students to new vocabulary and their application to the understanding.

Students may also need help reading and using their textbook effectively. The teacher can do this by providing and discussing with them suggestions and tips on how to study a textbook in which they follow the basic SQ3R study formula.

A business teacher designed *Tips on How to Study a Text* in which he followed the basic SQ3R:

Use the *SURVEY Q 3 R TECHNIQUE* to study a textbook. The steps are:

I.   Survey
II. Question
III. Read
IV. Recite
V.   Review

I. Survey
   A. Ask yourself these questions after you have looked at the chapter title:
      1. What do I know about this?
      2. What do I want to know about this?
   Your answers will help you establish purposes for reading the lesson.
   B. Look over the headings (boldface print) to see what main ideas are being discussed. Some people write down these topics as main headings of an outline, leaving space between these points to fill in details to be read later.
   C. Look at any pictures, graphs, or tables. These aids are included by the author to emphasize important points.
   D. Read the introductory paragraph and summary paragraph if included in the chapter.
   E. Glance over any key words or questions that might be at the end of the chapter.
   F. Ask yourself: "What do I know about this lesson at this point?"

II. Question
   Go back to the beginning of the chapter and *turn the first heading into a question.* For example, if the first heading was "Remedies for Breach of Contract," your question might be: "What are the remedies for breach of contract?"

   This step will arouse your curiosity, help you bring to mind information already known, and aid you in seeing important points being made, thereby making it easier and quicker to understand what you read.

III. Read

Read to the end of the first section to answer the question you have just asked.

IV. Recite
   A. Look away from the book, *after reading the first section,* and try briefly to recite, in your own words, the answer to your question. A good way to do this reciting from memory is to jot down brief phrases in outline form; or you can fill in the outline you might have started in the Survey step.
   B. Glance over the section again if you cannot recite the correct information.

Repeat steps II, III, and IV on each succeeding section heading. Turn the next heading into a question, read to answer that question, and recite the answer by saying it out loud or by jotting down brief phrases in outline form.

V. Review
   A. Look over your notes or main headings of the chapter after you have finished the lesson. Try to get a bird's-eye view of the points and their relationships. Check your memory of the content by reciting the major sub-points under each heading.
   B. Review 24 hours after you have read the lesson. Just refresh your memory of main points and sub-points you might have forgotten, because people often forget much in the first 24 hours. After studying something, this review is very important.
   C. Review a week later.
   D. Review periodically.

In the beginning of the school year go through these steps with the students several times to insure their independence in their implementation. Refer to the steps constantly thereafter during the school year.

Typing class, in which the goal is that the student learn to type quickly and accurately, involves specific reading skills. Verda Johnson points out that much of the reading done in typewriting classes is of a cursory nature. But she maintains that reading can be incorporated in beginning and advanced typewriting. She lists two reading objectives for beginning typewriting—reading for content, and reading to become word conscious. She adds an objective for the advanced typewriting class —research orientation—to help the student understand how to explore new ideas and to analyze findings. Johnson requires advanced students to do research papers.[2]

An analysis of the table of contents of the typical text in typing will give clues to many of the reading skills required of the student. The skill of following directions will be needed in the manipulation of the typewriter as well as in the techniques of typing many different kinds of copy. In addition, students must learn to

---

[2] Verda R. Johnson, "Teaching for Better Understanding in Typewriting," *Journal of Business Education* 41, No. 1 (January, 1966): 149–150.

read and to use the kinds of copy such as correspondence, forms, tabulations, and manuscripts in all of their variations.

Robinson, et al, sum up the importance of teaching reading in business education by stating

> The most important factor in the improvement of reading skills is the attitude of the teacher . . . Until business teachers, as well as other secondary instructors, fully realize their role in reading development, real progress will be hindered.[3]

VOCATIONAL SUBJECTS—INDUSTRIAL ARTS AND HOME ECONOMICS

Reading material in the vocational subjects is generally technical, terse, and factual. It employs a vocabulary peculiar to the tools, equipment, and processes required. Much of the content is comprised of directions and specific explanations. It closely resembles aspects of scientific and mathematical materials.

The vocational subjects require a wide range of reading skills. The student needs specific instruction in these skills if he is to become competent and independent with vocational subject material. Classes in the vocational subjects involve students who represent a range in reading competence from the severely disabled level to superior levels. Many have reading levels commensurate with the intermediate elementary grades. Therefore in reviewing the usual reading level of the student and the nature of the reading material in the vocational subjects, the teacher has a two-fold responsibility: one, to teach the processes and manipulate skills of the course and two, to teach the skills required for successful reading of the material.

The Skills of the Vocational Subjects

1. *Ability to master the vocabulary.* The vocabulary includes technical terms; abbreviations and symbols; and names of tools, patterns, plans, equipment, and materials.

2. *Ability to follow directions.* Many of these are minute, complex and must be followed exactly. The directions may include safety instructions, recipes, and the use of tools and equipment as well as the steps of constructing a project or completing a job.

3. *Ability to read diagrams, charts, pictures, patterns, cutaways, drawings, and plans.* Parts of this ability will include the recognition and understanding of symbols and the interpretation of the legend or the scale.

4. *Ability to gain and interpret information from technical magazines, catalogs, and journals.* This is an important skill since technology is constantly changing and the student must be able to independently acquire new and related information. In addition to the ability to use the index and the table of contents, the

---

[3] Richard D. Robinson, John Carter, and Don B. Hokanson, "Business Teachers are Reading Teachers," *Journal of Business Education* 44, No. 2 (February, 1969): pp. 201–202.

student will need to understand the ratios of quantity and quality and to note the pertinent clues to agencies which underwrite, approve, or rate materials and products, to use order forms, and to interpret the analysis of specification descriptions with prices.

5. *Ability to read for main ideas and specific details and then to see the interrelationship of the information.*

6. *Ability to read occupational information of a trade nature for information about careers, individual or avocational interests.*

General Techniques

The industrial arts and home economics classroom procedures lend themselves well to providing readiness for reading. Tools are demonstrated and materials handled before the student embarks upon his project. Vocabulary is introduced at these times, diagrams, patterns and illustrations are studied and the labeled parts identified. Processes are guided sequentially so that the student gradually develops his concepts and skills. The process of student readiness which is an intrinsic step in the vocational classroom procedure is also the first step of a content-directed reading lesson.

The vocabulary terms pertinent to the vocational subjects are similar to those found in other disciplines. There are basically two types: technical terms peculiar only to the field or a part of it, and common terms with a special meaning appropriate to a field. Technical terms are most often taught to the students since you know that such terms would probably be new to them. These terms usually designate materials, equipment and operations. On the other hand, common terms are often not taught because they are so commonplace and the student is usually able to pronounce them fluently. For instance, such terms as *edge, rim, face, cut, clip, trim, set, tap, hem, draw, turn, snip, vent,* and many others may be known by the student in a general usage, but not as they pertain to a specific process in the vocational fields.

Obviously, it is the responsibility of the vocational teacher to teach both the technical and the common terms. No other teacher is able to provide the contextual setting for the specific vocabulary usage. Levine speaks to this point when he says

> If the teacher of English were merely to attempt analysis of the oral elements of the technical terms, he would be giving little assistance to the shop teacher anxious to have his students read for understanding. The pupils could call out the words from the examination of radio as smoothly as the teacher and still be no farther into reading the question than when they first started the analysis of words like "modulating."[4]

Obviously, the student must become competent in the vocabulary if he is to succeed in the various vocational subjects. Also, in a longe range view, the student needs to know the vocabulary in order to react intelligently as an adult consumer, to

---

[4] Isidore N. Levine, "Solving Reading Problems in Vocational Subjects," in *Teaching Reading in High School: Selected Articles,* ed. Robert Karlin (New York: The Bobbs-Merrill Company, Inc., 1969), pp. 347–357.

retain the skills of following directions and to establish the foundation for those who wish to build toward a vocational future in the trades.

Suggested techniques for building vocabulary are:

1. As words are needed for specific concepts, they should be taught as part of the lesson procedure when they can be illustrated with material, tools, equipment, and operation.
2. Specific explanatory pictures, properly labeled, to show equipment and its parts as well as a schematic drawing to show the process.
3. Labeling tools and equipment in their appropriate storage places.
4. Construct a class dictionary which can be kept current by a committee of students as new words are introduced. This may be in addition to each student's individual notebook.
5. Incorporate the appropriate vocabulary in student projects. The introduction of the term, its concept and use for an immediate purpose and its reinforcement as the project is constructed, demonstrated and explained provide a real purpose for usage.
6. Use whatever textbook aids are available to help the student learn the term: glossary, contextual usage, diagrammatic illustrations.
7. Many incidental relationships to assist in more meaningful understanding can be found between technical vocabulary and student's background. For example:

    Toughness (steel)—resiliency of a young tree to withstand pushing with the feet while pulling with the hands

    Hardness (of steel)—similar in nature to the brittleness of glass

    Method of striking (arc welder)—described as to tickle it.
8. Use direct experiences such as films, field trips, patterns, and models.
9. Use comparison charts such as with similar types of cuts as a *chamfer* and a *bevel*.
10. Use oral questioning and specific reading assignments for reinforcement.
11. Organize terms into categories.

Comprehension in the vocational subjects is similar to the mathematics and science in that the material is highly factual and new knowledge depends on the students' knowledge of what has been studied before. Specifically, the student faces several different organizational patterns in the writings on vocational subjects.

The patterns occurring in the greatest frequency either singly or in combination are (1) explanation of a process, (2) vocabulary, (3) combination of verbal text and diagram, and (4) directions. In the first, explanation of a process, the student will find that the pattern is very similar to a main idea followed by details. The main idea is the process and the essential nature of it. The details would likely describe or list specific parts of the process in order, may state exceptions, cautions, and possibly give application. The student ability to outline or list sequentially would be of value. Structure words indicating sequence or order of importance may be used. In vocabulary, the meaning would be provided with possible applications. Diagrams may accompany the definition. The student's ability to read the diagrams and to note the definition in context is needed. The combination of verbal text and diagrams requires slow intensive reading in which the student must constantly shift his attention between the verbal text and the diagram. Such reading is often required in the explanation of a process. In following directions the specific procedures as already outlined would operate. Vocabulary understanding and diagram reading are likely to be components in the application of this skill.

Suggested techniques for comprehension are:

1. Teach comprehension skills directly as they are needed by the students.
2. Use repeated questioning to elicit specific information from the student.
3. Have the student verify information when possible in his projects by inspection, measuring and testing—(evaluate schematic diagrams, patterns and plans found in hobby magazines for accuracy and appropriateness of design, for advanced levels). See p. 286.
4. Alert students to and have them use aids from the organization of the textbook.
5. Use "job sheets" with specific instructions. Discuss with the students to see if they can visualize the process—have them explain it. See p. 287.
6. Have students assemble simple machinery according to printed directions. Have them follow a recipe.
7. Have students draw up plans, exchange them, and see if they are clear for another student to follow.

Wide Reading

There are many opportunities for students to read widely in each field. Catalogs, journals, advertisements, guides, instructional manuals, consumer guides—all require careful reading and at the same time do much to enrich the student's background. Each vocational class should have a library of related materials directly accessible. Bamman lists the reasons for setting up such a library:

1. Developing an appreciation for the advances in modern industrial products, for workmanship and design, along with developing his skill in the fundamental processes of interpreting drawings and illustrations.
2. Choosing a vocation in which he may determine his capabilities, limitations, and interests.
3. Planning and problem solving.
4. Making use of leisure time, both as a hobby and as the "handy man" about the home, through the use of detailed information.[5]

The library is valuable in stimulating interest and in student practice in skills of reference reading. Reports from consumer guides, of a new process or a new development in equipment, give a current vibrant aura to the classes. The material is relevant.

FOREIGN LANGUAGES

Reading skills in foreign languages equate largely with the skills required in the English classes. Not only do the students read to get ideas and understandings,

---

[5] Henry A. Bamman, Ursula Hogan, and Charles E. Greene, *Reading Instruction in the Secondary School* (New York: Longmans, Green & Co., 1961), p. 207.

UNIT 4
front and back neck facings

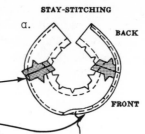

STAY-STITCHING

a.

BACK

FRONT

a—<u>Stitch</u> shoulder seams of facings.
Stitch 1/4″ from long <u>unnotched</u> edge.
<u>Press</u> <u>under</u> <u>edge</u> along stitching and stitch.
<u>Clip</u> neck edge to stay-stitching.

Technical vocabulary
facings
stay stitching
seams
hem

b—With RIGHT sides together, <u>pin</u> facing to neck edge, <u>matching</u> centers and seams. (Facing <u>extends</u> 5/8″ beyond center back opening edges.) Stitch neck edge.
<u>Trim</u> seam; <u>clip</u> curves.

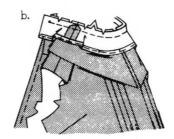

b.

General vocabulary
Students must understand if directions are to be followed correctly.
(Underlined).

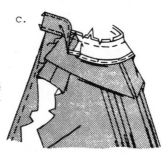

c.

c—Press facing out; press seam <u>toward</u> facing.

Facing side up, <u>understitch</u> close to seam line thru facing and seam.[6]

Following directions
Steps numbered. Help students to recognize each individual step.

Skills required:
Vocabulary
Following directions
Relating diagrams to directions
Reading diagrams

---

[6] *Sewing Direction Sheet,* Pattern Number 8924 (New York: Simplicity Pattern Co., 1970).

COMBINATION AWL and OFFSET SCREWDRIVER

MATERIALS: ¼″ Mild Steel Rod 8″ long

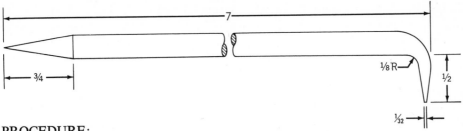

PROCEDURE:

1. File pyramid point on one end as shown in Fig. #1.

2. Round sharp edges forming pencil point as shown in Fig. #2. Emery if necessary.

3. Heat awl end in furnace and case harden.

4. With a hack saw cut stock to overall length of 7½″.

5. Heat screwdriver end in furnace. Draw metal to a taper by forging on anvil. Work no further than one inch in from end of piece.

6. Metal has fanned as it was drawn. Remove shaded section as shown in Fig. #3.

7. Draw file oblique surfaces of screwdriver blade tapering to a thickness of 1/32″ as shown in Fig. #4.

8. Further shape this end as shown in Fig. #5.

9. Place work in vise with 5/8″ of screwdriver blade extending above top of vise jaws and bend blade 90 degrees to main section.

10. Remove any scars with file and emery.

11. Case harden screwdriver end.

12. Polish with emery and crocus and buff by machine.

Fig. #1.

Fig. #2.

Fig. #3.

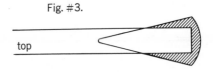
top

Fig. #4.

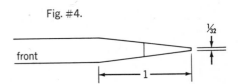
front

Fig. #5.

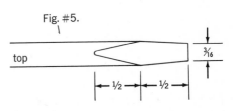
top

Students must apply the skills if following directions and reading diagrams.
Students must know vocabulary:
General words indicating action.
Technical words (It is likely that the student will know many of these words, however, the teacher should check them with the students).

but they have the added dimension of decoding the language, which provides practice in using the language. With a foreign language, the student may need to acquire a different phonetic system. In addition, several skills may be itemized: the ability (1) to read and memorize the vocabulary of a foreign language which requires the association of a foreign word or phrase with its English equivalent; (2) to read, that is translate, a selection given in a foreign language; (3) to comprehend and appreciate the common idiomatic expressions appearing in a foreign language; (4) to comprehend and be able to apply explanations and examples related to the grammar and the construction of a foreign language; (5) to read with comprehension English descriptions that deal with the people and the history of the country; and (6) "to think" in a foreign language while reading, writing, speaking or hearing it. This skill is especially fostered by the various language laboratory programs now available and in use in the schools.

The reading needs of a foreign language are much the same as they are for English. Preston states that it is doubtful that the student will be able to read the language with fluency and adequate understanding unless he knows over ninety-five percent of the running words at sight.[7] Therefore, the scope of the student's vocabulary is of fundamental importance. The various techniques of recognizing the meaning of the word are used—wide related reading, contextual usage, dictionary, structural analysis. The student should keep his own notebook—a dictionary of new words from his reading as well as those troublesome words which he finds difficult to remember. The notebook-dictionary should list the word, the contextual usage, meaning in context, and other "dictionary" meanings. Memorizing vocabulary, using words in both oral and written sentences, and repeating the meanings and examples of usage from memory are time-honored techniques and still viable.

Learning a language requires, as well, the mastering of its grammar. A comparative chart, evolved with the class, showing parallels and differences between English and the foreign language will be helpful to the student in noting the distinctive features of the foreign language. Such a chart may be a continuing activity, developing as different aspects of the language are studied throughout the year.

Lesson procedure when reading a foreign language follows the same steps as in English. Of particular importance is the preparation of the student for reading the selection—essential background pertaining to the setting, history, etc., needed for a complete understanding and appreciation of the selection. Students reading a selection in a foreign language also need to ascertain their purpose for reading, and to preview, using effective study techniques.

ART—PAINTING AND THE GRAPHIC ARTS

The reading skills relate to art instruction in three ways. Students need to (1) acquire the meanings of technical terms, (2) read and follow directions accurately for performing technical operations such as mixing paints and other processes, and

---

[7] Ralph C. Preston, "Give the Student Tips on How to Get the Most from Foreign Language Books," in *Improving Reading in Secondary Schools: Selected Readings,* ed. Lawrence E. Hafner (New York: The Macmillan Company, 1967), pp. 401–403.

(3) read with comprehension biographies and materials dealing with the description, history, and criticism of works of art. The first two skills and the type of subject content are similar to that found in science and the vocational subjects. The third skill and type of content relates closely to the social studies.

Though the art class is an active one in which students manipulate various media, a library of related art books should be in the classroom for supplementary reading and enrichment. This is a vital way of stimulating student interest in aspects or fields of art of concern to him. Also, the art teacher who knows the reading material is a prime resource to the student in guiding him to the book which he is capable of reading and which is about his specific interest.

MUSIC

Music, as a subject, divides into five areas as they pertain to clusters of reading skills. The first area is the student's ability to read musical notation and to interpret music symbols. Usually at the high school level little is taught in this area except to recognize various symbols and to distinguish one from the other. For instance, the student is taught the difference between a whole note and a half note and he is taught such musical symbols as the clef sign, key signature, rests, and so on. However, little is done to help him read music as he would read print—for meaning. That is, the student is not given instruction in being able to hear in his mind the melody from the printed representation of the music. In practice, then, the first area of music instruction resembles the symbolic aspect of mathematical vocabulary—the recognition of the parts and symbols that comprise a musical score.

The second area encompasses a technical vocabulary, usually consisting of Italianate words. Knowledge of this technical vocabulary also helps the student to interpret a musical score in both vocal and instrumental music. Words such as *andante, allegro, forte, pianissimo* comprise this type of vocabulary.

Musical theory is the third area. Usually, only a small number of students who wish to specialize in it embark on this more advanced level of music. This aspect of musical instruction is not taught in all high schools but is taught in some large city and suburban schools. Tirro points out rather picturesquely the intense nature of reading required of music theory texts.

> Music theory texts are almost in a class unto themselves. Very similar to an algebra text or a geometry problem book where each letter, number, and sign must be carefully considered, tasted, chewed, swallowed, and rechewed like a cow's cud, it becomes obvious that one does not really read a theory book; one grapples with it in a life and death struggle.[8]

The fourth area resembles the type of reading required of English and the social studies. It includes reading for background and enrichment to investigate

---

[8] Frank Tirro, "Reading Techniques in the Teaching of Music," in *Fusing Reading Skills and Content,* ed. H. Alan Robinson and Ellen Lamar Thomas (Newark, Delaware: International Reading Association, 1969), pp. 103–107.

aspects of musical history and the lives of composers. Historical content and biographical material are the key types in this area.

The fifth area involves the area of musical criticism. Current newspaper writing about musical events includes comments by music editors and critics. Obviously such material is written with a specific point of view. The reader must apply criteria of evaluating the criticism just as he would read critically in any subject. As applied to a critical analysis of either music or literature, the reader will need to check out the background qualification and point of view of the writer. The student will also check the use of words which may be used to present a specific impression as well as the writer's grasp of the subject.

PHYSICAL EDUCATION AND HEALTH EDUCATION

The physical education teacher can also be involved with the teaching of reading. In the event that he is charged with teaching a class in health he is dealing with scientific writing in textbooks and various pamphlets and current materials pertinent to current sociological and health problems. The physical education teacher usually has a strong liaison with students, and knows them well in other than just academic work. Along with this knowledge is often a strong rapport between teacher and students. Such a mutual feeling of trust and the insights deriving from a broader knowledge of the students places the physical education teacher in a prime position to motivate, counsel and direct the student toward improvement in reading. He can, as well, become an "ombudsman" for the student with other members of the faculty. He may give the student insight into acquiring reading skills by pointing out the parallel to acquiring athletic skills.

Physical education can also be an impetus to wide reading for further information and for pleasure. A departmental library of related materials makes books accessible to students who, though competent in sports, may not be competent in reading. Thus interest and practice in reading can be fostered. Books as well as sports might be discussed in class. One coach reported

> Suppose the coach is idolized by some boy in a depressed neighborhood. He might say, "Jim, come on into my office. I have this book. Can you look it over, read it, and see how you like it?" You like the kid. The kid thinks that now you talk to him! You might have given him a reading interest—a habit, maybe. You may have helped to keep him off the streets. It just might work. . . . I regard this as a very important part of teaching physical education and coaching. If you select books carefully, books about techniques, you're going to have more playing power in your boys. Television is bringing sports events to millions, many ill-informed persons. Through books, boys broaden their backgrounds and add to their enjoyment as spectators.[9]

---

9 Sanford Poltar, "Physical Education and Reading: Questions and Answers," in *Fusing Reading Skills and Content,* ed. H. Alan Robinson and Ellen Lamar Thomas (Newark, Delaware: International Reading Association, 1969), pp. 81–88.

There is not any subject in the curriculum that does not require the student to use the reading skills in some way. There is not any subject that does not use reading profitably for enrichment. The "moral" is that reading instruction must include content. Reading cannot be taught in a vacuum, or relegated to one subject. Rather, it permeates the curriculum.

SUGGESTED QUESTIONS AND PROBLEMS TO BE CONSIDERED IN REFERENCE TO YOUR CLASSROOM

List A (For readers who are training to be teachers)

1. In your subject determine for each lesson the technical vocabulary words the student must know. List also the general words used in a technical manner.
2. Compile a bibliography of references and trade books pertinent to your subject which you can have the students read for enjoyment and enrichment.
3. In your subject prepare visuals of diagrams and other graphic aids and plan how you would help your students in effective use of them.

List B (For readers who are teaching)

1. Have your students write a set of directions for doing some project. Discuss and evaluate the clarity of the directions.
2. Discuss with your students how they think reading applies to your subject. Make a list of the skills with them.
3. Have your students compile a pictorial dictionary of technical terms they must know for your subject.

CHAPTER THIRTEEN

The Complete High School Reading Program

Reading instruction must pervade the entire high school curriculum . . . a point that is emphasized throughout this book. Language is the basis of most of the learning that takes place. It is the basic tool of learning. Instruction in language coupled with adequate practice is needed in all subjects.

Instruction in the mechanics of reading the language—instruction in the recognition of graphic symbols and in the acquisition of meaning from these symbols—is required for student efficiency and competence. The ultimate goal is to enable the student to gain ideas independently through reading. He needs help in learning to sort and understand ideas in order to infer, conclude, evaluate and apply them. Competence in reading should be the prime consideration of all teachers.

PARTS OF A COMPLETE PROGRAM

When a high school reading program is either considered or planned, certain essential elements become apparent as the school philosophy is determined. If we accept the view that reading does indeed permeate the entire curriculum, five elements comprise the whole. They are:

1. Reading instruction is provided in each of the subject fields as it applies to each.
2. The central library of the school provides opportunity to the students for both research and pleasure from reading.
3. Supplementary classroom libraries must be available to provide opportunities for enrichment.

4. Elective courses are offered in the mechanics of reading for those students who wish to sharpen their reading-study skills.

5. Remedial courses are available for those students who need help in addition to the content reading instruction in each classroom.

Each of the five parts is interrelated. The school library is the nucleus of the program and should contribute to each of the other parts by providing materials for wide reading and thereby practical application of the reading skills. Obviously the reading research skills needed for research projects in the content disciplines would be taught by each classroom teacher with the librarian assisting in the student application of them. Finally, the library offers enrichment to the various disciplines. The library can be a partial source of classroom supplementary materials by lending books to a classroom while a specific topic is being studied. It contributes to interest in reading for the elective and remedial classes as well as in the content areas.

Supplementary classroom libraries offer opportunities for developing interest and enrichment. They are particularly effective because the books are readily available to the students, which tends to encourage wide reading.

CRITERIA OF A COMPLETE SECONDARY SCHOOL READING PROGRAM

The following guidelines for successful implementation of a complete reading program are grouped under three areas: philosophy, practice, and personnel.

Philosophy

1. Secondary school reading instruction should be an all-school program which involves all personnel. The program needs to be comprehensive. All opportunities must be utilized to teach the students to apply reading skills to various materials. The program should have the unity that comes with all teachers and personnel being involved in upgrading the student's use of this medium of learning. Adequate progress does not come as an isolated effort from a single teacher. We know that there is too little transfer by most students with this approach, and too little reinforcement. Transfer is assured and reinforcement becomes adequate as each teacher, whatever his content field, works with the same skills as they apply to a specific discipline.

2. The program must be guided toward the accomplishment of identifiable goals. The school staff must know what their objectives are. This is an obvious need for any successful program. The school staff must think about what they are to accomplish. Though they may express the goals in esoteric terms with a literary flavor, essentially the goals are derived from so simple a question as "What do we want the students to be able to do and to become as a result of our instruction?" The answer to this question will determine the emphasis and scope of the program. If the answer is to have the students read their textbook materials, then the program will evolve into largely a remedial one because the emphasis will be on those students who are not reading adequately—a large or small number depending on

the school. If the answer is to have all of the students become independent in using reading as a means of attaining information as well as of recreational pleasure, then the program will include all disciplines and all students.

3.   There needs to be a strong interrelationship between reading and the other aspects of the language arts. This criterion harks back to the fundamental goal of instruction—facility in language usage. It is implied that all teachers are teachers of language, albeit the language of their discipline. Therefore all language usage is employed—speaking, listening, reading, and writing—to help the student learn. Each aspect of language usage is interwoven with the others. Skills of reading can also be applied to speaking, listening, and writing. Again there is a unity which the teachers must help the student to utilize.

4.   Instruction in the skills of reading as well as in the goals of reading instruction must be continuous from grades K-12. Competence in reading grows as the student learns and practices continuously. It is a tool and one's skill in using it can always grow. The extent of growth can be fostered or hampered by many factors, but the capacity of growth in competence is infinite. Theoretically, growth should not stop as long as the student lives.

5.   Reading must be considered as a process rather than as a subject. One does not read "Reading." It is a process in the use of language which, in turn, is a medium of learning in the various subjects in the school curriculum.

6.   Instruction in reading must be systematic. Competence in reading does not develop by chance. There must be, as in all skills, a development in the application of the many skills of reading that starts simply and grows more and more complex as the student's mastery increases. The student should be paced by his own development. Further, the interrelationship of the skills must be made apparent to the student. For example, the skill of discerning main ideas and the skill of relating pertinent details to the appropriate main idea is the beginning of the skill of noting organization—outlining.

7.   The nature of the student, his social and personal development, and his mental capacity must be considered in relation to reading progress. In other words, reading instruction must be geared to the student. It must be related to him, not the other way around. Positive conditions should be capitalized upon and negative conditions corrected. The student must be known by the teacher as an individual human being, not merely as a name in the class grade book. Through classroom diagnosis the student has the right to expect an accurate and objective assessment of his assets and liabilities in the process of reading. The plan evolved *between* the student and teacher must use both his strengths and weaknesses. It must fit him individually, and he must understand its goals and design. It must incorporate student goals and its design must be comfortable and possible for him.

Practice

1.   An effective program provides for both instruction and application. The student needs to be shown how to use the reading skills effectively with whatever

material he is reading. Instruction in a skill, however, is not enough. He must practice the skill with various materials. Much of the practice should be supervised in order to insure developing competence. Subsequently and concomitantly there should also be independent practice in applying the skill.

2.   Meaning is emphasized as the student reads. The secondary teacher has the fundamental responsibility to help his students gain meaning from the reading material. He will need to insure adequate background, vocabulary, and comprehension of the main idea, related details, and the organization of the material. Then the student is more likely to be able to interpret and evaluate logically what he reads.

3.   All of the necessary study skills are taught as their use is required. In addition to vocabulary and comprehension, the student must receive instruction and guidance in how to study—how to attack an assignment, to conduct library research, and to understand the syntax of the language.

4.   Instruction should be differentiated and flexible in the classroom. The skills emphasized in the classroom must be a balance between those required by the assignment and the content, and those needed by the student. If the student, for instance, is adept in noting main ideas, the teacher will not find it necessary to teach this skill. The student will, however, use it. Or the teacher may find that a portion of the class needs such instruction. Procedure, then, is flexible to the point that such students receive the specific instruction.

5.   Continuous evaluation is conducted to measure student competence in the skills. Techniques of diagnostic teaching and informal inventories as well as standardized tests are used. The teacher should know at all times the strengths and weaknesses of his students individually, even when the total class load per day is large. Easy, effective and continual records must be kept.

6.   Adequate materials are needed for effective teaching. Though it has been established that the teacher is the key to teaching effectiveness, adequate materials to fit both the levels of competence and special interests of the students are necessary. A student cannot read with understanding materials which are above his level, but to read material below his level of competence is deadening to student interest and accomplishment. A variety of materials is needed in the classroom.

7.   Basic lesson procedures should use the fundamental steps of the directed activity. Adequate preparation for reading, and instruction in and application of the skills are essential to planning.

8.   A stimulating classroom environment is needed. The classroom should be filled with materials—exhibits, displays, books, models—appropriate to the discipline. The atmosphere that should emanate from the physical layout as well as the manner of the teacher should invite learning and the development of interests. This often works in subtle ways as some material catches the eye of a student and he sees the relationship of the material to his classroom study. Nothing is drearier than a barren classroom and an unenthusiastic teacher. Nothing does more to dampen an interest in learning.

Classroom teachers who "float" to different rooms for their various classes say that it is impossible to have enriching and stimulating materials about. Surely when a teacher finds himself in such a situation, providing supplementary materials is more difficult. However, they can be provided, though perhaps not as well as in a room in which the teacher is "permanently in residence." A bookshelf in a cabinet which can be locked when the class is not in session might be provided. A library cart could be used by the teacher to take the materials to the room each day.

Other teachers say that the materials would be defaced, destroyed, or stolen. Still others maintain that the need to maintain classroom order precludes additional materials and the activities involved. These situations do occur. Yet, when the materials are interesting to the students and when they are guided to be involved in setting up and maintaining such materials, little vandalism is likely to occur. One constructive procedure is to involve the students in the selection of the materials. Organize a selection committee which, with your help and that of the school librarian, will select and evaluate supplementary materials. Of course, the committee will solicit and consider suggestions and reactions of their classmates. Taking part in such an activity serves many purposes. Foremost is the interest engendered. Next, in that the students have a vital role in the selection, their care of the materials will be highly positive. Further, the very act of selection widens background and thereby provides enrichment.

Students learn when they are interested. It is then that they begin to take pride in the facilities of learning. A stimulating environment elicits interest.

9. Effective classroom teaching incorporates the concept of diagnostic teaching—classroom instruction which pertains to each of the various individuals and gives immediate reteaching when needed and appropriately uses the practice of daily diagnosis.

10. The teacher needs to preplan the learning experiences on both a short-term and a long-term basis. The long term planning includes the understanding, skills, and attitudes the teacher hopes to impart during the course. The short term planning is a result of diagnostic teaching.

Personnel

A total school reading program is as effective as the involvement of all the professional school personnel in its administration and functioning.

The classroom teacher is the most important person to the success of the school program. Each teacher's expertise with his discipline makes it possible for him to best teach the related reading skills. He is best able to help the students to apply the skills to a specific discipline. He can best differentiate instruction to special needs of the individuals within the class. He is therefore best qualified to give specific corrective help to students as the need arises.

The school principal sets the tone of the school and through his leadership engenders enthusiasm, or lack of it, in the school teaching staff. Through administrative considerations of scheduling and budgeting he can govern indirectly the effectiveness of teachers. Proper facilities, materials, and time are necessary ingredients. His concern is to provide help for the teachers in the forms of reading specialists to assist, inservice courses for an understanding of the reading process, support of the teachers in their efforts and explanations to the community. All of these contribute fundamentally to the success of the program.

The curriculum coordinator is the principal's delegate to plan and see to the execution of the program. He should be knowledgeable about reading and be able to give specific help to teachers.

The reading consultant, if he is a part of the school, should be a prominent member of the curriculum coordinator's team. Often the consultant in reading will be the coordinator's delegate charged with specific planning and administration of the program. Some reading consultants also spend part of their time as reading teachers for remedial students. At the same time they are still the coordinator's delegates and must work toward the improvement of curriculum and teaching.

The reading teacher is most often used to give additional specific help to the student in accordance with his level and needs. Sometimes he is assigned to teach general classes in reading—for those high school students who wish to re-fine their skills. There should be at all times a close liaison between the content teachers and the remedial teachers. Many times the lack of such coordination is a basic weakness. A unified approach with everyone working for the same goals is obviously more effective than each going his own way.

The guidance counselor is a resource to teachers in advising and alerting them to the problems, needs, strengths, weaknesses, and interests of the students. Special schedules may be arranged. Also pertinent information about the student, other than school information, can be provided which may give the teacher insights about the student as well as suggesting classroom approaches.

The school nurse can investigate the general physical condition of the student. Aberrations of vision and hearing which need correction can be noted and proper referral made.

The librarian obviously plays an important role—especially in the areas of the reading-research skills and in fostering wide reading. One librarian organized a committee of students, which was well publicized, to assist her in choosing new books for the library. This was an ongoing and active committee throughout the year. When the books were received she placed them on a table for students to browse. She believed that student involvement was of prime importance in stimu-lating wide reading and interest in the library.

The special media specialist is to help classroom teachers with the use of ma-terials—tapes, films, film strips, transparencies, etc., which can assist the student in his understanding of the printed page. Materials which enliven, clarify, and dramatize classroom learning can be provided. Background growth and enrichment are greatly enhanced by his services.

ORGANIZING THE READING PROGRAM

Organizing, enlarging, or adapting a high school reading program involves all of the school personnel under the leadership of the principal, the curriculum co-ordinator and the reading consultant/teacher. The leadership is usually channeled through a reading committee of teachers (usually one from each discipline and other interested personnel). It is particularly necessary to have teachers engaged in the structuring of the program since they will be responsible for its success or failure. Open lines of communication must be maintained between the committee and the educational staff.

In order for a reading committee to function effectively, the following factors must be considered:

1. Adequate administrative support and involvement.
2. Active teacher support and involvement.
3. Maintenance of open communication between the committee and all educational personnel as well as parents.
4. Planning the reading program to fit the curriculum organization and needs of the school.
5. Adequate budget.
6. Provisions for teacher inservice training.
7. Selection of adequate materials to fit the reading and learning needs of the students.
8. A comprehensive program to include all phases of reading at all levels of ability.
9. Developing community interest and support.

SUCCESS OF THE PROGRAM

The success of the program can be governed by extrinsic factors such as the interest of administrators, teachers and the community; budget; and the school philosophy. Even more important are the attitudes of the teachers toward the place of reading in the high school with the result that their classroom procedures are governed accordingly. For instance, are the teachers planning their lessons to:

1. provide for good motivation?
2. develop skill in adapting techniques and using materials to help students on various levels of ability?
3. extend help in developing a broad vocabulary?
4. use recommended reading procedure?
5. provide a balance among all the skills in their development in each discipline?
6. guide the students in purposeful reading?

The reading committee of a school may evaluate its program by asking the following questions:

1. What are the basic premises underlying the school reading program?
2. Do the teachers have a well-founded philosophy of reading instruction?
3. Is provision made to teach the reading skills sequentially, systematically and continuously?
4. Are thought and relationship questions used as well as fact questions?
5. Are the reading skills taught in the context of a story or subject matter, or are they isolated?
6. Is practice work related to a student's understood need?
7. Are reading materials of varying levels and topics available for student use?

8. Is there a well stocked school library with a qualified librarian?
9. Are there classroom collections of books parallel to the textbooks?
10. Is reading isolated from the rest of the curriculum—is it taught as a subject apart?
11. Is reading taught in all subjects, whenever the student uses printed materials?
12. Do teachers follow the steps of a directed reading activity?
13. Are the students reading books on their instructional level (material that is challenging but can be read successfully)?
14. Is instruction in reading differentiated to each student's needs or to that of the class as a whole?
15. Are we able to provide instruction in reading for the superior reader?
16. Are we able to provide instruction in reading for the disabled reader?
17. Is there provision for all types of classroom organization as needed for effective instruction?
18. Are teachers flexible in their classroom organization?
19. Do teachers continuously diagnose the needs and evaluate the progress of students in reading?
20. Do teachers know how to diagnose and evaluate?
21. Are the students enjoying reading; are they reading widely?
22. Do teachers have the necessary background to interpret the reading program to the public?
23. Are opportunities for in-service instruction provided for teachers?

The purpose of schools is to have the students become literate. The object of literacy is to enable the student to function constructively in society, both individually and in groups. Being able to read is a necessity for becoming a self-sustaining individual. Consequently, the thrust of all reading instruction is toward this end. It is, indeed, one of the prime charges given to our schools. All school personnel, therefore, are involved, as surely as they meet students each day, in their students' educational capacity.

SUGGESTED QUESTIONS AND PROBLEMS TO BE CONSIDERED IN REFERENCE TO YOUR OWN SCHOOL

List A (For readers who are training to be teachers)

1. Describe a school reading program in which you would like to teach.
2. If you had a problem reader in one of your classes, to whom would you go for assistance? Describe the type of assistance you would expect.
3. If you were asked to serve on a school reading committee, what would you envision to be your duties and responsibilities?
4. What would be your expectations in reading for the students in your classes? How would you use the school resources to meet their needs?

List B (For readers who are teaching)

1. Analyze your school reading program and determine how and where instruction in reading is provided and how and when provision for wide reading is provided.
2. Note a reading problem in your school and determine how it can be solved.
3. Survey the personnel roster for your school and determine who should be included in a school reading committee.
4. Note the various personnel assigned to your school and list the duties of each toward the implementation of a total school reading program.
5. As a basis for the work of your school reading committee, survey your department or school for (1) the apparent reading problems, and (2) suggestions for corrective action.

UNIT DEVELOPMENT

I. *Introducing the Unit*

A. Select a topic for study which may be divided into several problems for group and individual research.

1. Find out what the students know about it. (Determine what needs to be taught)

   a. List the facts on the blackboard.

   b. Discuss the sources of information.

   c. Decide on ways of judging the correctness of ideas such as contradictions or misconceptions.

   d. Have a record made of the information listed.

2. Find out what the students want to know about the topic.

   a. Use the same four points listed under #1 above.

   b. As the material is previewed, graphic aids and topical headings may alert students to information they wish to investigate.

   c. Note that very few questions may be forthcoming at this time. The suggestion can be made that other questions may come to mind as the topic is studied.

3. Help the students relate the topic to their experimental background. Relate the topic to present knowledge and understandings.

4. Use whatever materials may be available, appropriate, and necessary such as pictures, objects, models, current news,

CLASSROOM ORGANIZATION TO MEET SPECIFIC NEEDS

The entire class

Note: If multitexts are used, the teacher may survey by using an overhead projector to select pertinent features from each. This will help students with their specific textbook and provide an enriched introduction based on all of the textbooks.

READING SKILLS

A. Prepare (readiness) for reading

1. Explore the student's background of information. Probe with questions to help students remember information in their background.

2. Develop meaning to basic concepts (vocabulary).

3. Survey the scope of the topic. When using printed materials, use typographical aids.

4. Set up purpose questions.

UNIT DEVELOPMENT	CLASSROOM ORGANIZATION TO MEET SPECIFIC NEEDS	READING SKILLS
related stories or poems, TV and radio news or programs, and trips. B. The time needed for the introduction to a unit may require just one class period or a few days. This is the same as the introduction for an individual lesson procedure. The preparation depends upon (1) the length of the unit, (2) the fundamental nature of the material, and (3) the student's background in the data.		B. Diagnose student's proficiency in using the skills.
II. *Developing the Unit* A. Use basic materials to expand pupils' information about the topic. Initial reading will help the students to decide what problems they may wish to work on as well as to know more about the main topic. B. Determine the major problem and various sub-problems. The problem should be stated as questions rather than as topics in order to implement the application of the skills of interpretive and critical reading. Identify problems to be used for research by groups.	A. The entire class B. Possible grouping according to the need of students for instruction in specific skills.	A. Use the information gained through the diagnosis to determine the skills which need to be taught further and practiced. B. Teach the following skills, if needed, as basic materials are used: 1. Review and teach all of the skills common to the content area. 2. Develop specific vocabulary. 3. Use typographical aids. 4. Teach how to use graphic aids (maps, pictures, etc.). 5. Give instruction in setting up purposes for reading.
III. *Student-Teacher Planning for Research* A. Organize the groups (committees) according to interest indicated in each problem. (Students may also be assigned to specific groups if the teacher sees a student's social need which can be met.) B. Discuss and review resource material. 1. Have the students recall and determine what they know about resource materials. 2. Discuss sources of materials. a. Determine where the materials may be located.	A. Interest groups B. Social groups if indicated by needs of students C. Total class (prior to actual beginning of research by groups) D. Role of the chairman 1. Direct discussion. 2. Use the ideas of other participants—get all shades of opinion. 3. Help all participants to take part in the discussions. 4. Have a sense of organization.	A. Set up purposes (problems) to guide reading. B. Teach locational skills: 1. Use of library skills 2. Use of references 3. Use of parts of a book

b. Help students determine specific sources which may contain information about their problem.

Formulate answers to the question: How can we solve our problem?

3. Provide instruction in techniques of using various resource aids and resource materials, *i.e.,* card catalog, World Almanac, etc. The school librarian is a valuable resource person.

C. Set up standards for the group work.
1. Determine the role of the chairman, recorder, the process observer.
2. Organize the work of the group so that each participant has a job he can do.
3. Note effective work procedures—each student works so as not to annoy others, does not talk too loudly, works at the job at hand, does not waste time, works democratically, does some things even though they are not his first choice, does his own job, etc.

5. Lead the group in evaluating their work.
6. See that facts are well supported by research.

E. Role of the recorder
1. Maintain a record of group progress.
2. Assist leader in summarizing work completed.

F. Role of the process observer
1. Watches working of the group in accordance with standards of effective work.
2. Assist leader in planning for participation.
3. Assist group in providing information pertinent to group evaluation, such as reactions of group members.

G. Group member duties
1. Participates by reading, doing his part, and discussing with group.
2. Contribute ideas freely.
3. Accept decisions of the group.
4. Set standards for group work.

H. The students will need to delineate their problem—determine the scope and depth which they will need to develop.

A. Apply locational skills
B. Use skimming techniques.
C. Apply all skills for getting information common to research.
D. Use outlining skills.
E. Synthesize data from more than one source.
F. Organize data into a report.
G. Apply information to the problem. (Involves the use of interpretive reading skills.)

A. Interest groups conducting research
B. Possible social groups
C. Special need groups, as established groups of individuals needing further help in some research skill or grouping technique
D. Groups organize the assignments in accordance with standards and duties of members as listed in *III. Student-Teacher Planning for Research*

IV. *Conducting Research*
A. Have a variety of materials on differing levels of difficulty.
B. Encourage students to read widely and pool their information.
C. Keep a bibliography.
D. Teach the students to evaluate their group work; assist groups when necessary; help in further planning; try not to let group bog down.

The teacher may find it necessary to guide the pupils through their group work, at least at first. The teacher may pace students by requiring the recorder to give her an account of what was accomplished in each day's group

UNIT DEVELOPMENT

work and a statement of the next day's inten-
tions. In this way the teacher can keep a close
scrutiny of each group's progress and be prepared to assist if the group seems to be floun-
dering. When groups begin to work, students
should be directed to map first their total assignment within the time limit given and each
day think through what is to be done at the
meeting.

V. *Culminating the Unit*
A. Help the students prepare their presentations to the class.
1. Determine what to report.
2. Determine how to report.
Presenting information using types of
projects such as dramatizations, original
descriptions or stories, models, dio-
ramas, charts, pictures, collections, etc.
B. Develop standards for an audience such
as listening with a purpose, taking in outline the main ideas of the report, being
courteous to the speaker, etc.
C. Evaluate each group's presentation—
through discussion and questionnaire.
1. Did each group solve its problem?
2. Was the presentation well-organized
and interesting?
3. Were standards of group work maintained?
D. Evaluate the solving of the main topic.
1. Has the main problem been answered?
(Help students see the relationship of
each group's information to the main
topic.)
2. What improvements are necessary?

CLASSROOM ORGANIZATION
TO MEET SPECIFIC NEEDS

E. Entire class according to need for possible immediate evaluation. This may be
done at any time to help the students rethink the mode of work through group
processes.

A. Group participation in presentation
B. Group evaluation of its work
C. Total class evaluation of method of working; of need for further instruction in the
skills of reading, etc.; of the entire unit's
work.

READING SKILLS

A. Teach techniques of giving reports. Set up standards such as well-organized reports in student's own words.
B. Teach techniques of taking notes.
1. Main ideas and supporting detail outline
2. Listening for any key words and phrases
3. Listening for main ideas, structure of information in the report.

Note: The teacher should know what the groups are to do *before* they are to be expected to do it. The teacher should also know the references, see the
organization of the unit and ways it may be culminated *before* the pupils do the research.

Index